Voices of the Civil War

Voices of the Civil War · Chancellorsville

By the Editors of Time–Life Books, Alexandria, Virginia

Contents

Rapidan River

Ely's Ford

Ely's Ford Road

U.S. Ford Road

Wilderness Church

Orange Turnpike

Dowdall's Tavern

Bullock Road

Mountain Road

Chancellorsville

Plank Road

Brock Road

Hazel Grove

Fairview Heights

Orange Plank Road

Furnace Road

Unfinished Railroad

Catharine Furnace

Unfinished Railroad

Furnace Road

Catharpin Road

THE FIELD AT CHANCELLORSVILLE

The Battle of Chancellorsville centered on an obscure country crossroads just south of the winding Rappahannock River in a region of eastern Virginia known as the Wilderness. The artist's rendering depicts the densely wooded terrain over which the opposing armies maneuvered and fought in the spring of 1863.

U.S. Ford

Rappahannock River

River Road

Banks' Ford

Mine Road

Salem Church

Turnpike

Zoan Church

Tabernacle Church

Plank Road

Mine Road

Unfinished Railroad

Gordon Road

Into the Wilderness

Major General Joseph Hooker, the new commander of the Army of the Potomac who would direct Federal operations at Chancellorsville, got his celebrated nickname, it is said, because of a typographical error. Someone at a New York newspaper, about to print a report of a battle that had taken place during the abortive 1862 Federal campaign on the Virginia Peninsula, provisionally tagged the story "Fighting—Joe Hooker." The tag was not for publication, but it was printed by mistake and without the dash, so the headline appeared as "Fighting Joe Hooker." The nickname stuck and the general was known ever after as Fighting Joe. Hooker himself professed to loathe the sobriquet. It caused him "incalculable injury," he claimed, by making the public think he was "a hot-headed, furious young fellow, accustomed to making furious and needless dashes at the enemy."

At Stoneman's Switch, near Fredericksburg, Virginia, crates of hardtack, barrels of meat, and long boxes containing collapsible pontoons lie stockpiled along a railroad siding as part of the massive build-up for the Federal offensive in the spring of 1863.

Much of the Northern public seemed delighted, however, when President Abraham Lincoln appointed someone called Fighting Joe to command the army in January 1863. Maybe here was a bold warrior able to smash General Robert E. Lee's stubborn Army of Northern Virginia and send it reeling back toward Richmond. In any case, certainly Hooker could do no worse than his predecessor, Major General Ambrose E. Burnside, author of the catastrophic Federal defeat in December 1862 at the Battle of Fredericksburg.

Lincoln had put Burnside in command the previous November when Burnside's predecessor, Major General George B. McClellan, failed dismally to pursue the Confederates after the Battle of Antietam, giving the masterful Lee two months to reorganize his battered forces—and place them squarely in the Federal army's path near Culpeper, Virginia. Finally losing patience with McClellan's "slows," Lincoln fired him and turned to Burnside in the desperate hope that a change in command would produce some results.

At first Burnside moved swiftly and decisively. Choosing not to attack Lee at Culpeper, he marched the entire Federal army 40 miles southeast around the Confederate flank to the banks of the Rappahannock River across from Fredericksburg.

Burnside's plan called for crossing the river at Fredericksburg and attacking the town head-on, but he stalled, waiting for the pontoon bridges he would need. When the bridging gear finally arrived, Burnside stalled again —giving Lee time to catch up. Within days Lieutenant General James Longstreet had rushed southeast from Culpeper to Fredericksburg with his First Corps and had begun fortifying the heights behind the town. Racing after Longstreet came Lieutenant General Thomas J. "Stonewall" Jackson with his fast-marching "foot cavalry."

Dithering and unable to improvise a better plan, on December 12 Burnside at last moved most of his 120,000-man army across the river and, after another day's delay, ordered a series of suicidal assaults on the dug-in Confederates. The result was a dreadful butchery, with dozens of Union regiments torn to bits by massed Confederate fire as the Federals struggled to cross open fields toward the heights. "We might as well have tried to take Hell," one Union soldier said. The attacks, Longstreet coolly summed up, were "desperate and bloody, but utterly hopeless."

Having sacrificed more than 12,000 men for no gain whatever, on December 15 Burnside pulled his entire force back across the Rappahannock and into the camps around Falmouth. There things went from bad to worse. Appalled by the senseless killing, troops began to desert at a rate of more than 200 per day. Thousands more fell ill with scurvy and dysentery. Angry and dejected soldiers took to the bottle en masse. "I have seen a whole regiment so drunk," a Pennsylvania soldier wrote, "that they were hard put to find 15 sober men for picket duty."

Burnside made the situation worse by trying to launch another attack, sending his troops trudging westward up the Rappahannock on January 20 toward a pair of fords. There, in theory, they would cross the river and sweep in behind the Confederates. But then rain began to fall in torrents. "The bottom literally dropped out of the whole immediate country," one veteran wrote. Wagons sank up to their axles in mud, and cannon became so mired that in one case 150 men straining on ropes could not dislodge a single gun. After four days of agony, Burnside called off the thwarted attack.

The infamous Mud March sealed Burnside's fate, his officers complaining loudly to the White House and the War Department about his incompetence. Soon after, Lincoln relieved Burnside of command—and named Fighting Joe Hooker to take over.

To many in the army, Hooker was a dubious choice. A West Pointer, he had been brevetted three times for bravery during the Mexican War of 1846-1848, and he had proved a tough, reliable brigade and corps commander on the Peninsula and at Antietam, where he led the first furious attack on the Confederate left. But Hooker was also known for being inordinately ambitious and abrasive, and for singing his own praises to the press. He was, one critic said, "a veritable Bombastes Furioso." He was also said to be fond of the bottle, and he most certainly had a penchant for making blustery, unguarded remarks. Recently he had publicly condemned Lincoln's handling of the war and called for a dictator to take over.

Lincoln knew well all the negatives, but he had decided to gamble on Hooker's driving energy, his apparent eagerness to fight, and his proven flair as a combat leader. In a

forthright letter to Hooker, Lincoln chided him for his outspoken opinions—and then urged him on. "Only those generals who gain successes can set up dictators," the president pointedly wrote. "What I now ask of you is military success, and I will risk the dictatorship." Lincoln then added, "Beware of rashness, but with energy, and sleepless vigilance, go forward, and give us victories." Hooker carried the letter in his pocket and showed it to friends. "He talks to me like a father," he said. "I shall not answer this letter until I have won him a great victory."

But victories would have to wait, Hooker knew, until he had reorganized the demoralized army at Falmouth. To everyone's astonishment, Fighting Joe quickly proved himself an excellent administrator. He mandated new sanitary rules, requiring the use of proper latrines and making the troops clean up and air out their fetid huts. He cut desertions by setting up a liberal system of furloughs. He vastly improved the hospital services.

Hooker also won the men's hearts by forcing the army's vast but laggard supply corps to provide fresh vegetables, mostly onions and potatoes, twice a week. Most surprising of all, he ordered that fresh, chewable bread be delivered at least four times a week, to supplant the usual issue of maggot-infested, tooth-breaking hardtack.

Hooker also insisted that the men exercise. He called for long sessions of close-order drill, and he livened the drill with frequent parades, which he reviewed sitting ramrod straight on a large white horse. Within weeks of Fighting Joe's arrival, a Wisconsin officer wrote home that "the army is in excellent condition as far as the health and spirit of the men are concerned." A Maine captain recalled that "never was the magic influence of a single man more clearly shown."

Hooker also reorganized the army's command structure, dismantling the huge, unwieldy "grand divisions" invented by General Burnside and cutting them up into seven more-maneuverable corps, their commanders all reporting directly to him. To distinguish the corps, Hooker's able chief of staff, Brigadier General Daniel Butterfield, devised a system of badges—various geometric shapes cut from colored cloth—for the men and officers to wear on their caps or hats. The shapes indicated the corps, and the color designated the division within it. A red diamond, for example, was worn by soldiers of the 1st Division of the III Corps, a white diamond by those of the corps' 2d Division.

The emblems did wonders for morale, the men wearing them "like badges of honor." More vitally, the varicolored lozenges and stars and crosses would allow officers to immediately tell even in the heat of battle which units soldiers belonged to.

Even more important for the future, Hooker created a separate cavalry corps modeled on the wide-ranging Confederate legions headed by the famous Major General James Ewell Brown "Jeb" Stuart. Previously, the Union horsemen had been dispersed among the various infantry corps and divisions. Now all Federal troopers would be grouped in an independent three-division corps ready and able to act on its own.

To command the new Federal cavalry, Hooker named Brigadier General George Stoneman, a West Point classmate of Stonewall Jackson's. Stoneman shared some of Jackson's intensity if not his furious combativeness. And if less dashing than Stuart, he would soon be ready to throw a division of his horsemen against the enemy in the

first full-scale all-cavalry battle in the East.

Contemplating his reforms, Hooker was immensely pleased with himself and the situation. He had "the finest army on the planet," he told Lincoln, boasting to the president that it was not a question of whether he would take Richmond, but only when.

Lee's Confederates, camped about three miles away on the other side of the Rappahannock, were in far less happy shape. Fiercely proud of their victory at Fredericksburg, the troops were still freezing and half starved. An officer of a Louisiana brigade reported that of his 1,500 men 400 had no shoes and a great many were also bereft of shirts, socks, and blankets. As for overcoats, they were so rare as to be "objects of curiosity."

Food was desperately scarce, in part because a drought the previous summer had stunted crops. Also at fault were the Southern rail lines that, badly overstrained by the war, struggled to deliver what supplies there were. Shipments were so sporadic that Lee's commissary officers were forced to cut the meat ration to a miserable four ounces of bacon per man per day, and to reduce the sugar ration as well. Vegetables were so scarce that to avoid scurvy Lee ordered each regiment "to send a daily detail to gather sassafras buds, wild onions, lamb's quarter and poke sprouts." Some of Lee's less squeamish troops began to shoot and cook rats—which one of them optimistically claimed "tasted like young squirrel."

Almost as bad from a military point of view, the army's draft horses were in deplorable shape for lack of fodder, long since exhausted in northern Virginia. The animals would have perished by the thousands if forced to pull wagons and guns along muddy roads. This would have left the Confederate army, as Lee said, "destitute of the means of

transportation." In short, Lee could not for the moment move his army anywhere, to attack or even shift defensive positions.

Still more critical was a shortage of manpower. At full strength Lee's army was a scant two-thirds the size of Hooker's, and in February he was forced to send Longstreet marching off to southern Virginia with the 13,000 men of John Bell Hood's and George E. Pickett's divisions. A Union corps, it was reported, was moving down the Potomac, which might mean an attack on Richmond. Even after this danger proved illusory, Longstreet stayed south to collect supplies for the army.

These thronging problems made the tightly self-controlled Lee unusually ill tempered and snappish. When his daughter Agnes suggested she come for a visit, Lee wrote back saying, "The only place I am to be found is in camp, and I am so cross now that I am not worth seeing anywhere."

Lee did make one brilliant move, however, during the long winter. His artillery, especially with Longstreet gone, was badly outgunned by the Federals. Hooker had more than 410 cannon, Lee only about 220—and many of the Confederate pieces were old smoothbores. To try to make up for the shortfall, Lee consolidated his field pieces in independent battalions of about 16 guns each, or four batteries. This way he could order scores of guns massed quickly at any crucial spot to blast away at the enemy. In the great battle to come, Lee would use his ability to concentrate artillery fire with devastating effect.

The two armies, both engrossed in solving their various problems, had little contact through the late winter except for an occasional skirmish. Until, that is, the cavalry battle near Kelly's Ford.

The raid was the brainchild of Brigadier General William W. Averell, a division commander in General Stoneman's new Federal cavalry corps. In mid-March, with the roads firming up, Averell thought it would be a fine idea to test out his troopers by riding westward up the Rappahannock, crossing at Kelly's Ford, and driving away some Confederate horsemen known to be in the area.

Averell was also responding to a Confederate challenge. The leader of the Rebel cavalry regiments near Kelly's Ford was Brigadier General Fitzhugh Lee, a nephew of Robert E. Lee, whom Averell had known at West Point. A rival then—both were superb horsemen—Fitz Lee had recently led a sharp little raid across the river and taken 150 Federal cavalrymen prisoner. He had also left a note daring Averell to "return my visit." If he did, Averell was to bring along a sack of coffee, a rare luxury for the Confederates though plentiful in Union commissaries.

Averell mustered six regiments of Union horsemen and parts of two others, about 3,000 men in all, plus a battery of horse artillery. With the 4th New York Cavalry in the lead, the Federal force reached Kelly's Ford early on the morning of March 17.

At first the raid did not go well. Scanning the far bank, the New Yorkers spotted a spiked wooden barrier blocking the road. To help smash the obstacle, 20 dismounted troopers from the 16th Pennsylvania came up armed with axes and waded into the frigid river water. They were immediately driven back, however, by heavy fire from the Confederate defenders.

With that, Averell brought up two guns, which began blasting away at the Rebels. Under cover of the artillery fire, Lieutenant Simeon Brown and a detachment of 18 Rhode Island troopers rode into the ford, followed by the ax-wielding Pennsylvanians. Only three of Brown's brave Rhode Islanders made, it to the far shore, but they and the Pennsylvanians somehow managed to reach the barrier and hack it apart. In minutes, more men of the 1st Rhode Island had made it across and scattered the enemy pickets.

Fitz Lee, hearing of the fracas, swiftly rode forward from his headquarters at Culpeper, deploying his 800 troopers between Kelly's Ford and Brandy Station, a small town on the Orange & Alexandria Railroad that Lee assumed was Averell's target. As his skirmishers rode forward, however, Lee found to his surprise that Averell's men were mostly in defensive positions a mere mile and a half from the ford. Averell had decided not to charge blindly ahead into an all-out fight with Lee and his seasoned horsemen.

Averell also faced—though he did not know it—Stuart himself and the star artillerist Major John Pelham, the hero of a half-dozen previous battles, including Antietam and Fredericksburg, for his daring use of his guns.

Stuart and Pelham, who by chance had both been nearby on separate errands, arrived just as Fitz Lee ordered one squadron of the 3d Virginia Cavalry to dismount and fire at some Federals positioned behind a stone wall. The rest of the regiment, backed by the 5th Virginia, made a mounted charge.

Pelham, dashing up on his borrowed mount, joined in the charge of the 5th as the troopers were pouring through a gap in the stone wall. Just then a Federal shell exploded with a huge roar just above Pelham's head, hurling him from his horse. He lay on the ground apparently unhurt, his eyes open and his heart beating. But a fragment from the shell had pierced the back of his head. Car-

ried to Culpeper, the much loved and admired Pelham died only moments after surgeons located the tiny wound. His body, taken to Richmond, lay in state in the capitol before being returned to his native Alabama. "The gallant Pelham," Jeb Stuart said, "will be mourned by the nation."

Moments after Pelham was wounded, the Federals countercharged and retook the stone wall. At the same time Colonel Alfred N. Duffié, Averell's boldest subordinate, made a charge of his own, his troopers hurling back the Confederates and killing or capturing a good number of Lee's Virginians.

These successes, though, did not tempt Averell to pursue very far, and when he heard from a prisoner that he faced Jeb Stuart as well as Fitz Lee he "deemed it proper to withdraw." Bugles sounded recall and the Federals made their way back across the Rappahannock. Behind him Averell left a sack of coffee and a brief note: "Dear Fitz. Here's your coffee. Here's your visit. How do you like it?"

This rousing set-to took place on Saint Patrick's Day. Less than three weeks later, on the Easter weekend, President Lincoln sailed down the Potomac to visit Hooker and spur him on. The president was beset by criticism of his handling of the war, the roads were drying out, and Hooker had boasted that his force was ready.

To impress and entertain his guest, Hooker staged a pair of soul-stirring shows. First, 15,000 men of General Stoneman's Cavalry Corps paraded out on a large field for Lincoln to review. A couple of days later Hooker mustered two-thirds of his entire force for what was known ever after as the Grand Review— 85,000 infantrymen marching past the smiling president in massed formations two companies wide, battle-torn flags whipping in the breeze. The huge parade was, one officer said, "the most magnificent military pageant ever witnessed on this continent."

Hooker also had welcome news for the president. In a matter of days he would launch his great campaign. First to move would be General Stoneman with 10,000 of his troopers. They would ride well up the Rappahannock, cross that river, then ford the Rapidan and fall on the rear of Robert E. Lee's army, cutting its supply routes and communications.

This initial move was thwarted when torrential rains once again pelted down, swelling the rivers and making the upstream fords impassable for almost two weeks. But by April 25 Hooker had elaborated a new and still bolder plan. Three of his infantry corps would follow the cavalry upstream, cross at several fords, and double back toward a country crossroads called Chancellorsville, thus enveloping Lee's far left. At the same time other corps would remain around Fredericksburg to threaten Lee's right flank or move where they were needed most.

The plan, Hooker wrote the president, could hardly fail. His main fear, he said, was that Robert E. Lee and his army would at the first show of force retreat so fast as to "escape being seriously crippled." It was a curious notion to have about an enemy general who never before had panicked, or fled, or done anything but fight tooth and nail. This Lincoln knew, and Hooker's blithe confidence worried him.

But this time Lee's army, still lacking Longstreet's two divisions, numbered only about 60,000 men, less than half the size of the huge Federal force of 130,000. It remained to be seen what Lee would do as Fighting Joe sent six of his corps stepping out toward their first objectives on the morning of April 27.

CHRONOLOGY

December 13, 1862	*Battle of Fredericksburg*
January 26, 1863	*Hooker assumes command of the Army of the Potomac*
March 17	*Battle of Kelly's Ford*
April 5-10	*Lincoln visits Hooker; Grand Review of Federal army*
April 27	*Army of the Potomac begins to move*
April 28-29	*Federals cross Rappahannock at upper fords and south of Fredericksburg*
April 30	*Hooker's main force converges on Chancellorsville; Confederates move west to meet the threat*
May 1-4	*Battle of Chancellorsville*
May 1	*Hooker pushes east, then orders a recall*
May 2	*Jackson flanks the Federals and rolls up their right*
May 3	*Stuart renews attack; Hooker falls back north; Federals take Marye's Heights; Sedgwick repulsed at Salem Church*
May 4	*Lee turns on Sedgwick; Hooker decides to withdraw*
May 5-6	*Federals recross the Rappahannock*
May 10	*Death of Jackson*

ORDER OF BATTLE

ARMY OF NORTHERN VIRGINIA   (Confederate)

Lee   60,000 men

First Corps (Longstreet with Hood's and Pickett's divisions detached)

McLaws' Division	Anderson's Division
Wofford's Brigade	*Wilcox's Brigade*
Kershaw's Brigade	*Mahone's Brigade*
Semmes' Brigade	*Wright's Brigade*
Barksdale's Brigade	*Posey's Brigade*
	Perry's Brigade

Cavalry Stuart

Hampton's Brigade
F. Lee's Brigade
W. H. F. Lee's Brigade
W. E. Jones' Brigade

Second Corps Jackson

A. P. Hill's Division	Rodes' Division	Early's Division	Colston's Division
Heth's Brigade	*O'Neal's Brigade*	*Gordon's Brigade*	*Paxton's Brigade*
McGowan's Brigade	*Doles' Brigade*	*Smith's Brigade*	*J. R. Jones' Brigade*
Thomas' Brigade	*Colquitt's Brigade*	*Hoke's Brigade*	*Warren's Brigade*
Archer's Brigade	*Iverson's Brigade*	*Hays' Brigade*	*Nicholls' Brigade*
Lane's Brigade	*Ramseur's Brigade*		
Pender's Brigade			

ARMY OF THE POTOMAC   (Federal)

Hooker   130,000 men

I Corps Reynolds

1st Division Wadsworth	2d Division Robinson	3d Division Doubleday
Phelps' Brigade	*Root's Brigade*	*Rowley's Brigade*
Cutler's Brigade	*Baxter's Brigade*	*Stone's Brigade*
Paul's Brigade	*Leonard's Brigade*	
Meredith's Brigade		

II Corps Couch

1st Division Hancock	2d Division Gibbon	3d Division French
Caldwell's Brigade	*Sully's Brigade*	*Carroll's Brigade*
Byrnes' Brigade	*Owen's Brigade*	*Hays' Brigade*
Zook's Brigade	*Hall's Brigade*	*MacGregor's Brigade*
Brooke's Brigade		

III Corps Sickles

1st Division Birney	2d Division Berry	3d Division Whipple
Graham's Brigade	*Carr's Brigade*	*Franklin's Brigade*
Ward's Brigade	*Revere's Brigade*	*Bowman's Brigade*
Hayman's Brigade	*Mott's Brigade*	*Berdan's Brigade*

V Corps Meade

1st Division Griffin	2d Division Sykes	3d Division Humphreys
Barnes' Brigade	*Ayres' Brigade*	*Tyler's Brigade*
McQuade's Brigade	*Burbank's Brigade*	*Allabach's Brigade*
Stockton's Brigade	*O'Rorke's Brigade*	

VI Corps Sedgwick

1st Division Brooks	2d Division Howe	3d Division Newton	Light Division Burnham
Brown's Brigade	*Grant's Brigade*	*Shaler's Brigade*	
Bartlett's Brigade	*Neill's Brigade*	*Browne's Brigade*	
Russell's Brigade		*Wheaton's Brigade*	

XI Corps Howard

1st Division Devens	2d Division Von Steinwehr	3d Division Schurz
Von Gilsa's Brigade	*Buschbeck's Brigade*	*Schimmelfennig's Brigade*
McLean's Brigade	*Barlow's Brigade*	*Krzyzanowski's Brigade*

XII Corps Slocum

1st Division Williams	2d Division Geary
Knipe's Brigade	*Candy's Brigade*
Ross' Brigade	*Kane's Brigade*
Ruger's Brigade	*Greene's Brigade*

Cavalry Corps Stoneman

1st Division Pleasonton	2d Division Averell	3d Division Gregg
Davis' Brigade	*Sargent's Brigade*	*Kilpatrick's Brigade*
Devin's Brigade	*McIntosh's Brigade*	*Wyndham's Brigade*

Reserve Cavalry Brigade Buford

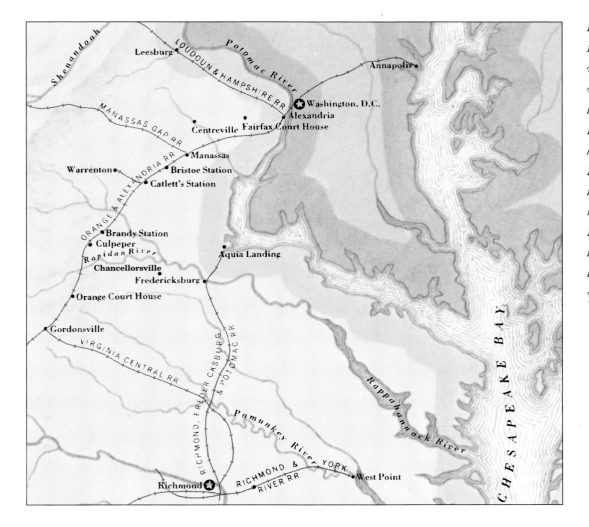

Following the Battle of Antietam in September 1862, Robert E. Lee's Army of Northern Virginia withdrew southward, deploying in two separate wings near Winchester and Culpeper. In November the new commander of the Union's Army of the Potomac, Major General Ambrose Burnside, shifted his forces east from Warrenton, intending to seize Fredericksburg and descend on a direct route south to capture Richmond. Lee matched the Federal movements in time to turn Burnside back in the first Battle of Fredericksburg in December. Both armies then went into winter camp on opposite sides of the Rappahannock River to await the return of warmer weather and a renewal of the fight.

PRESIDENT ABRAHAM LINCOLN

On January 26, 1863, President Lincoln relieved General Burnside and placed General Hooker in command of the Army of the Potomac. Lincoln's letter to the new commander was intended as a sober reminder of the challenges that lay ahead. Though well aware of Hooker's penchant for intrigue, the president hoped the new commander would use his energy and organizational skills to restore the army's flagging morale in time for the spring campaign.

I have placed you at the head of the Army of the Potomac. Of course, I have done this upon what appear to me to be sufficient reasons. And yet I think it best for you to know that there are some things in regard to which, I am not quite satisfied with you. I believe you to be a brave and skilful soldier, which, of course, I like. I also believe you do not mix politics with your profession, in which you are right. You have confidence in yourself, which is a valuable, if not an indispensable quality. You are ambitious, which, within reasonable bounds, does good rather than harm. But I think that during Gen. Burnside's command of the Army you have taken counsel of your ambition, and thwarted him as much as you could, in which you did a great wrong to the country, and to a most meritorious and honorable brother officer. I have heard, in such a way as to believe it, of your recently saying that both the Army and the Government needed a Dictator. Of course it was not *for* this, but in spite of it, that I have given you the command. Only those generals who gain successes can set up dictators. What I now ask of you is military success, and I will risk the dictatorship. The government will support you to the utmost of its ability, which is neither more nor less than it has done and will do for all commanders. I much fear that the spirit which you have aided to infuse into the Army, of criticising their Commander, and withholding confidence from him, will now turn upon you. I shall assist you, as far as I can, to put it down. Neither you, nor Napoleon, if he were alive again, could get any good out of an army while such a spirit prevails in it.

And now, beware of rashness. Beware of rashness, but with energy, and sleepless vigilance, go forward, and give us victories.

Hooker assembled his personal staff for a group portrait by photographer Timothy O'Sullivan. The senior officers, seated in front, are (from left) Colonel Henry F. Clarke (chief commissary), General Henry J. Hunt (chief of artillery), Colonel Rufus Ingalls (chief quartermaster), Hooker, and General Daniel Butterfield (chief of staff).

PRIVATE EDWARD W. STEFFAN

121ST PENNSYLVANIA INFANTRY, ROWLEY'S BRIGADE

Writing to his brother in February 1863, Private Steffan reflected the cynicism pervading the Army of the Potomac's rank and file in the wake of Burnside's disastrous assault on Fredericksburg and the subsequent Mud March. Promoted to sergeant, Steffan was captured during the campaign for Petersburg in October 1864 and spent the last months of the war in a Confederate prison camp.

This change in Army Commanders of which you speak, is it for better or worse? If I am not sadly mistaken it is the latter. I think the best change that they actually could make would be to exchange the pen for the sword and bayonet. The simple sentence, "The Pen is mightier than the Sword" would be very appropriate in this squabble which is the only term that can properly be attached to it. I once had an idea that they were making good progress, but that idea has since faded away entirely. They are now only slaughtering men for mere amusement it would seem. All those who participated in the Fredericksburg battle will testify to this. Hooker will now try his hand and I suppose make another blunder if even it is not. To be *stuck in mud* it may be something similar but I scarcely think that our *small* Company will participate in it. As you say McClellan is the man who has gained the entire confidence of the soldiers, and you would still think more so if you were down here among the old troops. The Reserves are and all swore that if they had been taken across the Rappahannock in this last move they would never have come over again, and I believe it too.

Hooker ordered each of the seven corps in his army to adopt distinctive insignia to be worn on the soldiers' caps as a ready means of identification. Designed by General Butterfield, the badges proved both utilitarian and a boost to morale. The three insignia above represent (from left) II Corps, I Corps, and V Corps.

Edwin Forbes, an artist working for Frank Leslie's Illustrated Newspaper, sketched Sergeant Major William J. Jackson in a Federal camp near Fredericksburg. Jackson's unit, the 12th New York, was among dozens of "two-year" regiments whose terms of service were due to expire in early May. The loss of these veteran soldiers was a matter of grave concern to Northern leaders.

"Hooker's popularity shows how closely the stomach and emotions are allied."

PRIVATE
JOHN W. HALEY
17TH MAINE INFANTRY,
HAYMAN'S BRIGADE

A 23-year-old mill worker from Maine, Haley had been in service for five months when Hooker took command. Haley recorded his impressions in a wartime diary (below, right)—notes he later reworked into a colorful memoir. Though skeptical of Hooker's bombastic pronouncements, Haley shared his comrades' appreciation of the army's improved rations.

And now it is "Fighting Joe" Hooker who is called upon to show his skill. With his habitual modesty, he has remarked that with a certain force he could "drive the Rebels to Hell or anywhere else." The administration's plan doesn't involve so extensive a campaign, only that we go as far as Richmond. General Hooker is at last in the position he has so long coveted (according to report).

Within a week a change was perceptible in our cuisine. Our larders began to fill and we had no occasion to patronize the sutlers, who no doubt wish Joe Hooker in the sultry locality to which he threatens to drive the Rebels.

Not only has the quantity increased, but the quality has improved and we enjoy all the variety afforded by government, of which we have previously been defrauded. Now we have more than we could possibly eat—no thanks to sutlers or commissaries. General Hooker had immense bakeries built, and in a few days we were enjoying delicious hot loaves of bread, the mere sight of which is better than a pound of the measly, wormy hardtack we had been served so long. Besides this, there are beef (fresh and salt), pork, beans, peas, rice, and potatoes, as well as other vegetables, pickles, candles, coffee, sugar, and condiments of all sorts, with the exception of Worcestershire sauce. Our diet is generous and our spirits rise high in consequence. We no longer desire death, nor suffer a weakness that makes the slightest labor a burden. General Hooker once remarked that "men who are fed well will fight well." This is excellent logic, and we like the first part of it immensely. Hooker's popularity shows how closely the stomach and emotions are allied.

The huts of a Federal winter encampment sprawl across a hillside near Stoneman's Switch, a mile from Fredericksburg. The group gathered in the foreground of Andrew J. Russell's photograph includes portly Chaplain Jeremiah Shindel of the 110th Pennsylvania, whose hat bears the white diamond insignia of the III Corps.

CAPTAIN ALEXANDER C. HASKELL
STAFF, BRIGADIER GENERAL SAMUEL McGOWAN

While Hooker's Yankees enjoyed their plentiful rations, Lee's Army of Northern Virginia was forced to get by on far less. Haskell, assistant adjutant general for McGowan's South Carolina brigade, was one of seven brothers who fought for the South. He served until the end of the war despite four wounds, one of which cost him his left eye.

That winter was probably the most dreary and miserable we had. It was the first picture the world had of the magnitude and the horrors of our strife, and took our people and our government unprepared. The suffering from cold, hunger, and nakedness was intense and widespread. There were thousands on duty in the perpetual snow and mud, without shoes, often no blanket, hardly any overcoats, and many without coats, nothing often but a ragged homespun shirt. Many received aid from home, but much of this was lost by defective transportation, and for the poor fellows from across the Mississippi nothing could come. . . .

It was at this date the Confederate Congress law was in force, taking away from officers the right to buy from the Commissary rations for their servants, allowing a ration for the officers alone. I went, one day, quite a distance to General Lee's Head Quarters on business. He chanced to come out just as I was taking my leave, and as it was the hour for dinner he politely insisted on my sharing the meal. Of course I could not decline. Entering the tent, there was before us a crude board table with camp stools around it; on it a beautiful glass dish of "Virginia Pickles" sent by some hospitable Virginia lady; the balance of the dinner was a plate of corn bread, or "pones," and a very small piece of boiled bacon. The grand old General said Grace, and as we took our seats he raised the knife saying, "Mike (that was the name of his faith-

ful Irish attendant) has harder work than we have in Quarters, and must be fed," he cut off a thick slice for Mike and, having laid it on the side of the dish, proceeded to help the rest of us and, finally, himself to each a slice but a fraction of Mike's.

LIEUTENANT COLONEL HILARY A. HERBERT
8TH ALABAMA INFANTRY, WILCOX'S BRIGADE

In the winter of 1862–1863, soldiers of the opposing forces encamped along the Rappahannock routinely traded coffee, tobacco, and newspapers and occasionally visited friends in enemy lines. Despite orders forbidding it, many commanders, such as prewar lawyer Hilary Herbert, saw little harm in the practice.

To Wilcox's brigade was assigned the duty of protecting . . . the line of that river for about two and one-half miles, from Taylor's house near Fredericksburg to Scott's dam up the stream. The 8th occupied about the centre of this line, and was encamped on the hill south of and over-looking "Banks' Ford." We were in plain sight of the enemy. A battery of two guns, not more than three-quarters of a mile off, could have fired a shell into my camp at any moment during the winter; so too the enemy's pickets and ours, occupying as they did opposite banks of the narrow river, could at any time have killed each other. But we were now real soldiers on both sides and well knew that mere picket shooting helped neither side and was only murder; so by a sort of tacit consent we dropped everything of the kind. Pickets talked with and bantered each other across the river. One day a Yankee came down to the other side of Banks' Ford to water his horse and called out to one of my men, also on picket duty:

"Hello, Johnny, have you any horses over there?"

"Yes, lots of them," was the reply.

"We were now real soldiers on both sides and well knew that mere picket shooting helped neither side and was only murder."

"Well, bring one over; I can beat you running."

"Well," said the reb, "you ought to, for you have had more practice."

I often rode up and down that river, as officer of the day, during that period and had the Federal pickets on the other side to salute me, and of course always politely acknowledged the salute. But the extreme friendliness of our soldiers on picket brought its embarrassments with it. I remember one night David Buell, then Ordnance Sergeant of the regiment, and afterwards my law partner and brother-in-law, came to me and said:

"Colonel, my brother Seth is across the river and I want to see him."

Buell was a New Yorker from the Valley of the Genesee, and had not been long in the South when the war began. I replied:

"Well, Buell, I have no authority to give you permission to see him."

"I know that, Colonel, (I had now been promoted to Lieutenant-Colonel) but I just wanted you to say that if I went you would not find it out."

Having no sort of doubt as to Buell's loyalty my reply was, "I do not see how I could find it out."

Buell went over to see his brother Seth, and reported to me the conversation, part of which was amusing. Seth wanted to give David some good U.S. blankets, insisting that he must need them very much. David replied, "We have plenty of good U.S. blankets captured from you—our regiment sent a wagon load of them to Richmond to save until next winter."

Decades after the war, a beech tree near Banks' Ford still bore the initials "TAS" carved in its bark by a picket of the 10th Alabama. The soldier was most likely Private Thomas A. Smith of Company H, who had recently recovered from wounds received at the Battle of Glendale in June 1862. Smith survived the remainder of the war unscathed and surrendered with Lee's forces in April 1865.

ROBERTA CARY CORBIN

In December 1862 Lieutenant General Thomas J. "Stonewall" Jackson established winter quarters at Moss Neck, a sprawling estate 10 miles southeast of Fredericksburg, transforming the quiet, stately grounds into a bustling military camp. The lady of the house, Roberta Corbin, whose husband, Private Richard Corbin, was away fighting with the 9th Virginia Cavalry, welcomed the excitement Jackson's presence brought. Later she would fondly remember that winter-long visit.

I think General Jackson remained at Moss Neck until he went to Hamilton's Crossing. Imagine the transformation of our quiet country homestead! Thousands of soldiers in sight, the hills echoing with the noises of army life, fife and drum, brisk tattoo and reveille, the sound of many axes, the crashing of great trees as they fell—all became our daily fare of strange experience. The great forests surrounding Moss Neck were literally mowed down. Almost instantly there sprang into life settlements of log huts, with here and there dotted white tents among them. The smoke curled upward from many camp fires. It was a moving scene, a panorama of busy life and activity. How the sounds of camp life haunt me still! The hum of voices, the music of the bands, especially the "Stonewall Brigade Band," stationed right in front of the house! Sometimes amid the bustle of this active life of the soldiers would steal out through the dim twilight a dirge from a band at the burial of some poor soldier whose mortal career had ended, sometimes doubtless from lack of woman's nursing. They were laid to rest far from home and mother.

I can never hear to-day that old hymn tune, "Mear," without the chill of unutterable sadness creeping over me. There were bright sides to the story, however, and many pleasant episodes. Often there would be a fine dress parade or grand review, when the whole neighborhood would come to witness the drill. As a rule, however, the ladies remained at home, for the "corduroy" roads were dreadful. The soldiers often gave the Rebel yell, and anything from "Old Jack" to a rabbit would set them off. The bad roads did not keep the homesick fellows from visiting, and all the neighbors kept open house. It was my delight to give them the treat of a good supper now and then. The clanking of spurs often mingled with music and dancing, and good old war time songs of "Lorena," "Her Bright Smile Haunts Me Still," "Ever of Thee," and other ballads filled many an evening and soothed many a lonely heart.

Now while our men were quietly resting around Moss Neck General Hooker's army was encamped at Farley Vale, home of S. Wellford Corbin, on the other side of the river, in King George County. From our garden hill could be seen their tents, and we could also hear the music of their bands. I have sat for hours listening to the fine music of those Northern bands and seeing their balloons sailing through the air. Wonderfully near they seemed! . . .

During the winter I had ample opportunity to see and know some of our most distinguished officers; Generals Lee, Stuart, A. P. and D. H. Hill, and others. Often seated by my window, I saw General Lee ride by like a crusader of old, General Stuart with his plumes waving in the wind, Von Borcke upon his huge horse (selected on account of his immense size), and other distinguished personages. I became well acquainted with General Jackson. I saw him almost every day. He and the old Sorrel and "Uncle Jim" were most familiar object[.] Uncle Jim was his well-known body servant, and the little sorrel his much-used steed. General Jackson was not only a great soldier but a man as loving and as tender as a woman in his sympathies and interests. "The bravest are the tenderest, the loving are the daring." He was very fond of children, especially of little Jane Wellford Corbin, our only child, who was at this time about five years of age, winning in her ways, and the pet and darling of the whole staff. Indeed, she was beloved by all our army friends. General Jackson would send for her to come to the office and see him in the mornings. She would play there for hours at a time. She would sit on the floor, cut paper dolls, and entertain the General with her childish prattle.

One favorite amusement of his as well as of hers was her folding a piece of paper and cutting a long string of dolls all joined together in ranks which she called her "Stonewall Brigade." I can imagine a smile and a merry twinkle in his eyes as he scanned these miniature soldiers, funny little bow-legged fellows they were. I have some of them now between the leaves of my old Bible. I am sure any of the old veterans would laugh to see their diminutive representatives.

Stonewall Jackson's forage cap, a gift from his wife, Anna, bears a band of gold braid believed to have been attached after his death. The original cap band (lower left) so displeased the general that he removed it. "I like simplicity," he wrote his wife. Jackson gave the braid to little Jane Corbin (above); she died from scarlet fever the morning after the general left his winter quarters at Moss Neck.

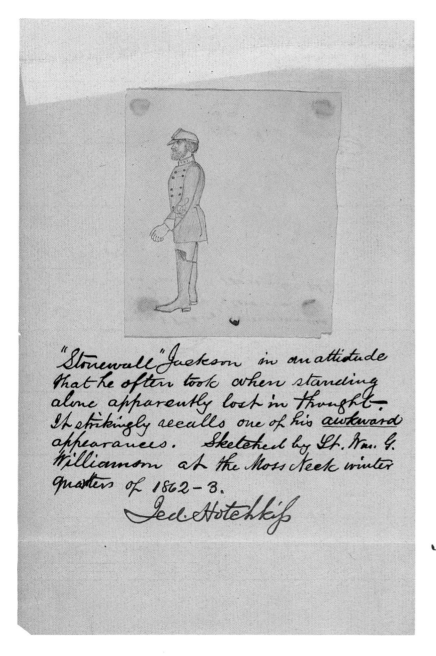

"Stonewall" Jackson in an attitude that he often took when standing alone apparently lost in thought. It strikingly recalls one of his *awkward* appearances. Sketched by Lt. Wm. G. Williamson at the Moss Neck winter quarters of 1862-3.

Jed. Hotchkiss

Stonewall Jackson strikes a pensive pose in a sketch by Lieutenant William G. Williamson, an engineer on Jackson's staff. The drawing, made during the winter of 1862–1863, was later annotated by Jedediah Hotchkiss, Jackson's cartographer.

Janie particularly admired the new military cap with its broad gilt band, not long before sent to the General by Mrs. Jackson, and she also admired the new uniform which I have heard was given to him by Gen. J. E. B. Stuart, which was worn the day of the battle of Fredericksburg, making him thus unconsciously a target for the enemy. One day he took the end of his pen knife, and, ripping the band from the cap, he pinned it round the child's hair like a coronet. He said: "Janie, it suits a little girl like you better than it does an old soldier like me." She came running in, her eyes sparkling, to show it to mother and to tell what he said. Afterwards she wore it in the same ornamental way when she was dressed for the evening. Regally she wore her crown: the gold of the band blended with the gold in her hair. Dear little girl, we did not dream that for this gift of General Jackson her name would become historic. The incident has been mentioned in many a history as an evidence of his great, loving heart and regard for little children.

LIEUTENANT THOMAS F. GALWEY
8TH OHIO INFANTRY, CARROLL'S BRIGADE

Hooker's decision to host a grand celebration on Saint Patrick's Day of 1863 met with enthusiastic approval from the thousands of Irish Americans serving in the Army of the Potomac, among them 17-year-old Lieutenant Thomas Galwey. Like Irish brigade commander Thomas Meagher, Galwey was a zealous member of the Fenian Brotherhood—an organization of militant Irish nationalists that maintained a circle within Hooker's army.

The day dawns clear and pleasant. General Meagher's headquarters are a sight. An arbor of cedar and pine branches has been constructed in front of his tent. This arbor forms a sort of porch or vestibule to the tent. At either side of the porch stands a table with an immense pile of cakes. In the middle, elevated on a pedestal, is a huge tub made of pork barrels and painted green. It is surrounded with a festoon of flowers and *shamrogs*. This tub is full of good *usquebaugh* (Irish whisky), and a ladle hangs temptingly at its side. Here the General and others of the upper-crust are hospitably seen, and they no doubt are innocent of any shyness at their introduction to the green tub. I was guest of friends in the brigade. The whisky had been spiced, and I was satisfied with one large cup draught.

It was at the race course, however, that the greatest merriment prevailed. Here were assembled officers of all ranks, including myself, and

soldiers from each corps of the army, on foot and on horseback. Nor were they all Irish. On the contrary, St. Patrick's Day seemed always in the Army of the Potomac to be of nearly as great importance as the Fourth of July among all but a few of the bluest of Yankees.

The morning was given up to the sack races, mule races, pig chases, and what not. About noon the great event of the day occurred. This was the steeple-race, and entries were made by several officers not of the Irish Brigade. By this time the concourse was crowded. Generals Hooker, Butterfield, Meade, and other senior officers were in the judges' stand. General Meagher, who presided over everything, was conspicuous in his Irish sporting gentleman's dress. He wore a white hat, blue swallow-tail coat with immense metal buttons, buckskin knee breeches and top boots, and he carried a heavy dog whip, with the air of one used to the sport.

The gentlemen who were to ride were in full jockey dress and were as jaunty as well could be. One of the most conspicuous of the jockeys, by his appearance and the easy grace of his horsemanship, was Captain

In this sketch by artist Edwin Forbes, mule jockeys attempt with varying degrees of success to negotiate a water hazard in one of several races held during the Saint Patrick's Day festivities at Falmouth, Virginia. The races were run over a course featuring five-foot-high hurdles and five-foot-wide, water-filled ditches. Hosted by the Irish Brigade, the March 17 celebration ended with a ceremony featuring prizes for the most skilled horsemen.

Jack Gossin of General Meagher's staff. Until the beginning of the war he had been an officer of Prince Lichtenstein's Hungarian Hussars of the Austrian Cavalry but, at General Meagher's invitation, had resigned to come over to America to fight under the green banner. Jack Gossin was the model of an Irish soldier-of-fortune—tall, splendidly shaped, with a pleasant if not handsome face. He was a fine horseman, yet withal something of a fop. He wore a green silk vest, with white sleeves, a green skull cap, white breeches, and top boots. He won the first race, riding General Meagher's own white horse and taking the jumps in

"St. Patrick's Day seemed always in the Army of the Potomac to be of nearly as great importance as the Fourth of July among all but a few of the bluest of Yankees."

grand style amid shouts of applause from all sides. The next race was won by Count "Somebody or Other," an officer of the 4th Regular Artillery. And so it went on until towards dark.

In the meantime General Hooker became uneasy at the assembling of so large a body of men, far away from their commands. An alarm was sounded. The report spread far and near through the immense throng of unarmed officers and soldiers, that the enemy was preparing to attack. Some had the report one way and some another. Meanwhile from all sides came the clear tones of bugle and rattle of drums, and within a few minutes we were all on the way back to our various camps. The enemy did not attack, however.

LIEUTENANT JACOB B. COOKE
1ST RHODE ISLAND CAVALRY, DUFFIÉ'S BRIGADE

The fine showing of General William Averell's troopers in the clash at Kelly's Ford on March 17, 1863, did much to lift the spirits of the Union cavalry. Led by French-born Colonel Alfred Duffié, the 1st Rhode Island spearheaded one of the charges, sustaining 42 of the 78 Union casualties in the fight. Twenty-year-old Lieutenant Jacob Cooke came through unhurt, but later that year he was severely injured by a kick from his horse and was compelled to resign from service.

The rebel guns in front of us had remained quiet for a while when suddenly they began a rapid and annoying fire, under cover of which a column of cavalry was seen advancing in column of fours. Prisoners stated that the command was composed of the First and Fourth Virginia, seven hundred strong, including the famous Black Horse Cavalry, accompanied, if not led, by Stuart himself. The woods from which the Confederates emerged were less than a quarter of a mile distant, and a line of fence ran across the fields from the road on our right.

The rebels advanced at a trot, under fire of our two guns, which were unable to do much execution on account of defective ammunition, until they came to the fence, where they halted for a moment to allow of its being torn down by dismounted men; they then advanced, deploying into squadrons. In the meantime the First Rhode Island and Sixth Ohio had again formed on the right of the battery, in *echelon,* for the purpose of supporting it, for its capture was evidently the purpose of the Confederates. When our squadrons had been halted and dressed, for we were maneuvered as if on parade, the order was given to "Advance carbines!" As the Confederates advanced, having now changed from the trot to the gallop, our men were anxious to open fire upon them, but although there were one or two men who indulged in such cries as "Come on, come on, you sons of guns, we can't reach you there," but one man discharged his carbine, whereupon Colonel Duffié, who was sitting quietly on his horse on the right, commanded, "Steady men; don't you stir; we fix 'em; we give 'em hell!" A moment afterwards the orders were given, "Sling carbines! Draw sabres!!" Empty scabbards fell back with rattle and clang, and a line of cold steel flashed in the waning sunlight. On came the "rebs," now changed from the gallop to the charge, yelling and cheering, and firing an occasional shot from carbine or pistol. Captain Rogers, who was in command of the First Rhode Island, said to Major Farrington, "Shall I not go, Major?" "No!" replied the Major. Still we remained quiet. I turned in my saddle and looked at the men behind me. Never shall I forget their appearance. Every sabre was grasped as with a hand of iron; every eye was looking straight to the front; every knee was gripping its owner's saddle as with a vise. They

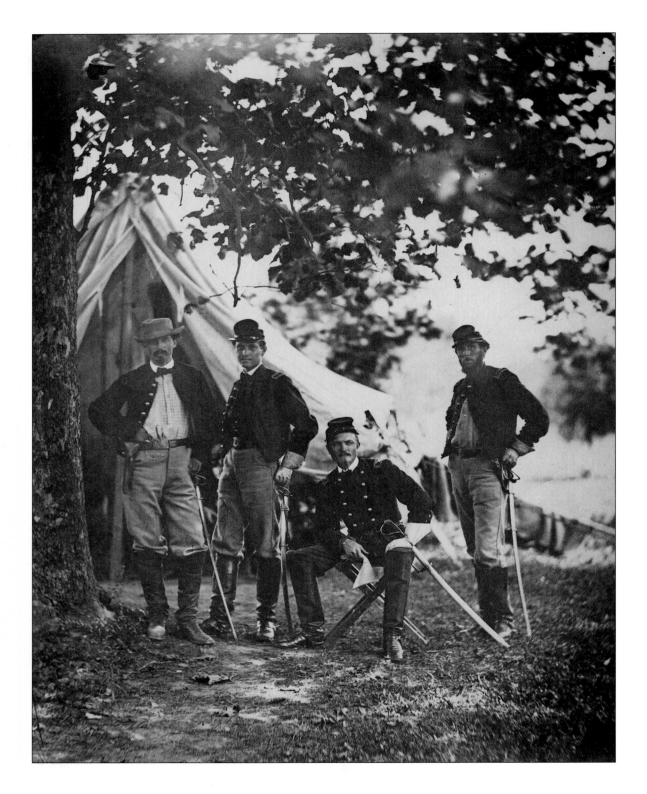

Confederate cavalry general Fitzhugh Lee (above) helped bring about the battle at Kelly's Ford by issuing a challenge to his old friend William Averell (seated, left), commander of a Union cavalry division. The two men had been classmates at West Point. Averell secured a victory of sorts, and many considered the battle a turning point in the fortunes of the Federal cavalry in the East. Whatever advantage that was gained, however, was largely tossed aside several weeks later when the bulk of Hooker's cavalry arm went off on Stoneman's ill-fated raid.

sat indeed like a veritable stone wall; they appeared as immutable as fate. Turning again to the front I could see that the first squadron of the charging "rebs" was wavering; files of men were breaking off from the right and left. I exclaimed to myself, with I am afraid a big, big D, "We've got them." Again Captain Rogers said to the Major, "Shan't I go?" Again Major Farrington replied, "Not yet; wait a minute." Waiting a few seconds longer, till the "rebs" were within a hundred feet of us, the Major said "Go!" Then came the ringing order from Rogers, "Charge!" At them we went as if shot from a catapult. But they could not stand the cold steel. They broke and ran in wild disorder, leaving a number of dead, wounded and prisoners, among the former being the gallant General Pelham. Sergeant Fitzgerald, of Troop G, First Rhode Island, was killed, shot through the heart. We pursued the fleeing "rebs" but a short distance, when we returned to our battery.

Photographed in New York following his resignation from the U.S. Military Academy, John Pelham became one of the finest artillery commanders in the Confederacy—known throughout Lee's Army as the Gallant Pelham. The death of the young major at Kelly's Ford occasioned widespread grief. General Jeb Stuart issued an order stating that Pelham's "noble nature and purity of character are enshrined as a sacred legacy in the hearts of all who knew him."

CAPTAIN WILLIAM W. BLACKFORD
Staff, Major General J. E. B. Stuart

John Pelham's comrade and friend Captain Blackford recounted the circumstances leading up to the major's death at Kelly's Ford. Though Pelham's guns were not actively engaged in the fight, he hastened to the field and joined Fitz Lee's cavalry in a countercharge against Averell's Yankee horsemen. While urging on the Southern troopers, Pelham was knocked from the saddle by an exploding shell, a fragment of which pierced his head and inflicted a mortal wound.

During the winter Pelham and I had become more intimate than we had ever been before. Our tents were next each other and we had built our stables together. Pelham had some fine horses and, like myself, liked to see them well cared for. I had five and he had three. . . .

Pelham and I had been reading aloud to each other Napier's "Peninsula War," and the day he left us to go to Orange C. H. on a little pleasure trip I marked the place we stopped and I have never had the heart to read more in it since. A sudden advance of the enemy was made just as he reached there and he went out to the field and was killed at the very opening of the engagement.

He had been wanting to go to see some friends in Orange for some time, and the night before he persuaded the General to let him go, nominally under orders to inspect the Horse Artillery. Fitzhugh made out the order and gave it to him, and fearing that Stuart would countermand it, he concluded not to wait for breakfast the next morning but to get his breakfast at the camp of a battery on the road; so he was off before daylight. General Stuart loved him like a younger brother and could not bear for him to be away from him. So the next morning at breakfast the General asked where Pelham was, and when he heard he was gone, and expected to breakfast at the camp on the road he told Fitzhugh to order him back.

These and the curious combinations of little incidents which follow show on what slight circumstances important events sometimes hang. Any one of these might have been different and Pelham would not have met his death at that time.

Fitzhugh wrote the order and the courier started. But Pelham knew the General well, and feared he would do exactly this thing; so when he got to the camp of the battery he did not tarry but took a cup of coffee and pushed on. The courier did not overtake him until he had nearly

Alfred R. Waud sketched the review of Brigadier General John Buford's cavalry division on April 9, 1863—one of a series of military pageants held during President Lincoln's visit to Hooker's army. The two officers riding behind General Buford (foreground) are Irish-born Captains Joseph O'Keeffe and Myles W. Keogh.

reached Orange C. H. late in the evening, and of course he had to go there to sleep that night. The next morning a locomotive came in from Culpeper C. H. for ammunition with news that the enemy had advanced his cavalry in some force, and Pelham, knowing Stuart would sanction such a violation of orders, jumped on the engine and returned with it. The troops had marched out to meet the enemy before he arrived and with great difficulty Pelham borrowed a horse and followed.

. . . If Pelham had stayed for breakfast at headquarters or at the horse artillery camp as he intended; if the locomotive had not come for the ammunition; if Pelham had not gotten a horse . . . Pelham would not have lost his life when he did. What a pity it was that none of these things had happened differently. His remains were sent home to Alabama, and lay in state several days in the capitol in Richmond, where many people went to see them and place flowers on the bier.

"There was evidence of the greatest enthusiasm on the part of both Officers & men, & of unbounded confidence in their Commander."

DOCTOR ANSON G. HENRY

A longtime political supporter and close friend of Abraham Lincoln's, Doctor Henry had settled in the Oregon Territory, where he served as an Indian agent and newspaper publisher. During a visit to Washington in April 1863, Henry accepted the president's invitation to accompany him on an inspection tour of General Hooker's Army of the Potomac.

We started for Genl. Hookers Head Quarters at Falmouth on Saturday the 4th inst. and returned last Friday evening. Our party consisted of the President & Lady, Myself & two friends from the Pacific, (Mr Crawford & Mr Brooks of Cal.) and at my suggestion Mr Bates of the Cabinet was invited half an hour before we started, and very gladly accepted the invitation. Mr. Bates is an old friend of mine, and is one of the purest and best men in the world. We were the Guests of Genl. Hooker at Falmouth for six whole days. . . . I feel very sure that we have got the right man at last, and one that will take his army into Richmond before the end of 90 days, but not *through* Fredericksburgh, for he will find a way to get round that strong hold, & put an overwhelming force between their army & Richmond. He has the finest army ever marshaled upon one field in the world—There were some 15,000 well mounted, & well equiped Cavalry passed in review, *three* hundred pieces of field artilery with six good Horses to each Gun, & every thing else complete, with about 150,000 of the finest looking, & best diciplined Infantry that was ever seen in one army. Handled as

I am confident they will be by Genl. Hooker, they will be able to march, not only to Richmond, but to New Orleans if necessary. There was evidence of the greatest enthusiasm on the part of both Officers & men, & of unbounded confidence in their Commander. Mr. Lincoln's visit will add intensity to their zeal and confidence. Any one that will read the Presidents letter to Genl. McClellan after the battle of Antietam, will not hesitate to say that he exhibits more Generalship than has ever been shown by any one in the field, and that if his suggestions had been carried out by McClellan the war would have been ended & "Little Mc" would have been a great Hero for Mr Lincoln would have never claimed the Glory. Now he is a dead Lion, if not a disgraced officer. Genl. Hooker showed me the letter Mr Lincoln wrote him, when he tendered him the Command, & which ought to be printed in letters of Gold—It will be read by our posterity with greater veneration for its author than has ever been shown for any thing written by Washington, or any other man. It breathes a spirit of Patriotic devotion to the country, and a spirit of frankness & candor worthy of Mr Lincolns character, and is peculiarly his own. We are all more hopeful than we have ever been.

PRIVATE WILLIAM B. SOUTHERTON
75TH OHIO INFANTRY, MCLEAN'S BRIGADE

The review of Hooker's forces on Falmouth Heights was intended to impress both friend and foe with the might of the Union war machine. Southerton, a farm boy from Athens County, Ohio, shared the opinion of many Northern observers that the Army of the Potomac would prove victorious in the coming campaign.

Our corps was marched over beyond the spur of the ridge. Each regiment, its flag rippling gracefully as it bent to the wind, advanced in a double line, a quarter of a mile long! Bands played. Men cheered. The wide cove was black with soldiers. The hard damp earth throbbed with the pounding of their marching feet. This was something special! A review of the entire Army of the Potomac!

My company was the flanking one of my regiment, my place was near the end of the line. I was close to the reviewing officers. They were all mounted on the finest horses, beautiful horses! President Lincoln, his black military cloak billowing slightly as he reached forward to adjust the reins of his horse, reminded me of a Quaker. His expression was kindly, yet firm and serious, even sad.

General Hooker, mounted on a bay, was next to the president. He beamed with satisfaction and pride as our corps marched by. His blue eyes sparkled with confidence. He held his chin up a little too high to suit me.

How proud we were of General McLean! Our regiment had bought his horse, a dappled gray. We thought the world of General McLean. General Barlow, and General Howard were there. Buglers and drummers played better than ever before. Such a great army! Thunder and lightning! The Johnnies could never whip this army!

Circling around the cove once, disbanding at the ridge, that was all there was to it. No demonstration of guarding, defending or attacking a position, maneuvers an army would be compelled to make under attack, nothing to show how orders would be given or carried out. The only order: "Fall in!"

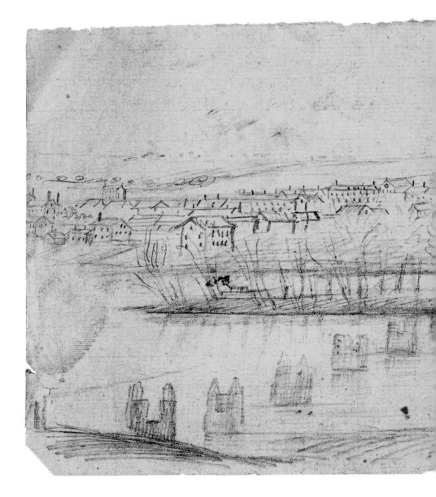

NOAH BROOKS
CORRESPONDENT, SACRAMENTO DAILY UNION

Arriving in Washington in December 1862 to cover the war for his California newspaper, Noah Brooks quickly made a reputation as one of the capital's most energetic and opinionated journalists. An outspoken admirer of Abraham Lincoln, Brooks accompanied the presidential party to Falmouth and took the opportunity to examine the war-ravaged Confederate stronghold at Fredericksburg.

The day after the cavalry review, a small party of us went down to our pickets opposite Fredericksburg to take a look at the rebels. . . .
The banks of the Rappahannock descend in abrupt terraces and steeply to the river in front of the Lacy House, and for a considerable distance up and down the stream, where the pontoon bridges were thrown across the narrow current, the banks were cut down in deep roads, and the batteries where the enormous siege guns were mounted bear upon the ruined city opposite and upon the plain below the town. The painfully famous plain, which was a slaughter pen for so many men, lies beyond and below Fredericksburg, and with a good glass we could see the ridges where the unnamed graves are made. Beyond rise the two ridges of woody hills which our forces so vainly attempted to scale upon that dreadful day and where thousands fell a useless sacrifice. The smoke from rebel camps rises peacefully from behind the ridge, and a flag of stars and bars is floating over a handsome mansion among the heights just above that stone wall where the rebels slew our men by hecatombs. Almost all else bears no sign of the enemy supposed to be lying in force on and behind the wooded ridge of hills beyond Fredericksburg. But while we look a small squadron of infantry wheel over the hill, as if on review, and then disappears again, its traitorous arms gleaming distantly in the broken sunshine as it sinks behind the hill.

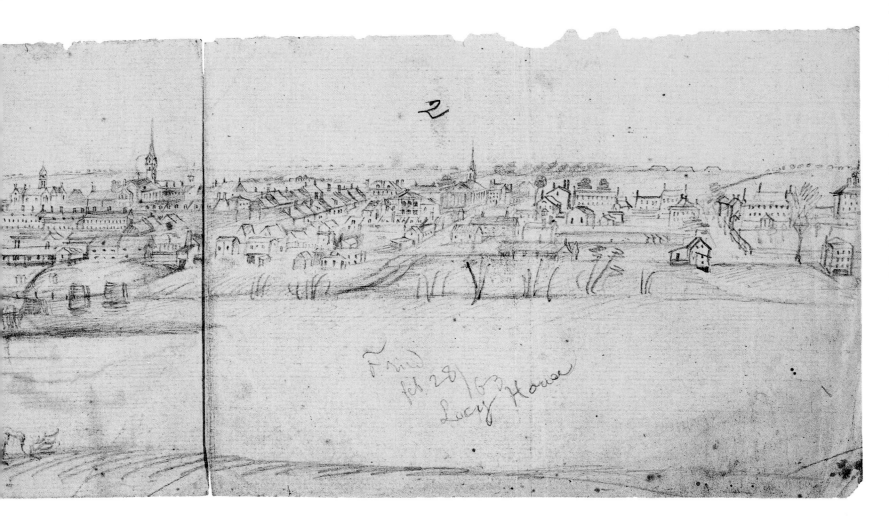

The town of Fredericksburg is well-built and ancient in appearance, but scarcely no building in sight from where we stood was free from battle scars. Bomb, shot, shell, and cannon ball have made many hideous holes in the walls of the doomed city, and even from the tall and graceful spire of one of the churches were flying the torn sheets of tin which flying shot had ripped off, and huge rents and fissures gaped from every wall. Near the river bank, which is low and sloping, a tall chimney stood solitary and alone, the house to which it once belonged having been burnt or torn down, and at its lonely fireplace two secesh pickets were toasting their shins by a cheerful fire. Presently, attracted by our little party's appearance, they got up, when I was galled to notice that while one wore the "grayback" garb of Secessia, the other was comfortably clad in a United States blue military overcoat. Federal clothes on rebel backs is no novelty, but it is never a comfortable sight

Private John Keyser of the 24th New Jersey made this sketch of Fredericksburg from a vantage point near the Lacy house—an imposing mansion that served as a Federal headquarters. Heavily damaged in the grim battle the preceding December, the town would be the scene of more fighting as Hooker attempted to force a way across the Rappahannock.

to a sensitive loyalist. They yelled at us and made menacing gestures, but we could not understand what they were at. Later in the day the wind went down and they bawled to our sentries that we had been beaten at Charleston. A rebel officer, dressed in dark clothes, with his badges on his coat collar, attended by an orderly, came down to the water's edge, doubtless to see if Uncle Abraham was of our party. Failing to see him, he bowed politely and retired.

CAPTAIN JAMES K. BOSWELL

STAFF, LIEUTENANT GENERAL THOMAS J. JACKSON

Two weeks before the armies took the field in the spring of 1863, Captain James Boswell—chief topographical engineer on Stonewall Jackson's staff—penned a letter to his aunt expressing his conviction that the Confederacy was on the verge of a great victory. On the evening of May 2, 1863, Boswell was instantly killed by the same volley that mortally wounded General Jackson; the unmailed letter was found on his body.

Hd. Qrs. 2nd Army Corps, Engr. Dept.
Near Fredericksburg, April 21st, 1863. . . .
. . . Our family has suffered very much since the commencement of this war. Fauquier has been in possession of the enemy for at least one-half of the time, during the past year, and they have committed very much excesses, and have been most tyrannical in their will; yet the spirit of the people is unbroken, and will continue so no matter how long this war may last. I was at Spring Farm about a month since; grandma, Aunt Mary, Cousin Mildred, Sister and Tom are there at present, and all in good health and spirits, though they have suffered many annoyances from the close proximity of Hooker's army; they may be considered in the lines of the enemy, though they very seldom see any of them now; the country is so entirely stripped as to hold forth no

inducement to the miserable thieves which compose the cavalry of the army of that mushroom hero. All the negroes have gone off except old Frank, two old women and a girl of 12 years. Still they seem to live quite comfortably. Grandma looks better than she has done for several years, and bears her losses without a murmur. This is the case, as far as I have been able to observe, throughout this Confederacy, everyone seems perfectly reconciled to any personal loss, so that we accomplish the one great object, whipping the Yankee cut-[throats]. . . .

The army in Va. is in the finest condition possible, and there are more men for duty than at any time last summer, despite the numerous and bloody battles which they have fought. With such a cause and with such troops, commanded by our noble Genl. Lee, with such associates in command as Jackson, Longstreet, Ewell, Hill & Hood there is not the slightest chance of failure; there is not a man in this army who is at all familiar with its numbers, and organization, who feels the slightest doubt of our ultimate triumph. The attack at Charleston, despite the immense preparation of the enemy, has proved a perfect failure, and the enemy are about to give it up in disgust. All their efforts against Vicksburg seem perfectly unavailing, and if Genl. Johnson's [Johnston] army in Tenn. is as strong as ours in Va. and will whip Rosecrantz, as we are sure to do Hooker, I doubt not that the present campaign will lead to a perfect Confederate triumph, and that we may safely conclude that this campaign will close the war. The North is evidently rapidly awakening to the folly of attempting to conquer a people who have shown the courage, endurance and heroism which have been exhibited by the people of the South, since the commencement of this war. . . . and a few more brilliant victories, such as Manassas and Fredericksburg, will I doubt not decide a majority of them to accept peace on almost any terms. . . .

. . . Since the 24th of Feby., 62, I have been constantly with [Genl. T. J. Jackson] as chief engr. of his Army Corps. During that time I have been with him in ten bloody battles and a large number of skirmishes, and have been very much exposed, but thanks to a kind Providence, have never received a wound. Strange as it may seem, not one of Genl. J's staff has ever been killed, though I doubt not they have been as much exposed as the staff officers of any Major Genl. in the army. I suppose his prayers have shielded us; for if there is a man in the world whose prayers are those of the righteous, that man is Genl. Jackson. I do not believe there is a more truly consistent Christian in the world [than] he is; and to his piety I doubt not may in a great measure be ascribed the universal success which has attended his arms.

Three officers of the 4th Georgia Infantry—(from left) Captain Howard Tinsley, Major William H. Willis, and Lieutenant Eugene A. Hawkins—posed for an ambrotype portrait shortly before the Battle of Chancellorsville. Tinsley emerged unhurt, Willis was wounded in the engagement, and Hawkins died in the Battle of the Wilderness the following year.

BRIGADIER GENERAL E. FRANKLIN PAXTON
BRIGADE COMMANDER, ARMY OF NORTHERN VIRGINIA

Nicknamed Bull for his stocky build, Paxton became one of Jackson's most trusted subordinates and, since November 1862, commander of the Stonewall Brigade. In a letter to his wife, Paxton hinted at a premonition that he would not survive his next battle. On May 3 he was killed leading his brigade against the Union line.

The roads are now in pretty good condition, and if the enemy wish to make the attack, there is, I think, no reason now for deferring it on account of the roads. But, darling, there is no telling when it will be. The future, ever a mystery, is more mysterious now than ever before. Our destiny is in the hands of God, infinite in his justice, goodness and mercy; and I feel that in such time as he may appoint he will give us the blessings of independence and peace. We are a wicked people and the chastisement which we have suffered has not humbled and improved us as it ought. We have a just cause, but we do not deserve success if those who are here spend this time in blasphemy and wickedness, and those who are at home devote their energies to avarice and extortion. Fasting and prayer by such a people is blasphemy, and, if answered at all, will be by an infliction of God's wrath, not in a dispensation of his mercy.

The future, as you say, darling, is dark enough. Though sound in health and strength, I feel that life to many of us hangs upon a slender thread. Whenever God wills it that mine pass from me, I feel that I can say in calm resignation, "Into thy hands I commend my spirit.". . . And now, darling, good-bye. When we meet again, I hope you will have a better husband—that your prayer and mine may be answered.

"I dont wish to cross that river agin for it is a hard place to tackel you can bet."

LIEUTENANT FRANK HASKELL
STAFF, BRIGADIER GENERAL JOHN GIBBON

With General Hooker's army poised to take the offensive, the Union commander was forced to adjust his plans to the vagaries of the weather. Lieutenant Haskell, a lawyer serving on the staff of the 2d Division of the II Corps, expressed a ruthless determination to vanquish the Southern forces in the coming campaign.

The mud has no bottom,—the army cannot move for some days yet at all events,—the newspapers to the contrary notwithstanding. The army is in excellent condition as far as the health and spirit of the men are concerned. I believe we shall strike some good blows when the time comes.

We can see the tents and camps of the enemy for miles, thick upon the other side of the Rappahannock,—we will disturb them soon however, and give their vile bodies to the buzzards and crows. It would give you a disagreeable feeling could you see the camps of the armies here at present. Where less than a year ago was one of the loveliest vallies human eyes ever saw, with farms and homes, hill and dale, woodland and meadow, all populous with the image of God, now is desolate and unsightly waste, without trees, fences, or plantation, and few homes,—these deserted and nearly ruined—but bristling with two mighty armies, thirsting to cut each other's throats! Thank God that the desolation of war comes no nearer to you. . . . humanity bleeds at this war,—but,—who made it? Who trampled the ensign of Peace and Security in the dust? By God's help they shall pay the penalty of their sin. May I be one of the instruments of their desolation, and punishment, and to bring it about, that the places . . . know them no more forever, and to teach such as they how sacred a thing is the Constitution, and how terrible is the wrath of the offended Republic. I could not be out of such a war as this.

PRIVATE JOHN S. ROBINSON
27TH CONNECTICUT INFANTRY, BROOKE'S BRIGADE

Not all Federal soldiers were eager for the fray, as Private Robinson revealed in an April 2, 1863, letter to his nephew. Recently returned to his company from an assignment as assistant teamster of the brigade, Robinson passed through the fight at Chancellorsville without a wound but succumbed to chronic diarrhea in a Baltimore hospital on June 18.

Newton I received your letter on the 28th of March. But i have not had time to write until today & now i will write you a few lines. I am well and harty and hope this will find you the same. I have left off driveing team. I am with my company now. We are in the same old camp yet and i hope we shall stay hear until our time is up. There is [no] excitement down hear just [now] but there may be before long for the mud is a drying up fast & it will soon bea dry enuf to march & I think they will try to cross the river when they move agane. We know we can cross but we may get drove back agane.

I dont wish to cross that river agin for it is a hard place to tackel you can bet. I hope when we move that we shall move back toards Washington. We have only two months and a half longer to [serve] where ever we go and then we shall move toards New Haven that will sute mea you can bet. I should like your pickture very much and i will send mine to you

I cannot stay to write much more this time so i will soon close my letter.

Give my respects to all and tell them i am tough as a [k]not.

From your uncle J. S. R.

Write soon

On the 23d of April (the day she was five months old) General Jackson had little Julia baptized. He brought his chaplain, the Rev. Mr. Lacy, to Mr. Yerby's, in whose parlor the sacred rite was performed, in the presence of the family, and a number of the staff-officers. The child behaved beautifully, and was the object of great interest to her father's friends and soldiers. . . .

The next Sabbath was a most memorable one to me, being the last upon which I was privileged to attend divine service with my husband on earth, and to worship in camp with such a company of soldiers as I had never seen together in a religious congregation. My husband took me in an ambulance to his headquarters, where the services were held, and on the way were seen streams of officers and soldiers, some riding, some walking, all wending their way to the place of worship. Arrived there, we found Mr. Lacy in a tent, in which we were seated, together with General Lee and other distinguished officers. I remember how reverent and impressive was General Lee's bearing, and how handsome he looked, with his splendid figure and faultless military attire. In front of the tent, under the canopy of heaven, were spread out in dense masses the soldiers, sitting upon benches or standing. The preaching was earnest and edifying, the singing one grand volume of song, and the attention and good behavior of the assembly remarkable. That Sabbath afternoon my husband spent entirely with me, and his conversation was more spiritual than I had ever observed before. He seemed to be giving utterance to those religious meditations in which he so much

MARY ANNA MORRISON JACKSON
WIFE OF LIEUTENANT GENERAL THOMAS J. JACKSON

The campaigns of 1862 and the hard winter following the Battle of Fredericksburg had separated General Jackson from his wife for a year, and he had yet to see the baby daughter born to them during that time. Eagerly anticipating their arrival in the spring of 1863, Jackson wrote, "I am beginning to look for my darling and my baby. . . ." Seen here with her daughter, Julia, in a photograph taken some years after her husband's death, Anna remembered that visit in April as the family's happiest time together.

Julia Laura Jackson's christening on April 23, 1863, at the age of five months was attended by her father's officers, who later gave her this silver mug in remembrance of the baptismal day. The mug's oval cartouche bears the engraving "Julia L. Jackson from the General Staff Officers of her Father.— Maj. Harman, Maj. Hawks, Col. Allan, Col. Pendleton, Dr. McGuire."

"It was during these last happy days that he sat for the last picture that was taken of him—the three-quarters view of his face and head—the favorite picture with his old soldiers, as it is the most soldierly-looking."

delighted. He never appeared to be in better health than at this time, and I never saw him look so handsome and noble. . . .

General Jackson did not permit the presence of his family to interfere in any way with his military duties. The greater part of each day he spent at his headquarters, but returned as early as he could get off from his labors, and devoted all of his leisure time to his visitors—little Julia sharing his chief attention and care. His devotion to his child was remarked upon by all who beheld the happy pair together, for she soon learned to delight in his caresses as much as he loved to play with her. An officer's wife who saw him often during this time wrote to a friend in Richmond that "the general spent all his leisure time in playing with the baby.". . .

It was during these last happy days that he sat for the last picture that was taken of him—the three-quarters view of his face and head—the favorite picture with his old soldiers, as it is the most soldierly-looking; but, to my mind, not so pleasing as the full-face view which was taken in the spring of 1862, at Winchester, and which has more of the beaming sunlight of his *home-look*. The last picture was taken by an artist who came to Mr. Yerby's and asked permission to photograph him, which he at first declined; but as he never presented a finer appearance in health and dress (wearing the handsome suit given him by General Stuart), I persuaded him to sit for his picture. After arrang-

Wearing the braid-trimmed uniform given him by the dapper Jeb Stuart, Stonewall Jackson sat in unaccustomed finery for a photographer at the request of his wife, Anna. Taken in the hallway of the Yerby house, the photograph became a favorite among members of Jackson's command.

Situated six and a half miles southeast of Fredericksburg, the house owned by Thomas Yerby and his family provided the setting for the nine idyllic days Jackson spent with his family in April 1863. Also known as Belle Voir, the house with its sweeping grounds had been used as a hospital during the Battle of Fredericksburg in the winter of 1862.

ing his hair myself, which was unusually long for him, and curled in large ringlets, he sat in the hall of the house, where a strong wind blew in his face, causing him to frown, and giving a sternness to his countenance that was not natural. . . .

My visit had lasted only nine days, when early on the morning of the 29th of April we were aroused by a messenger at our door saying, "General Early's adjutant wishes to see General Jackson." As he arose, he said, "That looks as if Hooker were crossing." He hurried down-stairs, and, soon returning, told me that his surmise was correct—Hooker was crossing the river, and that he must go immediately to the scene of action. From the indications he thought a battle was imminent, and under the circumstances he was unwilling for us to remain in so exposed a situation as Mr. Yerby's. He therefore directed me to prepare to start for Richmond at a moment's notice, promising to return himself to see us off if possible, and if not, he would send my brother Joseph.

After a tender and hasty good-by, he hurried off without breakfast. Scarcely had he gone, when the roar of cannons began—volley after volley following in quick succession—the house shaking and windows rattling from the reverberations, throwing the family into great panic, and causing the wildest excitement among all the occupants of the place. My hasty preparations for leaving were hardly completed when Mr. Lacy, the chaplain, came with an ambulance, saying he had been sent by General Jackson to convey his family to the railroad station as speedily as possible, in order to catch the morning train to Richmond. My brother Joseph, seeing General Jackson's need of his services, had requested that Mr. Lacy should be sent in his stead as my escort. He brought a cheerful note from my husband, explaining why he could not leave his post, and invoking God's care and blessing upon us in our sudden departure, and especially was he tender and loving in his mention of the baby.

Collision at the Crossroads

General Hooker's scheme for his attack on Robert E. Lee's Confederates was daring, complex, and Hooker was convinced, as brilliant as the battle plans of the great Napoleon himself. First he would detach a third of his army, three entire infantry corps, and send them on a wide flanking move more than 20 miles up the Rappahannock to cross at Kelly's Ford. Once across the river, the three corps would turn abruptly left and march back southeast toward Fredericksburg, fording the Rapidan River and massing around a country crossroads known as Chancellorsville, after the Chancellor house, the white-columned mansion and sometime inn that sat by the road.

At the crossroads the flanking force would meet up with Major General Darius N. Couch's II Corps, which would cross the Rappahannock after the advancing columns had cleared the downstream fords of enemy pickets. If all

....

From the buttress of the ruined railroad bridge spanning the Rappahannock at Fredericksburg, men of William A. Barksdale's Mississippi brigade pose defiantly for their enemies across the river during the informal truce before the Battle of Chancellorsville.

went well, Hooker would have more than 70,000 men poised to smash the exposed left flank of Lee's army.

To mask this huge envelopment and confuse the enemy, Hooker designed a pair of deceptions. Major General John Sedgwick would take his VI Corps along with Major General John F. Reynolds' I Corps across the Rappahannock just south of Fredericksburg and deploy as if to attack Stonewall Jackson's troops on the Confederate right. At the same time Major General Daniel E. Sickles' III Corps and a II Corps division led by Brigadier General John Gibbon would stay in their camps across the river, looking threatening— and ready to move wherever needed.

The huge maneuver began on the morning of April 27 as the three corps making the longest flanking march moved out, flags fluttering and drums beating a smart cadence. Well fed and drilled through the late winter, the men were mostly cheerful and glad to be going somewhere at last. Even the roads were in good shape, as one Connecticut soldier noted optimistically, "too wet for dust, too dry for mud."

Leading the long Federal column was the XI Corps, commanded by Major General

Oliver O. Howard, a 32-year-old West Pointer from Maine. A conscientious officer, Howard was nonetheless young and inexperienced in command. Among several of his corps' regiments that were made up largely of German immigrants he was also an object of ridicule —in part because, being a puritanical Yankee, Howard strongly disapproved of the beer and schnapps the devoted, hard-fighting volunteers thought they deserved after a tough day's work.

Behind Howard's troops came the XII Corps, led by Major General Henry W. Slocum, an older West Pointer and veteran commander. Last in line was the V Corps, commanded by Major General George G. Meade. Sleepy-eyed, dour, and often irascible, Meade was not much loved by his men either—his aides called him Old Snapping Turtle—but he was a thorough professional whose troops had attacked with skill and courage at the doomed Battle of Fredericksburg in December, punching the only hole made all day in the Confederate defenses.

As the three corps marched on, it became hot, and some of the foot-slogging troops collapsed by the side of the road. Others lightened their backbreaking 60- to 80-pound packs by flinging away coats, blankets, tents, and other gear—not thinking that heavy rains might fall later. The entire force spent the night of the 27th near Hartwood Church; by late on the 28th Howard's men had reached Mount Holly Church and had begun to cross the river at Kelly's Ford on pontoon bridges brought up by army engineers.

By morning on the 30th the three corps were across the Rapidan and were moving in tight columns down roads cut through a dark, desolate tract of second-growth pine and tangled underbrush called simply, and

ominously, the Wilderness. About noon General Meade and parts of his V Corps emerged into the large clearing at Chancellorsville, followed at about 2:00 p.m. by Slocum and later by some of Howard's troops, now bringing up the rear. The men were exhausted but proud of what they had so far accomplished and full of faith in their leader. "Since we crossed the Rappahannock in such style, fording the Rapidan shoulder deep by moonlight, Hooker's stock is rising," wrote a New York soldier to his mother.

Hooker's plan seemed to be working to perfection. With only some of Jeb Stuart's troopers and a few other Confederate skirmishers anywhere about, the roads to Fredericksburg were wide open. "This is splendid, Slocum," exclaimed General Meade. "We are on Lee's flank and he does not know it." He suggested they immediately press on and get at Lee's army.

Meade was astonished by Slocum's response. "My orders," Slocum said, "are to take up a line of battle here, and not to move forward without further orders." Evidently Hooker wanted to wait until still more troops —Couch's II Corps and Sickles' III Corps— had made it across the Rappahannock by way of the United States Ford. Hooker seemed to think that the flank march had, in effect, already won the battle. Riding up to the Chancellor house on the evening of the 30th, he proclaimed that "the operations of the last three days have determined that the enemy must either ingloriously fly" or "give us battle on our own ground, where certain destruction awaits him."

Unaware that by Hooker's account his fate was sealed, General Lee was nevertheless becoming nervous. As early as April 16 he had sensed there was "some movement in agita-

tion" in Hooker's camps, and he was deeply worried that his army, still lacking half of Longstreet's corps, was too depleted to fight off the huge Federal force.

More worrisome still as the days dragged along, Lee's scouts were unable to tell where Hooker might be preparing to strike. On April 28 Stuart reported that "a large body of infantry and artillery was passing up the river," but he could not say how big it was or where it was headed, because Federal corps, moving northwest beyond the river in wooded country, had been largely screened from view.

By early on April 29, however, Lee knew where one threat lay. The Rebel commander could easily see the Federals, General Sedgwick's VI Corps followed by Reynolds' I Corps, streaming across the Rappahannock south of Fredericksburg. Immediately the combative Major General Jubal A. Early deployed his division of Jackson's corps along the Old Richmond road and a railway embankment while his forward skirmishers fired away at the Union troops.

Soon in motion, too, was Jackson, who had been enjoying a rare visit from his wife, Anna, whom he had not seen for a year, and their five-month-old daughter, Julia, whom he had never seen before. As soon as couriers brought news of the Federal crossing, Jackson embraced Anna and the baby and arranged for them to head home. He then instantly turned to business, moving Brigadier General Robert E. Rodes' division to Early's right and ordering Major General Ambrose Powell Hill and Brigadier General Raleigh E. Colston to hurry back from their positions downriver to support Early and Rodes.

But then Sedgwick's troops, although seemingly ready to attack, unaccountably failed to move. Lee had already heard from

Stuart that about 14,000 men—it was Howard's XI Corps—had been spotted crossing
the Rappahannock the night before. Then
toward evening on the 29th couriers brought
more news: Large numbers of both Federal
cavalry and infantry had crossed the Rapidan
at Germanna and Ely's Fords. As Lee well
knew, the roads from there ran through the
Wilderness toward Chancellorsville.

Still, on the evening of the 29th, Lee was
not sure where the main threat lay and dispatched only Major General Richard H.
Anderson's division to guard the roads leading into Fredericksburg from the west. By
noon on the 30th, however, Anderson could
see the massive Federal force bearing down
on Chancellorsville. Quickly sending a warning to Lee, he deployed his division on a rise
near the Zoan and Tabernacle Churches that
offered superb fields of fire on the two main
roads heading eastward, the Plank road and
an old route called the Turnpike.

Concluding at last that the main threat was
on his left, Lee with astonishing boldness
risked everything. In the famous Special
Orders No. 121, he ordered Jackson to march
three of his divisions westward at dawn the
next day, leaving only Jubal Early's single
division to watch Sedgwick's huge host. In
addition, Major General Lafayette McLaws
was to place a single brigade on the ridge
behind Fredericksburg and march the rest
of his division with all speed after Jackson.

When all units arrived, Lee would have
about 40,000 men to face Hooker's huge
right wing of 70,000. Faced with this situation, most generals would have tried a speedy
retreat, risky as that would have been. But
Lee evidently never considered retreat for a
minute. "It must be victory or death," he
told McLaws, "for defeat would be ruinous."

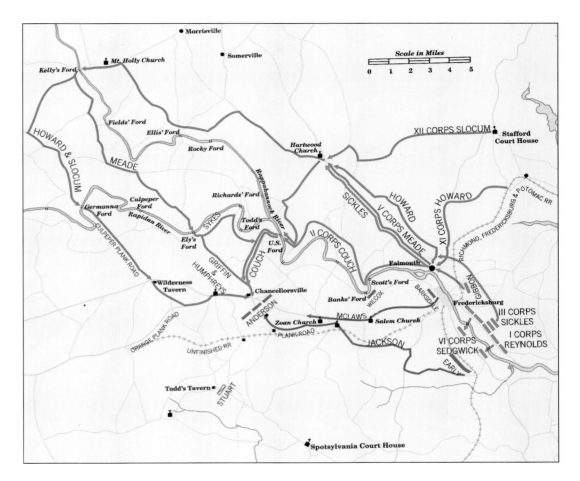

*Hooker opened the campaign by sending the V, XI, and XII Corps across the Rappahannock and Rapidan in
a wide flanking movement to get well around Lee's left. Converging on Chancellorsville, they were joined
first by the II and shortly after by the III Corps, both of which had crossed at the closer-in United States Ford.
Lee, preoccupied by the two Federal corps still remaining at Fredericksburg, was slow to see the danger at
first, sending only one division to counter the massive Federal concentration to the west. Soon, however, he
ordered most of his army under Jackson to march west, leaving only a small force to guard Fredericksburg.*

"Some of the boys looked like moving vans on legs, they took the gol-darndest loads."

PRIVATE WILLIAM B. SOUTHERTON
75TH OHIO INFANTRY, McLEAN'S BRIGADE

Part of Howard's XI Corps, the 75th Ohio Infantry left its comfortable winter encampment at dawn on April 27. Despite their months of inaction and over-loaded knapsacks, Private Southerton and the rest of the XI Corps managed to cover 14 miles that day. The next day's march would take them to Kelly's Ford, on the Rappahannock River, as Hooker's army continued its bold maneuver around Lee's left flank. After his capture at Gainesville, Florida, in August 1864, Southerton spent the rest of the war in prison.

Late in April a bright day came, a brisk wind blew, knolls were dried off, tips of pine trees glistened in the sunshine, spicy freshness of spring everywhere. But the ground was still soft and soggy. In the afternoon of April 26th, as I was catching up on the entries in my notebook, a burst of excitement drew my attention. An orderly dashed up, handed a paper to our officers, and rode on. Regiment to break camp and move out at daybreak.

What scurrying to get everything ready! Usual utensils; eight days' rations; crackers or hard bread; bacon and raw pickled pork wrapped up in paper; coffee, flour, brown sugar, salt, each tied up in a small cloth bag like a marble bag. Cartridge belts and boxes were loaded, twenty or more rounds of ammunition carried in clothing pockets. At daybreak pup tents were unbuttoned from the roof of one's shack, rolled with the gum blanket and the bundle strapped across the shoulders above the haversack.

"Gather up everything you want! We're not coming back!"

Frying pans and coffee pots clinked and rattled. Knapsacks were stuffed with extra clothing, including sometimes an overcoat. Some of the boys looked like moving vans on legs, they took the gol-darndest loads. Including the rifle, each man carried from sixty to eighty pounds. Some tucked away a prized daguerreotype, a breast-pin, a pocket knife. I hung onto my notebook and metal pencil. And my watch went down into my deepest pocket.

It was about 5:30. The world was taking on the peaceful dawn-look. My corps went out first. A few pieces of artillery lumbered past, then my regiment started out. Harness creaked as mules lunged and strained to pull our loaded wagon over the soft road. Ammunition, tools, extra rations, medical supplies, piled so high in the wagons, I didn't see how the canvas tops were ever stretched over. And hundreds of pack-mules went with the expedition. Some were loaded with reserve ammunition, some with officers' tents. Oh, golly! what loads were strapped upon them!

Out on the Warrenton road, in the general direction of the Rappahannock, upstream. I was puzzled. Lee and Fredericksburg were to the south. I paid little attention, though, for I was glad to get away from the monotony of camp life, and I felt safe with such a display of force.

Chilling mists began to creep over the valley during the afternoon. Clouds hovered lower and lower, and streaks of muggy fog. A swishing rain set in. Knapsacks, overcoats, blankets, became soaked and heavy. We slogged along, wearily and silently.

"Here it goes!" Perly King threw away his overcoat, and lively cheers broke out.

"Here goes mine!" Jake whirled his soggy coat above his head and with a fling he threw it to the edge of the road. Many threw knapsacks, skillets, cups, coats, into the bordering woods.

"Watch me hit that tree!" Nathaniel Green threw away the twenty rounds of ammunition he carried in his pockets. I emptied my sagging pockets, as many others did.

Shouts and cheers arose to the rear of us, when we resumed the march shortly after a rest at Hartwood Church. Our boys were singing The "Battle Hymn of the Republic," and we picked up the chorus.

"It's General Hooker! General Hooker's coming!"

Our lines swayed to the soggy berms to let the general and his staff pass. They were riding fast. Mud splashed in brown arcs in every direction. Our boys threw their caps high into the air, shouted hurrahs to the general. Hooker's bright blue eyes sparkled with pride and confidence. He waved his black hat high overhead. His thick blond hair jolted in rhythm to the galloping of his horse.

On April 29 artist Alfred Waud sketched troopers of the 8th Pennsylvania Cavalry fording the Rapidan River at Ely's Ford, watched by Rebel cavalry pickets on the far slope. The Confederate horsemen rode off for Chancellorsville, five miles to the southeast, while the Pennsylvanians secured the crossing for the infantry columns of Meade's V Corps. One of only four cavalry regiments held back with the army's main body, the 8th would lose more than 100 men on May 2.

PRIVATE JUSTUS M. SILLIMAN
17TH CONNECTICUT INFANTRY, MCLEAN'S BRIGADE

Marching with the XI Corps in the western arm of Hooker's offensive, the 17th Connecticut helped screen the Federal advance from Kelly's Ford south to Germanna Ford on the Rapidan. A farmer from New Canaan, Connecticut, Private Silliman survived the fight at Chancellorsville but was severely wounded and captured two months later at Gettysburg.

Our road now lay through the richest and most beautiful portion of Va. the farms were well fenced and smooth as a floor, rich and well cultivated. there was great quantities of grain growing. the country had apparently been undisturbed by either army as the farms were well stocked and had a thriving appearance though not showing that energy and enterprise exhibited at the north.

We marched several miles up the river and then making a turn to the left marched in nearly an opposite direction and down the river. We occasionally passed a well stocked slave shanty filled with grinning contribands who seemed glad to see us. there were two very intelligent darkies who stood near a well and gave us water as we passed. they said they had seen six rebel cavalrymen pass the house that morning on their way down, said they appeared in a great hury.

At one house we passed there was quite a collection of very substantial looking females on the piazza near the road. one of the younger ones who was knitting vigorously at a stocking said she guessed we must be the last of them and asked if there was any more coming. we told her there was any quantities of them behind us and that we were only scouts and skirmishers in advance of the main army. her exclamation was, "What a great gob of men." this little affair kept up our spirits for a time but we soon had a damper in the shape of a drizzling rain.

MAJOR HEROS VON BORCKE
Staff, Major General J. E. B. Stuart

When word of enemy activity reached Confederate cavalry commander Jeb Stuart at Culpeper, the general hastened to confront the threat but found the Federals positioned between his force and the rest of Lee's army. Major von Borcke, the stocky Prussian soldier of fortune who was one of Stuart's favorite staff officers, shared his commander's surprise at the Yankees' daring maneuver.

*I*t was about three in the morning when I was awakened by the General himself, who informed me he had just received intelligence that the enemy were approaching the river at several points with a strong force composed of infantry, cavalry, and artillery, and that we must hasten to the front without delay. The words were no sooner spoken than the bugle sounded to horse, and a few minutes after we galloped away from the camp, where all were busy with preparations for moving at a moment's notice. We reached the famous plateau near Brandy Station a little after daybreak, and found there W. Lee's brigade in line of battle, and two batteries of artillery in position. Fitz Lee's command arrived soon afterwards; and on this spot, so favourable for defence, Stuart decided to await the enemy's advance, making all preparations for a desperate resistance. A dense fog, which clung to the plain, precluded all observation of the hostile movements; but our pickets, which by this time had been forced back from the river and were receding towards us before vastly superior numbers, reported that a large body of troops of all arms had passed over to our side of the Rappahannock, and, to judge from the sounds which reached them, still more were crossing on several pontoon-bridges. . . .

Hour after hour passed away in this trying state of uncertainty, until at last, towards mid-day, the fog cleared away, and we were enabled to discover that our antagonists had for once completely deceived us. The advance in front had only been made by some cavalry to occupy our attention while the main body had marched in the direction of the Rapidan river. With his accustomed quickness, Stuart divined at once the intentions of the Federal commander, and, leaving one regiment behind to watch the movements of the hostile cavalry, we directed our march with all rapidity towards Stevensburg and Germana Ford on the Rapidan, trusting to be able to throw ourselves in the way of the enemy before he could reach the latter important point, where our engineers had just been completing a bridge. Unfortunately we were too late; and on reaching the intersection of the road, near the free negro Madden's house, previously mentioned, we found the greater part of the Federal troops had passed already, and could see, at a distance of not more than three hundred yards, the dense masses of their rear-guard marching steadily along.

An elderly civilian lies dead on the porch of a burned-out house in this hastily executed drawing by Alfred Waud, who accompanied the lead elements of Hooker's advance. Although the victim's name and the circumstances of his death are lost to history, the man was probably killed during the skirmishing along the banks of the Rapidan between Confederate pickets and troopers of Colonel Thomas C. Devin's brigade.

"Towards mid-day, the fog cleared away, and we were enabled
to discover that our antagonists had for once completely deceived us."

LIEUTENANT JULIAN W. HINKLEY
3D WISCONSIN INFANTRY, RUGER'S BRIGADE

On April 29 the Federal XII Corps led the advance on Germanna Ford, which was guarded by a screen of 150 Confederate troops. Brigadier General Thomas H. Ruger deployed a line of skirmishers, whose fire cowed the Rebels on the far bank, leaving Hinkley and his comrades to face the more daunting challenge of fording the Rapidan.

We arrived at the ford in about four hours, without alarming the enemy. A portion of the Regiment were deployed as skirmishers under cover of the woods, three or four hundred yards from the riverbank. At the word of command they moved on the run down to the river. Here each man hastily found for himself such shelter as he could, behind trees and brush, and opened fire on the enemy who were occupying some buildings on the opposite side. As we approached the river about a dozen Confederates started to run up the hill back of their position, in an attempt to escape. Our men were excellent marksmen, however, and after two had been killed and several others wounded, the rest of the enemy hastened back to the shelter of the buildings. Occasionally some fellow would fire at us from a window, but the puff of smoke from his gun would make him immediately the target for every musket within range, and that practice was soon discouraged. In less than ten minutes from the time when the skirmish commenced, the Southerners had hung out a white rag and surrendered. The swift-flowing Rapidan, nearly three hundred feet wide, separated them from us, but we compelled them to wade over. In this way, without a casualty to ourselves, we bagged 101 prisoners, and not a man escaped to the enemy to give warning of our approach.

We had just secured our prisoners when General Slocum came up. He immediately took in the situation, and ordered us to cross the river and secure the heights on the other side. We had had a good time laughing at our prisoners as we made them cross over to us, with the water up to their armpits; but when we had to go in ourselves, it did not seem so funny. It was still early in the spring, and the water was icy cold from the melting snow in the mountains. Moreover, the current was so swift that some mounted officers and cavalry who went in ahead of us could scarcely keep a footing. If a horse stumbled, he was washed off his feet in an instant and carried down stream. In fact, one man was drowned in such an accident, and several others had narrow escapes. We prepared for crossing by placing our ammunition and provisions, and such valuables as would be injured by the water, on the ends of the muskets or on our heads, and plunged in. We had the small men distributed among the large ones, and in this way crossed without serious trouble.

LIEUTENANT D. AUGUSTUS DICKERT
3D SOUTH CAROLINA INFANTRY, KERSHAW'S BRIGADE

At dawn on April 29, boatloads of Federal troops began crossing the Rappahannock at Fredericksburg, and the alarm was spread through the Southern camps. By afternoon two pontoon bridges were in place, allowing still more Yankee troops to gain the river's west bank. Rather than contest the enemy crossing, Lee decided to lure the Federals into a repeat of Burnside's costly assault of the preceding December.

On the morning of April 29th the soldiers were aroused from their slumbers by the beating of the long roll. What an ominous sound is the long roll to the soldier wrapped in his blanket and enjoying the sweets of sleep. It is like a fire bell at night. It denotes battle. It tells the soldier the enemy is moving; it means haste and active preparation. A battle is imminent. The soldiers thus roused, as if from their long sleep since Fredericksburg, feel in a touchous mood. The frightful scenes of Fredericksburg and Mayree's Hill rise up before them as a spectre. Soldiers rush out of their tents, asking questions and making suppositions. Others are busily engaged folding blankets, tearing down tents, and making preparations to move; companies formed into regiments and regiments into brigades. The distant boom of cannon beyond the Rappahannock tells us that the enemy is to cross the river again and try conclusions with the soldiers of Lee. All expected a bloody engagement, for the Federal army had been greatly recruited, under excellent discipline, and headed by Fighting Joe Hooker. He was one of the best officers in that army, and he himself had boasted that his was the "finest army that had ever been organized upon the planet." It numbered one hundred and thirty-one thousand men of all arms, while Lee had barely sixty-thousand. We moved rapidly in the direction of Fredericksburg. I never saw Kershaw look so well. Riding his iron-gray at the head of his columns, one could not but be impressed with his soldierly appearance. He seemed a veritable knight of old. Leading his brigade above the city, he took position in the old entrenchments.

Brigadier General Joseph B. Kershaw was a veteran of the Mexican War, a talented lawyer, and a member of the South Carolina state legislature. His sterling performance in every campaign of the war's eastern theater won him the admiration of his troops and the respect of his superior officers.

LIEUTENANT COLONEL RUFUS R. DAWES
6TH WISCONSIN INFANTRY, MEREDITH'S BRIGADE

Following the initial failure of Reynolds' I Corps to secure a crossing of the Rappahannock, two regiments were sent across downstream of the Rebel position, with instructions to flank the enemy rifle pits. Accompanied by their division commander, General James S. Wadsworth, the Federals succeeded in their desperate task, as Dawes related in a letter to his family.

We left camp at noon of the 28th, camped same night near the river four miles below Fredericksburg. About 11 P.M. same night started again for the river hoping to surprise the Rebels by a "coup de main." by rushing two regiments over in boats, storming & carrying the rifle pits, thus clearing the way for a pontoon bridge. For this perilous duty the 6th & 24th Michigan were selected. An honor most high. We moved along so slowly in the fog & rain and so much noise was made by the donkeys of the pontoon train that we had little hope of surprising. Sure enough when, near daylight we got the pontoons about half launched in the river. Crack, smash, whiz, ping, came the musketry volleys of long lines of Grey Backs in the pits. *Such* a skedaddling of negroes, horses, extra duty men of the pontoons never before was seen. Our Generals looked blank. It seemed that the Rappahannock must run red with blood, to force a crossing. Our regiment was in the advance. . . .

We double quicked up in face of their bullets, down on our faces, and lit into them in quicker time and better style than any other regiment in the U.S.A. can. The 24th Michigan and the 14th Brooklyn Zouaves were brought rapidly into line on our right and left and for ten minutes we kept up a tremendous musketry fire. But it was demonstrated that we could gain nothing that way. The rebels were on higher ground & in rifle pits, and it was destruction to lay under their fire. So we moved back in good order, out of range. Our pontoon boats were in

Two officers of the 8th Louisiana Infantry—Lieutenant Colonel Alcibiades DeBlanc (far left) and Lieutenant Robert S. Perry—were among the troops of Brigadier General Harry T. Hays' Louisiana brigade who defended the line of the Rappahannock River south of Fredericksburg. Hays was ordered to hold his position when Lee began shifting his forces to confront the Federal threat at Chancellorsville. The two men survived the battle, but later, during the July 2 assault on Cemetery Hill at Gettysburg, DeBlanc was gravely wounded and never returned to the field. Perry, captured in November 1863 along the Rappahannock River, sat out the rest of the war in captivity.

the river enough of them to carry about four hundred men. They lay about 150 yards width of the river from the Rebels in their pits. It was death to go near them. A desultory musketry skirmish was kept up for two or three hours. I had several narrow "clips." At nine o'clock, Gen. Reynolds [sent] down that the 6th and 24th *must cross* and carry the pits. Such a feeling of horror [came] over us. To be shot like sheep in a huddle & drown in the Rappahannock was the certain fate of *all* if we failed, of *many* if we succeeded. . . . Troops were moved down along the edge of the river and batteries planted on the hills back to fire at the Rebels as hard as they could, while *we* ran into the boats, rowed them across the river, scrambled up the bank and drove the rebels out with the bayonet, or held ground if we could until the boats could bring more troops to help us. After these dispositions had been made, we moved down over the open field in line of battle, truly the forlorn hope of the army. The rebels opened fire on us, and our men along the river, and the Batteries returned their fire. We moved down in line until

within two hundred yards of the boats, then by the right of Companies to the front, double quicked and into the boats the men plunged and down on their faces. The storm of bullets was perfectly awful. "Heave her off" "Down hon her" "The first man up the bank shall be a General" "Show the army why the old Sixth was chosen to lead them." It was the fiercest regatta ever run in this country. It was no time to quail or flinch one halt or waver was destruction. I stood up in the bow of the boat I commanded, swinging my sword in one hand and cheering on the oarsmen, holding my pistol in the other to shoot them if they wavered or flinched. Across the river, we tumbled into the mud or water waist deep, waded ashore, crawled & scrambled up the bank. Nobody could say who was first. . . . Crack—crack, for two minutes and the Rebels were running like sheep over the field or throwing down their arms as prisoners. I took the flag swung it as a signal of our victory, and such a shout of triumph as went up from the thousand anxious spectators on the north bank of the river it was good to hear.

"To be shot like sheep in a huddle & drown
in the Rappahannock was the certain fate of *all* if we failed,
of *many* if we succeeded."

Rowed across the Rappahannock River by oarsmen from the Engineer Brigade, New York and Pennsylvania troops from Brigadier General David A. Russell's brigade spearhead the VI Corps' crossing of the river a mile and a half south of Fredericksburg on April 29. "The boats gallantly vied with one another in the struggle to be the first to land," General Russell reported; "in five minutes after landing we had possession of the enemy's outer line of rifle-pits."

LIEUTENANT STEPHEN M. WELD

STAFF, BRIGADIER GENERAL
HENRY W. BENHAM

The Harvard-educated scion of a prominent Massachusetts family and a veteran of earlier campaigns, Lieutenant Weld was shocked by the drunken and boisterous behavior of his commanding officer during the perilous crossing of the Rappahannock. Unwilling to serve with General Benham any longer, Weld requested a transfer soon after the incident he describes and was reassigned to the staff of Major General Reynolds, commander of the I Corps.

The weather was perfect, and could not have been better. A very thick fog hung over the earth completely hiding every object a few yards distant. The boats were drawn by teams to within a mile of the intended crossing place. From here they were carried on poles to the river's bank, there being 75 men to each boat. This was done in order to get near the enemy unheard, and take them if possible by surprise. At 10 P.M. last night we left our camp, and went to General Sedgwick's headquarters, who had entire charge of the movements at the two lower crossings and who had the 1st, 3d and 6th Corps under his command. He and General Benham made their arrangements, and to *assist* General Benham, General Sedgwick sent an aide with him. While giving him some instructions a short time after, General Benham abused him shamefully without the slightest cause. Soon after he got himself into a scrape with General Brooks, and then with General Russell, whom he placed under arrest. I was asked by two officers, General Russell being one, whether General Benham was not drunk. I said he was not, as I knew he took wine only and not any liquors. Then, too, I was accustomed to his swear-

ing, etc., and thought nothing of it. Pretty soon a captain came riding along on horseback, and General Benham opened on him, yelling out in a loud tone of voice and Goddamning him. This, too, right on the bank of the river and when he had just been cautioning every one to keep quiet. I said to the general, "Don't call out so loud, sir, the enemy can hear you." He still kept on, however. All this time he was lying flat on the ground, complaining of fatigue. He then sent me off to find a Captain Reese, and when I came back he was gone, having left directions for me to stay where his horse was. I did not see him then for some time, when he came back on a borrowed horse and reeling in his saddle. He said to me in a thick voice, "Go tell General Sedgwick that General Russell has disobeyed my orders," and kept repeating it. I went off with the message to General S. During this last hour, everything had been going wrong. There was no one to attend to the matter and General B. confused and confounded everything. The enemy knew of our presence, and were signalling all along their line. And so it was until 4 or 5 o'clock in the morning, when men were put into the pontoon boats and pushed over, several shots being exchanged, with a loss of six wounded for us. Our men went right over and drove the enemy. Meanwhile, I was on the go to General Sedgwick with any number of messages from General B. When I came back about 6 o'clock, I found General B. drunk as could be, with a bloody cut over his left eye, and

In a photograph by Captain A. J. Russell, brawny General Henry Benham (right), commander of the army's Engineer Brigade, dwarfs his fellow brigadier, military-railroad construction chief Herman Haupt. In a lengthy report to General Hooker, Benham denied that he had been intoxicated during the Rappahannock crossing on April 29, noted that he had not slept for 42 hours before the crossing, and explained his seemingly irrational conduct as "a certain earnestness of manner in me."

Alfred Waud sketched Federal soldiers from Wadsworth's division of the I Corps resting beside their stacked muskets in the abandoned Rebel rifle pits on the west bank of the Rappahannock. Across the river the remaining two divisions of Reynolds' corps hold a reserve position, awaiting orders to move over the recently completed pontoon bridges. Reynolds would occupy the bridgehead until May 2, when his corps was ordered to rejoin Hooker's main force on the battlefield of Chancellorsville.

Brothers Floyd and Addison Ashley (left) served in Company C, 50th New York Engineers, one of the units entrusted with the responsibility of constructing pontoon bridges for Hooker's crossing of the Rappahannock. A. J. Russell photographed men of another engineer regiment—the 15th New York (below)—as they rested beside a campfire on the Confederate side of the river. The bridges behind them had enabled Sedgwick's VI Corps to take position for an attack on the Rebel defenses.

"He reeled in his saddle, and in trying to shake hands with General Pratt, he fell right off his horse on to the ground."

the blood all over that side of his face and forming a disgusting sight altogether. He had fallen down and cut his face. Soon after he reeled in his saddle, and in trying to shake hands with General Pratt, he fell right off his horse on to the ground. I saw him do this. The soldiers picked him up, and he mounted again, and rode round among the men, swearing and trying to hurry matters, but only creating trouble and making himself the laughing-stock of the crowd. Finally three bridges were got across and then we started for the two lower bridges where an unsuccessful attempt had been made to cross in the morning. The general had got moderately sober by that time, and began to feel slightly ashamed of himself. I never in my life have been so mortified and ashamed as I was this morning. I shall leave his staff as soon as possible, and I don't see how he can escape a court-martial and dismissal from the service.

SERGEANT MICAJAH D. MARTIN
2D GEORGIA BATTALION, WRIGHT'S BRIGADE

Initially deployed to guard the Confederate front at Fredericksburg, Brigadier General A. R. Wright's Georgia brigade was ordered west at midnight on April 29 to bolster the threatened position at Chancellorsville. Sergeant Martin and his comrades made a circuitous 27-mile march through rain and mud before halting astride the Plank road on the morning of April 30. Though Wright's soldiers were exhausted, he ordered them to begin digging in, and by May 1 they had erected a formidable line of rifle pits to confront the Yankee advance.

It commenced raining about dark and we spent a miserable time by our half-burning fires until midnight, when orders came to fall in, being ordered to Chancellorsville. Posey's and Mahone's brigades had been forced to fall back before superior numbers and we were ordered to reinforce them. We trudged through the mud and darkness as well as we could. There was nothing to disturb the silence except the occasional clanking of some soldier's tin cup against his canteen; or perhaps a half-muttered curse as some unfortunate fellow would slip and fall full length in the soft mire. Daylight found us far advanced on the plank road. It was a pleasant morning. The birds were warbling their sweetest notes in welcome of the budding spring. The rain had ceased and the dark clouds had disappeared from the horizon. All was lovely and bright, and I asked myself if such a lovely day was soon to witness scenes of death and carnage. We advanced within a mile of Chancellorsville, when the scouts brought in word that it was already occupied by a large force of the enemy. General Wright immediately determined to fall back and send for reinforcements, so we fell back three miles and took position on both sides of the plank road, concluding to await the enemy's advance. We waited until one o'clock, but they did not come, when General Wright sent a small squad of cavalry to the front to look for them. The cavalry had not been gone more than forty minutes when they came dashing back as fast as their horses could run, and about twice their number of Yankee cavalry pursuing them, while at the same time a squadron of the Yankees were charging across a field to intercept their retreat. It was an exciting race and I feared that our boys would be captured, but their horses were fast enough to save them. They passed where the body in the field would strike the road about the time the Yankees were still a hundred yards from the road. As they were only two hundred yards from us, they halted and fired a volley into the Yankees, killing two of them. The Yankees left in a run without returning the fire. . . .

We worked all night throwing up breast-works—ready for the enemy's advance next day.

LIEUTENANT ABNER R. SMALL
16TH MAINE INFANTRY, ROOT'S BRIGADE

While Wadsworth's troops maintained their bridgehead on the Confederate side of the Rappahannock, most of the I Corps remained on the river's east bank. When Colonel Adrian Root massed his brigade to observe National Fast Day, the tempting target drew a flurry of shells from the Rebel guns.

Thursday was Fast Day, proclaimed by the President. I don't recall that any of us indulged in fancy humiliations. We had a holiday that we hadn't expected; no marching, no fighting; we loafed happily in the spring sunshine under the green trees. A congratulatory order from Hooker was read:

"With heartfelt satisfaction the commanding general announces to the army that the operations of the last three days have determined that our enemy must either ingloriously fly or come out from behind his defenses and give us battle on our own ground, where certain destruction awaits him."

We hoped that all this was true. We were glad to know, at any rate, that a large part of the army had marched unopposed northwestwards, crossed the Rappahannock and the Rapidan, and was now in a position to flank the rebels and force them out of their intrenched lines.

Preparatory to the general slaughter soon expected, the chaplains of our brigade proposed to hold divine service. Accordingly, about four o'clock in the afternoon, the brigade was formed in a hollow square, the chaplains gathered in the center, and the holy work was begun. All was quiet across the river as the innocent twelve-hundred-dollar shepherds expounded to their lambs the cause of God and the glorious Republic. They were eloquent in their appeals to patriotism, and pictured in glowing colors the glory that would crown the dead and the blazons of promotion that would decorate the surviving heroes. They besought us all to stand firm, to be brave; God being our shield, we had nothing to fear.

Whoosh! Suddenly interrupting, there came a great rushing sound. Crash! A great crackling and bursting rent the air. The explosions of shells, the screams of horses, and the shouted commands of officers were almost drowned out by the yells and laughter of the men as the brave chaplains, hatless and bookless, their coattails streaming in the wind, fled madly to the rear over stone walls and hedges and ditches, followed by gleefully shouted counsel:

"Stand firm; put your trust in the Lord!"

"Come back and earn your twelve hundred dollars!"

The scare was soon over, but no persuasion could induce those chaplains to come back and confess their surrender to the weakness of the flesh. I wouldn't say that they were other than good Christian men trying to discharge their duties under peculiarly trying circumstances; I would only suggest that there was a practical deficiency in their training for the field. The danger was real enough. A few men of our brigade were wounded, and a few among other troops near by were killed.

LIEUTENANT CHARLES A. FULLER
61ST NEW YORK INFANTRY, CALDWELL'S BRIGADE

Couch's II Corps crossed the Rappahannock at United States Ford. At 10:00 p.m. on April 30 the corps halted within half a mile of the crossroads at Chancellorsville. As Lieutenant Fuller recalled, the recent presence of Federal cavalry horses made his unit's bivouac an uncomfortable one.

Towards sundown we were put in motion, making our way to the river's edge, and crossed it on a well-laid pontoon. We ate our supper on the other side of the river, and then advanced a few miles into the country, and halted for the night along side an open piece of woods, not far from the Chancellorsville house. We went into this piece of woods to spread our blankets to bivouac for the night. Our

Sketching by moonlight, Edwin Forbes showed columns of Union troops snaking across the pontoon bridges at United States Ford on the evening of April 30. Forbes added the notation "There is very little fighting going on today. Gen. Hooker seems to be acting on the defensive for the purpose of drawing the enemy from his position."

cavalry had been on this ground before, and they had responded affirmatively to the calls of nature, so that we soon discovered we were treading on mounds not as large, but as soft, as the one into which Peter Stuyvesant fell, according to the narrative of Irving. I remember, after spreading my own blanket, that my hand dropped down outside of it, and went slap into one of those mounds. I further remember that I was not the only Sixty-firster that imprecated in strong Saxon. But there we were, and there we lay till sunrise.

Union Probes and Rebel Response: May 1

Once General Lee had made the daring decision to shift virtually his entire army westward to fight Hooker's flanking force at Chancellorsville, Lee's most trusted lieutenant, Stonewall Jackson, wasted little time getting things moving. Jackson himself awoke shortly after midnight on May 1, then had the troops roused at 2:00 a.m., silently, with no bugle calls that would alert the Yankees camped only a few hundred yards away on the banks of the Rappahannock.

Within minutes General Rodes' division, leading the Confederate column, had begun to march. "On we went through mud and over stumps, stumbling about in the dark," wrote one of Rodes' soldiers, "to the great danger of our heads and shins."

Jackson, astride his undersized horse, Little Sorrel, rode on toward the Tabernacle Church to join General Richard Anderson, already dispatched there with his division to set up a defensive line. Arriving about 8:00 a.m., Jackson found Anderson's men busy digging trenches—a sensible move in the face of a huge enemy force.

But Jackson, intent as always on hitting the enemy no matter what the odds, ordered the troops to pack their shovels and be ready to attack. Lafayette McLaws' brigades, which had marched from Fredericksburg during the night, were deploying on Anderson's right. At 11:00 a.m. the two divisions—only about 14,000 men in all—started down the Plank road and the Turnpike to assault the oncoming 70,000 Federals.

Belatedly ordered by Hooker to begin the great advance, the Union troops started up the same roads at the same time, Slocum's XII Corps pushing ahead on the right along the Plank road and Major General George Sykes' division of Meade's V Corps moving up the Turnpike. On the Federal left, Meade's other two divisions also set out, following the River road between the Turnpike and the Rappahannock.

The Federal columns almost immediately ran into McLaws' and Anderson's skirmishers, with Confederate rifle fire crackling from the woods and little hills that fringed the roads. A number of ferocious fights erupted, including a seesaw battle between Sykes' men and Mahone's brigade, who retreated and then, supported by two brigades from Anderson, assailed the Federal column on both flanks.

The gunfire did not at first seem to worry Hooker, who ordered Major General Winfield Scott Hancock and his division to hurry up the Turnpike to support Sykes. This Hancock did, gaining a strategic position atop a ridge in open country. Slocum also gained ground while Meade on the Federal left was speeding ahead unopposed.

Then, astonishingly, at about 2:00 p.m. Hooker sent orders telling his corps commanders to stop the advance, break off contact with the enemy, and fall back to the areas around Chancellorsville that they had occupied the night before. Meade immediately exploded, "My God, if we can't hold the top of a hill, we certainly cannot hold the bottom of it!" The combative Slocum was even more furious, shouting, "Nobody but a crazy man would give such an order when we have victory in sight!"

What had occurred was an acute failure of nerve on the part of the Federal commanding general. Hooker, despite his army's overwhelming strength, had quailed at the enemy opposition and decided to go over to the defensive.

Debate over Hooker's stunning reversal began at once. Some blamed it on his fondness for the bottle, but several of his generals later testified at an inquiry that Hooker was not drunk. In fact, said General Couch, he might have performed better if he had "continued in his usual habit" and downed a drink or two.

Part of the answer certainly is that Hooker, having made his great flanking move, expected Lee to retreat. But Lee's instinct, like Jackson's, was always to attack. Hooker, uncertain of his ability to command an entire army despite all his bluster, gave way to panic at the signs of resistance. Hooker's own explanation, given weeks later to a friend, was simply, "for once I lost confidence in Hooker."

When the Union forces withdrew, the Confederates followed gingerly, suspicious of a trap, although McLaws' brigades, now backed by A. P. Hill's division of Jackson's corps, pressed some distance down the roads toward Chancellorsville. At the same time Jackson pushed several brigades up the Plank road, one of which, under General Ambrose R. Wright, veered left along an unfinished railroad, pushed past the Catharine Furnace ironworks, and briefly collided with forward elements of the XII Corps.

At dusk Lee and Jackson met near there in a pine grove to decide what to do next. The Federals had to be dealt a heavy blow, and quickly. Lee himself had done some scouting along with his engineers, and a frontal assault through the swamps and thickets of the Wilderness on the fortified semicircle Hooker had drawn around Chancellorsville seemed suicidal.

As the two trusted friends sat on a log talking, Jeb Stuart rode up to report that some cavalry scouts had discovered that the flank of Oliver Howard's XI Corps, holding the Federal far right, was "in the air," that is, unprotected by any hill or swamp or other natural feature. Both Lee and Jackson immediately recognized the possibility of a flank march that would put their troops in a position to attack the Union army from the rear —but how could they get an attacking force that far to the west?

Lee's sketchy pocket map of the area was little help. But well before dawn, information about the area had been provided by scouts and local people, among them the owner of Catharine Furnace, who knew all the local roads. Sketching furiously, Jedediah Hotchkiss, Jackson's cartographer, produced a map showing a largely concealed route leading down the Furnace road and then back up the Brock road that stretched all the way to the Federal right flank and beyond.

The two Confederate commanders consulted again. Lee looked at Jackson. "What do you propose to do?" he asked. "Go around here," said Jackson, pointing to the route on Hotchkiss' map. "What do you propose to make this movement with?" asked Lee. "With my whole corps," answered Jackson.

It was an audacious plan because it would leave Lee with only two divisions, Anderson's and McLaws', to face the entire main body of Hooker's force. After considering for only a moment, however, Lee gave his assent. "Well," he said, "go on."

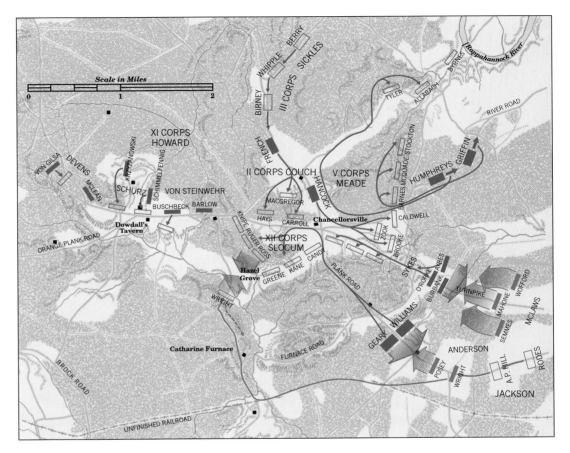

Early on May 1, with the bulk of his army concentrated around Chancellorsville, Hooker's plan seemed to be unfolding like clockwork. The Federal commander confidently ordered Slocum's XII Corps to advance down the Plank road, while Meade's divisions pushed east along the Turnpike and the River road. But Lee had brought his forces up quickly. Around midday, George Sykes' Yankees on the Turnpike were hit hard by Mahone's Rebels, who were soon reinforced by two of Anderson's brigades. This, along with the Confederates' aggressive posture on the Plank road and the arrival of Jackson's divisions, prompted a suddenly cautious Hooker to order a recall, setting the stage for Lee's bold countermove.

"If there is any poetry in fighting it is Infantry fighting Cavalry."

PRIVATE WESTWOOD A. TODD
12TH VIRGINIA INFANTRY, MAHONE'S BRIGADE

Advancing east astride the Turnpike, Sykes' Regular Army division found its way blocked by General Mahone's Confederate brigade. Private Todd was justifiably proud of the Southerners' determined stand against the veteran Yankees to their front—Regulars of Colonel Sidney Burbank's brigade—but the Federal retreat was in fact due to orders from Hooker, who wanted the Regular division to consolidate with the main Union force around Chancellorsville.

The following morning my company was ordered to deploy on each side of the main road to protect the flanks of a company of cavalry with which we were ordered to advance up the road to flush the game as it were. We had not gone far when I heard a rifle shot and then I heard the gallant Hill Carter, Jr., of Shirley, who commanded the cavalry, halloo out to us, "Hurry up boys and get a shot at the Yankee Cavalry." If there is any poetry in fighting it is Infantry fighting Cavalry.

A brisk fire was kept up between the cavalry on both sides. I couldn't see the Yankees from where I was; being almost the shortest man in the company I was at the extreme left of the line, which threw me a considerable distance from the road. The Federal Cavalry fell back before ours, and presently we emerged from the woods into a large field where we soon dispersed the Cavalry and came upon their Infantry skirmishers in beautiful line. And now ensued the most satisfactory fighting in which I had any share during the war. I am free to say that at Seven Pines, Malvern Hill and Manassas, my brigade had "made no leather" out of the Yankees, but now we had a fair, square stand-up, open field fight. Our company fell in with the rest of our regiment, which now came up in beautiful style, deployed as skirmishers in front of the brigade, and the whole line went forward with a yell. We

were fighting Sykes' Regulars. They stood up well for some time, but we steadily advanced, and when we got to close quarters, they began to give way and retire sullenly. We reached a rail fence, which ran along a slight ridge, on which were a few stunted oaks. From this position we poured into the enemy a hot fire which made them break and run. A Yankee who had fallen about fifty yards in front of me held up his handkerchief as a signal of surrender. I suppose he thought we might fire on him, but I hope we did not have a man in our army so cowardly as to fire on a fallen foe. One Federal Officer, a Captain or Lieutenant, behaved with splendid courage. He kept up his part of the line, when nearly all the rest had left. I don't think he was more than a hundred yards from my right. I fired at him several times, but missed him. Lieutenant Hill Carter rode up and asked me to let him fire my rifle at the officer, whose example alone kept his men from running. He dismounted and fired my rifle. He handed my gun back to me with the remark that he had hurt himself more than the Federal officer. The gun had kicked him. Poor Carter was mortally wounded a few hours later. I did not know him personally. He exposed himself unnecessarily that day. He was a gallant fellow, and deserves to be remembered. But to resume the fight, in a short time the whole skirmish line of the enemy was driven back. We had thrashed a line of Regulars in handsome style. Their line of battle now advanced. The field was wide enough for me to see the regiments. They came up in fine order. Our skirmish line, which was by this time in great disorder, many men

Private Henry T. Booker fought at Chancellorsville in the ranks of Company A, 12th Virginia Infantry, the unit that covered the deployment of the six Virginia regiments of Mahone's brigade. Booker had been wounded at Crampton's Gap during the Antietam campaign, but he was not among the 86 casualties suffered by the 12th Virginia on May 1. He survived to surrender at Appomattox.

CORPORAL J. ANSEL BOOTH
140TH NEW YORK INFANTRY, O'RORKE'S BRIGADE

The brigade of Colonel Patrick H. O'Rorke—a brilliant young West Pointer who had formerly commanded the 140th New York—successfully covered the withdrawal of Sykes' division, despite the heavy fire of Rebel artillery and the presence of enemy troops on the flanks. Corporal Booth, one of O'Rorke's soldiers, was a 35-year-old farmer from Monroe County who described the fight in a letter to his mother. Booth also sent periodic accounts of his unit's experiences to the Rochester Democrat & American.

A mile or so from camp we were formed in line of battle in a piece of woods, but the rebel guns had our exact range, a number of shells were exploded in our very midst. Within 20 ft of me a shell cut off a good sized limb of a tree, not far above the ground.

The 146th were drawn up in the rear of the 140th; right behind me, an explosion made the very ground tremble. I turned to see and it seemed as if a dozen men were struck down just as a tuft of grass is flattened when struck by a gust of wind. One or two were killed, several wounded, so reports said. Of course we were got out of that place quickly.

Going on about a mile further on the double quick, for the rebel guns commanded the road completely, we were filed left, out of the road into a cornfield. Just as Com. D were leaving the road, Capt. Lieper of Com. E. next in advance of Com. D was struck senseless by a fragment of a shell, and a Mr. Gardner of the same Com. instantly killed.

One or two Brigades were in advance of us; had opened the battle and drove the rebs a mile or two back to a more commanding position. As we moved over the ground, I saw where a number of shells had buried themselves in the earth, two or three dead men, and some few wounded.

We moved up to within supporting distance of the Brigades engaged, and lay down on our faces. Here we lay for an hour or more, when, it being evident that the rebel position could not be taken without bringing on a general engagement, our forces were withdrawn.

The rebs followed us closely; we reached camp at 4 P.M. and about 5 P.M. were attacked by them. The attack was most gallantly repulsed, and as suddenly as it was made.

But the 146th lost quite severely for a little thing. For a while the bullets flew over our heads like hail-stones, but it was the impression of outsiders that they were sent back by the Brigade quite faster than they were sent in.

GENERAL MAHONE.
Ent'd according to Act of Congress in the year 1866, by M. B. Brady, in the Clerk's Office of the Dist. Court for the So. Dist. of N. Y.

Brigadier General William Mahone, whose defense blunted the Federal foray on May 1, weighed barely 100 pounds and was known for his eccentricity and hypochondria. But he proved to be one of the finest brigade commanders in Lee's army.

having been killed or wounded, waited for orders to fall back. As to resisting their serried ranks with our then disorganized ranks, it was simply impossible. But not receiving orders to retreat we blazed away at them. They did not reply; the game was too small. At last Lieutenant Macon Martin, of my company, gave the order to fall back, and none too soon, for eighty of our regiment were captured in the retreat. Martin ordered us to fall back obliquely to the left towards the woods. When we got to the high rail fence on the edge of the field, I was so tired I could hardly climb it, my tongue was out, and I was encumbered with my blanket and haversack, to which I always clung. I managed, under the powerful incentive behind me, to mount the fence, and drop over.

"The only friends I had left were one day's rations in my haversack, gun, 60 rounds of cartridges, and my revolver."

Curtis was out as Sergeant of the picket; these were driven in so furiously that the most of them lost everything that did not tenaciously cling to them. Some of them came in leaving knapsacks, haversacks, overcoats, blankets, guns, caps, everything. Curtis lost knapsack, haversack, overcoat, housewife,—everything but what was hanging to him at the time the firing began.

During . . . one of the halts I laid up my knapsack—the roadside for a mile had been lined with them, with overcoats and blankets—under a tree all in good style, thinking perhaps, we might return in such shape that I could recover it. But we did not and I was minus knapsack, overcoat, blanket, poncho, shirt, stockings, towel, housewife, 5 days rations, hard tack, sugar, meat—the only friends I had left were one day's rations in my haversack, gun, 60 rounds of cartridges, and my revolver. For the first time I found myself in *light marching* order.

Alfred Waud entitled his May 1 sketch of the Federals pushing down the Turnpike "Victorious advance of Genl. Sykes," but General Hooker squandered his chances for success by failing to dispatch reinforcements. "Without support, my position was critical," Sykes reported. "Still, I determined to hold it as long as possible."

This swallow-tailed pennant was the headquarters flag of Major General Oliver O. Howard, commander of the XI Corps. On the late afternoon of May 1, Howard established his headquarters alongside the Plank road, some two miles west of Chancellorsville, in a white clapboard structure known as Dowdall's Tavern (top). The former hostelry was in fact the residence of the Reverend Melzi Chancellor, pastor of Salem Church.

PRIVATE HENRY MEYER
148TH PENNSYLVANIA INFANTRY, CALDWELL'S BRIGADE

The May 1 engagement east of Chancellorsville was the baptism of fire for the 148th Pennsylvania, a regiment attached to Hancock's division of the II Corps. Meyer recalled his apprehension as Hancock's troops came under fire while supporting Sykes' abortive advance on the Turnpike. A year later Meyer was wounded at Spotsylvania and suffered the amputation of his lower left arm.

Going into battle is a serious matter, an ordeal which the bravest dread. Outwardly, some may not exhibit a sign of fear, but it requires all the will power a brave man is able to put forth to stand in ranks to be shot at—one feels as though he were suspended over eternity by a slender thread. Some boasted they were not afraid, but they were mere cowardly blow-horns who always slunk out of ranks, or hid behind rock or trees in the rear when the bullets began to whistle. . . .

With their names and place of residence legibly written on the fly leaf of diary or Bible, or stamped on metallic badges securely fastened to their clothes, for the purpose of identification in the event of being left dead upon the field, steadily our rather sad looking boys moved in the direction of the firing in front. Notwithstanding the seriousness of the occasion, we could not refrain from smiling at the sight of the myriads of

Ft. Hookers Head Quarters at the Chancellorsville House.
May 1st 1863. Edwin Forbes.

cards strewn all along the whole breath of the road, and among the bushes along the sides, lying thick as autumnal leaves. The troops that passed along the road before us to enter the battle flung away their decks of cards for the reason that none of the boys would have a report go home, in case they should be badly wounded or killed, that there was found on their person a deck of cards. Other scenes, productive of graver thoughts now presented themselves. Streams of wounded soldiers were coming back from the battle then in progress; wounds of all descriptions met the view; some of the men dragged themselves along by the aid of rude crutches; some came with a shattered arm dangling by their side and others more seriously hurt, were brought in on ambulance or stretcher.

We were formed in line of battle on a hill about one and a half miles from Chancellorsville in the direction of Fredericksburg, on the right of the Turnpike, and at right angles to it, facing east. As we filed into position we observed one of our skirmish lines ascending, at a slow pace, a hill to our left and front, firing as they advanced. We noticed some dropping down killed or wounded. This was our first view of a battle, and to us inexperienced soldiers it was magnificent. The rebel batteries sent shells over us, above the tree tops in the direction of Chancellor House; the roar of the artillery, the unearthly screech of the shells overhead, and the explosions which followed, all that was magnificent, too. Later on, however, their batteries got the range of our position and when shells began to smash things right in our midst it became decidedly unpleasant. Our military ardor which had been raised to a high pitch by the carnival of war around us, cooled very rapidly under the potent influence of the bursting shells.

Special artist Edwin Forbes depicted the fight on May 1 from two different perspectives at the Chancellorsville crossroads. At left, in a view looking northwest across the clearing around the Chancellor house (large two-winged structure in the center distance), entrenched Federal batteries brace for a Confederate attack while supporting infantry files into position. In the sketch below, looking south from a point just northeast of the Chancellor house, troops of the II Corps march at a double-quick down the United States Ford road and onto the Turnpike to bolster Sykes' embattled division, fighting along the far line of woods.

"I retired from his presence with the belief that my commanding general was a whipped man."

MAJOR GENERAL DARIUS N. COUCH
CORPS COMMANDER, ARMY OF THE POTOMAC

A West Point classmate of George McClellan's and Stonewall Jackson's, Darius Couch was a cautious but reliable officer whom one subordinate described as looking "more like a Methodist minister than a soldier." Disgusted with Hooker's mismanagement, Couch requested a transfer from his command of the II Corps after Chancellorsville.

When the sound of their guns was heard at Chancellorsville . . . General Hooker ordered me to take Hancock's division and proceed to the support of those engaged. After marching a mile and a half or so I came upon Sykes, who commanded, engaged at the time in drawing back his advance to the position he then occupied. Shortly after Hancock's troops had got into a line in front, an order was received from the commanding general "to withdraw both divisions to Chancellorsville." Turning to the officers around me, Hancock, Sykes, Warren, and others, I told them what the order was, upon which they all agreed with me that the ground should not be abandoned, because of the open country in front and the commanding position. An aide, Major J. B. Burt, dispatched to General Hooker to this effect, came back in half an hour with positive orders to return. Nothing was to be done but carry out the command, though Warren suggested that I should disobey, and then he rode back to see the general. In the mean-

time, Slocum, on the Plank road to my right, had been ordered in, and the enemy's advance was between that road and my right flank. Sykes was first to move back, then followed by Hancock's regiments over the same road. When all but two of the latter had withdrawn, a third order came to me, brought by one of the general's staff: "Hold on until 5 o'clock." It was then perhaps 2 P.M. Disgusted at the general's vacillation and vexed at receiving an order of such tenor, I replied with warmth unbecoming in a subordinate: "Tell General Hooker he is too late, the enemy are already on my right and rear. I am in full retreat.". . .

. . . Continuing my way through the woods toward Chancellorsville, I came upon some of the Fifth Corps under arms. Inquiring for their commanding officer, I told him that in fifteen minutes he would be attacked. Before finishing the sentence a volley of musketry was fired into us from the direction of the Plank road. . . . Troops were hurried into position, but the observer required no wizard to tell him, as they marched past, that the high expectations which had animated them only a few hours ago had given place to disappointment. Proceeding to the Chancellor House, I narrated my operations in front to Hooker, which were seemingly satisfactory, as he said: "It is all right, Couch, I have got Lee just where I want him; he must fight me on my own ground." The retrograde movement had prepared me for something of the kind, but to hear from his own lips that the advantages gained by the successful marches of his lieutenants were to culminate in fighting a defensive battle in that nest of thickets was too much, and I retired from his presence with the belief that my commanding general was a whipped man.

A quiet and studious 20-year-old, Major Richard Channing Price (left) served as assistant adjutant general on the staff of his cousin, Confederate cavalry commander Jeb Stuart, who valued Price's "ready pen and fine perception." During the artillery duel on May 1 a fragment of shell struck Price behind the knee, severing an artery, but he insisted on remaining at his post. Had a tourniquet been available the major's life would most likely have been saved; but late that night the heavy loss of blood proved fatal.

Lieutenant Thomas Randolph Price Jr. (left) was with his younger brother, Channing, when the adjutant succumbed to his wounds. Three months before the Battle of Chancellorsville, Thomas Price had joined Stuart's staff as an assistant engineer, but his tenure there would be brief. On May 21 the New York Times printed excerpts from the lieutenant's diary, which had been lost during a Federal cavalry foray. Price's less than flattering description of his commanding officer gave Stuart no choice but to order his transfer.

CAPTAIN MARCELLUS N. MOORMAN
LYNCHBURG BEAUREGARDS BATTERY,
VIRGINIA HORSE ARTILLERY BATTALION

An 1856 graduate of the Virginia Military Institute, where he served as captain of a cadet company, Moorman (above) commanded one of four batteries attached to Major R. F. Beckham's battalion of horse artillery and was highly regarded by his superior officers. General Mahone described Moorman as "cool, prompt, energetic and attentive to every obligation of duty." On the evening of May 1, two of Moorman's guns were caught in a deadly cross fire from Federal batteries.

My battery, of the Stuart Horse Artillery Battalion, was on the extreme left of our troops, then confronting Hooker's army, near the old Catherine Furnace. Late that afternoon we were ordered to shell a piece of woods in our front. In order to do this we were turned into a very narrow old road, through a dense forest which ran perpendicular to the woods about to be shelled. The leading guns coming up, I at once rode forward to find a position, as I was still so closely confined with the scrub oak, that I could not unlimber. As I reached the guns in front, the Federal artillery opened, apparently all over the woods. Unable to move forward, I returned to my guns, where I found Generals Jackson, Stuart and Wright shrapnel and canister raining around them from the enemy's guns. Stuart remarked: "General Jackson, we must move from here." But, before they could turn, the gallant Channing Price, Stuart's Adjutant General, was mortally wounded and died in a few hours. My battery lost six men without being able to unlimber. We retired from this point and bivouacked for the night.

CAPTAIN ALEXANDER C. HASKELL
STAFF, BRIGADIER GENERAL SAMUEL McGOWAN

Marching westward at 4:00 a.m. from its positions south of Fredericksburg, A. P. Hill's division of Jackson's corps had arrived within two miles of Chancellorsville by nightfall. Uncertain of what lay in his front, Hill directed the brigades of Henry Heth, James Lane, and Samuel McGowan to advance on the crossroads. Captain Haskell, McGowan's assistant adjutant general, spearheaded the movement with a portion of the brigade and soon determined that a large Federal force was massed in the vicinity of the Chancellor house.

As we neared Chancellorsville, the report came in that Hooker had abandoned Chancellorsville. General A. P. Hill, our Division Commander, thereupon ordered General Heth to go across to the Pike road and press through Chancellorsville, while the balance of the Division pushed forward on the Plank road. Our Brigade, now McGowan's, was head of Heth's force and he rode with General McGowan and myself. Soon enough came in from the skirmish line to show that Hooker had *not* abandoned Chancellorsville. It was dense black-jack scrub forest and observation was very difficult. I reported to McGowan and to General Heth. The latter had just come from the Western Army and did not wish to do anything that looked over cautious and said that he had his information and orders from General Hill, and he would press through Chancellorsville. Of course we all wished to do that, but could we?. . . Heth then ordered McGowan to form his Brigade, five Regiments, in line of battle and press forward. There was an open old field before us about a quarter mile before we reached the forest around Chancellorsville. I put in my last appeal, for much was at stake. I said, "General Heth, let me go forward with two Regiments. If the enemy have gone, we can sweep through as your advance guard; and if they are there, the rest of your command will be saved for the general fight." To my delight he consented, and in a jiffy I had the 14th in line of battle on the right of the road, Orr's Rifles on the left, I on horseback in the center of the road, and we swept forward as if on dress parade, really not having an idea we would meet anybody until we got well into the forest. We had hardly got half way across the field when rifles and cannon opened on us. Soldiers will see a joke even in battle. At the first volley my good mare made a skip from the road and landed behind the 14th. The brave fellows laughed and cheered for the old Queen that "had sense.". . .

I instantly gave the order to reform the line of battle, and rode to a little hill to my right and from there had a free view of a point in Hooker's line. On the bare hill that was open to view were his three lines of battle entrenched by earthworks. There he was, with his mighty force protected and ready. I sat on my horse yearning and praying that somebody would come. I could not leave my men, but surely our own forces had seen and heard our charge and must know that Hooker was still there. Well, the old story of Blue Beard rushed over me, the picture of the sister in the tower. "Oh, they will come! I see dust. It gets thicker, and I hear the hoofs and see the men!" Here came old Stonewall Jackson, my beloved Commander, A. P. Hill, and a long retinue of staff and couriers behind them, at full gallop. My heart was relieved. I rode forward and met them. General Jackson, with his quiet intent face, "Captain Haskell, what is it?" Ride up here, General, and you will see it all. There he sat on his horse, with his field glass before his eyes, studying. Presently he let the the glass down and took up his reins. The shells were bursting around us, but like Master, like horse, and the old nag of many battles stood quiet. "Hold this position," he said, "until 9 o'clock tonight, when you will be relieved by General Fitzhugh Lee." Then he approached yet nearer and, leaning over, said in a low voice, "Countersign for the night is, Challenge, Liberty; Reply, Independence." I took a little note book out of my pocket, and wrote it in pencil in a ragged hand, for my horse was not as steady as General Jackson's, "Challenge, Liberty; Reply, Independence."

LIEUTENANT CLAY MACCAULEY
126TH PENNSYLVANIA INFANTRY, TYLER'S BRIGADE

Having earlier been held in reserve near Chancellorsville after the recall from the River road foray, Brigadier General Andrew A. Humphreys' division of Meade's V Corps was shifted north on the afternoon of May 1 to cover the bridgeheads on the Rappahannock. Though weary from marching, the soldiers in Humphreys' two brigades were confident that the Union was on the eve of a decisive victory. Recently promoted from brigade ordnance sergeant to company second lieutenant, Clay MacCauley shared this optimistic view.

Friday became a day for our division which none of us will ever forget. Already we had been pretty well used up by our night marching and hard work. But on that day was a grand climax. We made a quick-time reconnoissance to Banks's Ford, five miles away on the rebel right. Reaching that, we were suddenly about-faced, and returned on a double-quick to our starting-place. It seemed at times in that movement that human endurance could last no longer. Upon our return fierce skirmishing on our centre at Slocum's corps, of which we had some leaden tokens, was not at all cheering under the circumstances. At last, however, our tribulations seemed to have passed. Before nightfall we were in position on the extreme left, on a high bluff in a beautiful wood, our own left resting on the river-bank, covering our army's important line of retreat and supply, the United States Ford on the Rappahannock. Then we concluded that our army was finally in position, and that our division had been assigned to a place wholly free from peril of balls or assault. Nothing of the enemy could be seen or heard at our front. We threw up intrenchments and began to "take things easy." We were a comfortable crowd that 1st of May evening, tired though we were. We could hear distant skirmishing. We were nearly three miles away from the point of rebel resistance to Hooker's advance, and on impregnable heights. Over our pipes we talked of the day's events. There was, first, our commander's great boast in General Order No. 47, which had been read to us that morning, to the effect that we had "completely surrounded the rebels," and that they would

"either have to fly ingloriously or come out from their breastworks, where destruction was certain," and that "the operations of the Fifth, Eleventh, and Twelfth Corps were a series of splendid achievements." This was very flattering and reassuring. Then we had considerable fun over an incident which fell to us in our swift reconnoissance on the river road to Banks's Ford. We had passed through a rebel camp, apparently hastily deserted at our approach. Tents had been left standing, fires burning, clothing, food, and utensils scattered about on the ground, two caissons broken down and deserted in the road, and ammunition upset and left by men too much in a hurry to gather it up. I am saying only what we thought. I do not know that we had frightened anybody, but the supposition that our coming had set them to going made us feel comfortable. In this cheerful mood at length we fell into a well-earned sleep on the soft leaves under the great trees that bright and perfect May-day night.

A cloth haversack (right) is stenciled with the name of James P. Tilton, a corporal in the 129th Pennsylvania, of Tyler's brigade. Tilton was mustered out on May 18 at the conclusion of his unit's nine-month term of service.

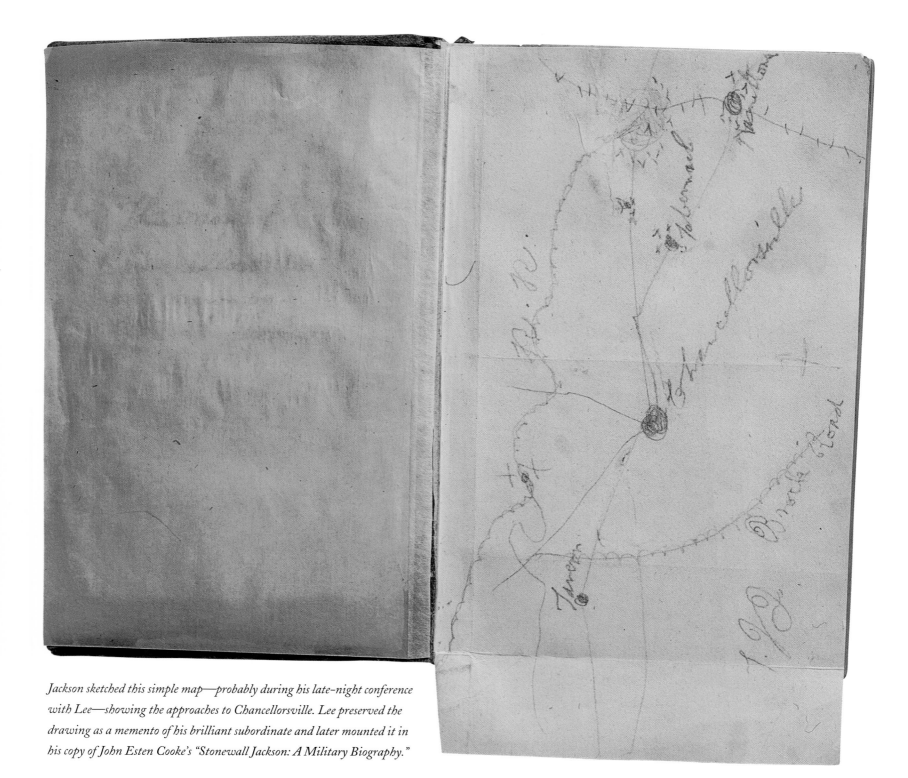

Jackson sketched this simple map—probably during his late-night conference with Lee—showing the approaches to Chancellorsville. Lee preserved the drawing as a memento of his brilliant subordinate and later mounted it in his copy of John Esten Cooke's "Stonewall Jackson: A Military Biography."

"Who can tell the story of that quiet council of war between two sleeping armies?"

LIEUTENANT JAMES P. SMITH
STAFF, LIEUTENANT GENERAL THOMAS J. JACKSON

Formerly a corporal in the Rockbridge (Virginia) Artillery, James P. Smith—whose photograph and jacket appear below—served as one of Stonewall Jackson's aides-de-camp at Chancellorsville and witnessed the famous council of war between Jackson and Lee. Smith was later attached to the staff of General Richard S. Ewell, but he resigned in December 1863 to accept a promotion and reassignment.

Capt. Smith

A little after nightfall I was sent by General Lee upon an errand to A. P. Hill, on the old stone turnpike a mile or two north; and returning some time later with information of matters on our right, I found General Jackson retired to rest, and General Lee sleeping at the foot of a tree, covered with his army cloak. As I aroused the sleeper, he slowly sat up on the ground and said, "Ah, captain, you have returned, have you? Come here and tell me what you have learned on the right." Laying his hand on me, he drew me down by his side, and, passing his arm around my shoulder, drew me near to him in a fatherly way that told of his warm and kindly heart. When I had related such information as I had secured for him, he thanked me for accomplishing his commission, and then said he regretted that the young men about General Jackson had not relieved him of annoyance, by finding a battery of the enemy which had harassed our advance, adding that the young men of that day were not equal to what they had been when he was a young man. Seeing immediately that he was jesting and disposed to rally me, as he often did young officers, I broke away from the hold on me which he tried to retain, and, as he laughed heartily through the stillness of the night, I went off to make a bed of my saddle-blanket, and, with my head in my saddle, near my horse's feet, was soon wrapped in the heavy slumber of a wearied soldier.

Some time after midnight I was awakened by the chill of the early morning hours, and, turning over, caught a glimpse of a little flame on the slope above me, and sitting up to see what it meant I saw, bending over a scant fire of twigs, two men seated on old cracker boxes and warming their hands over the little fire. I had to rub my eyes and collect my wits to recognize the figures of Robert E. Lee and Stonewall Jackson. Who can tell the story of that quiet council of war between two sleeping armies? Nothing remains on record to tell of plans discussed, and dangers weighed, and a great purpose formed, except the story of the great day so soon to follow.

Jackson's Flank March and Attack: May 2

After concluding their momentous conference, Stonewall Jackson left Lee to get his divisions moving. About 7:00 a.m. the lead regiments filed past Lee's headquarters. Then Jackson appeared, the two men talked briefly, and Jackson cantered on along the Furnace road. The two daring generals never saw each other again.

Jackson spurred ahead to join General Robert Rodes' division in the lead and to urge the troops to hurry. "Press on, press forward!" he called out over and over, leaning forward on his horse, his cap as usual pulled down almost over his eyes. "Permit no straggling. See that the column is kept closed. Press on, press on!"

Speed was indeed essential. To work his way around to Hooker's right, Jackson had to march his 26,000 soldiers almost 14 miles on a roundabout route along narrow dirt roads that, he hoped, were hidden from the Federals. And he had to do it well before nightfall, to allow time to deploy and launch his surprise attack. The weary, underfed troops trudged on as best they could, the column heading west and south on the Furnace road, then eventually north on the Brock road with few delays.

Jackson's march had in fact been spotted by Union lookouts at Hazel Grove, a small rise southwest of Chancellorsville. Given the news, Hooker soon concluded—correctly for once—that Lee might be trying to flank him, and he sent a message to General Howard, the XI Corps commander, urging him to "take measures to resist an attack from the west." But then Hooker did nothing to harass Jackson's column until midday, when he finally gave Sickles' III Corps permission to "advance cautiously."

The combative Sickles did more than that, launching an attack that swiftly overran what amounted to Jackson's rear guard, the 23d Georgia at Catharine Furnace, and threatened to roll up the rear of Jackson's column. Soon, however, a Rebel counterattack threw the Federals back.

This commotion actually aided Jackson. Combined with reports that the long Confederate column snaking west included numbers of wagons, it somehow convinced Hooker that Lee's entire army was retreating. Out on the Union right, where the blow was to fall, senior commanders dismissed the warnings of Jackson's approach that came in thick and fast from Federal pickets throughout the afternoon.

By the time the Confederate troops reached the Orange Turnpike and started deploying, less than three hours of daylight remained, but Jackson never thought of postponing the attack. Quietly, with orders murmured in undertones, the officers marshaled the troops into two long lines straddling the Orange Turnpike, Rodes' division in front, Raleigh E. Colston's next, with A. P. Hill's still forming up in the rear. Finally, at 5:15 p.m. by his pocket watch, Jackson turned to Rodes and said simply, "You can go forward, then."

Minutes after Rodes' troops moved they were spotted and fired on by startled Union pickets. The surprise over, the attackers screamed the bloodcurdling Rebel yell, dashed forward through the dense underbrush, and smashed into the camps of Leopold von Gilsa's brigade. Some of the Union troops formed ranks and got off a volley or two, but most were taken in the flank by blasts of gunfire and fled without firing a shot.

Shortly the Federal retreat turned into a rout, and terrified men streamed through the forest in chaos. By dusk the Confederates had raced ahead in their wild charge more than two miles, but by then many units had become mixed, and the exhausted and famished men were unable to find their officers or regiments. Slowly the attack shuddered to a halt.

Well after dark, as his officers desperately tried to sort out their disordered ranks, Jackson did something incautious but perfectly in character. Not satisfied with his brilliant victory, he rode ahead to scout out a side track of the Plank road that he could use to launch a night attack and, he hoped, utterly destroy the enemy. As he rode back about 9:00 p.m., jittery troops of the 18th North Carolina mistook his party for Federal cavalry and fired wildly into the dark. Jackson was hit three times, two bullets shattering his left arm, which was amputated shortly after he was taken to the rear.

Meanwhile a courier had reached General Lee with the news that Jackson had been shot by his own troops. Lee gave a moan and seemed on the verge of tears, the courier recalled, then asked not to hear any of the details. "It is too painful to talk about," Lee said. "Any victory is dearly bought which deprives us of the services of General Jackson, even for a short time." But then Lee turned to business, confirming the appointment of Jeb Stuart to take over Jackson's corps and sending Stuart firm orders to hit the Federals with everything he had the next morning.

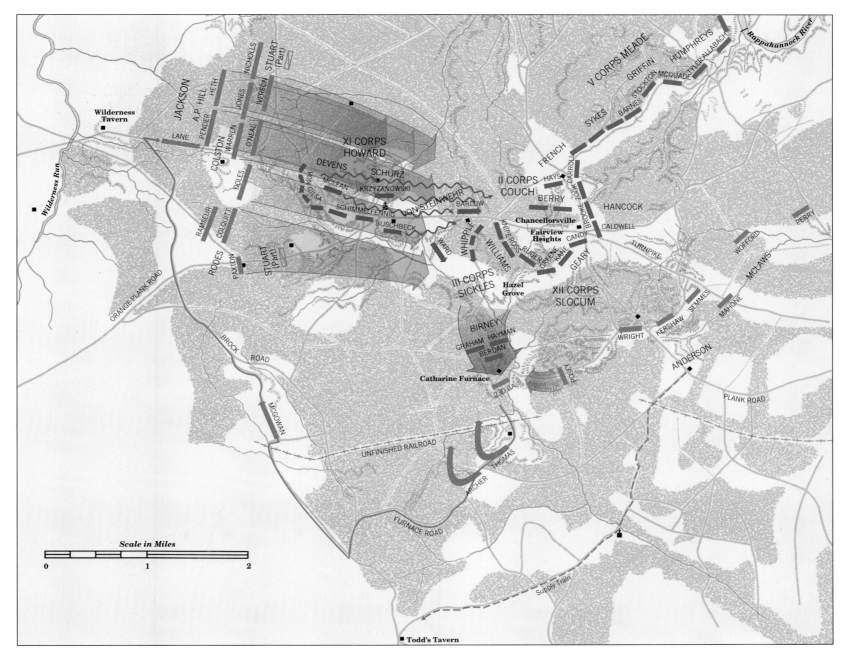

On May 2 Jackson, with 26,000 men, marched 14 miles around to the open Federal right flank, leaving Lee with only 14,000 soldiers to contain Hooker's 70,000. Although the Federals spotted the Confederate column, Jackson was still able to complete the march and then fall on and rout Howard's totally unprepared XI Corps.

LIEUTENANT WILLIAM M. NORMAN
2D NORTH CAROLINA INFANTRY, RAMSEUR'S BRIGADE

Temporarily detached from Rodes' division during the fight on May 1, Brigadier General Stephen D. Ramseur's four North Carolina regiments were reunited with the division the following morning and prepared to join Stonewall Jackson in his envelopment of the enemy right. A company commander in the 2d North Carolina, Norman correctly surmised the general purpose of the risky maneuver.

At daylight on the morning of the 2nd of May we were relieved and went to the rear about one mile to where the roads forked. Here were Generals Lee, Jackson, A. P. Hill, Stuart, and many major generals holding a council of war and planning our attack. Generals Lee and Jackson seemed to be very busily engaged in laying and arranging some broom straws on one end of the box, where some bacon and crackers were placed for their breakfast. At last General Lee gave the straws a stroke and knocked them all off. Rising to his feet and shaking hands with Generals Jackson, A. P. Hill, and some others, he sat down to eat his breakfast, after asking a blessing. General Jackson, I suppose, had already eaten, for he immediately mounted his horse and, uttering a few words to some of his aides, rode off up the road. In a few moments Jackson's corps was in motion. No one in the ranks knew anything about where we were going but supposed it to be one of Stonewall's flank movements.

LIEUTENANT J. F. J. CALDWELL
1ST SOUTH CAROLINA INFANTRY, McGOWAN'S BRIGADE

Disengaging from their position southeast of Chancellorsville, McGowan's South Carolina brigade fell into line with the rest of A. P. Hill's division in the rear of the long column snaking through the wilderness that screened their movement. When they gained a clearing near Catharine Furnace the Confederates briefly came under Yankee artillery fire, but Jackson's flank march continued.

At daylight the next morning, everything was astir. Blankets were rolled up; the coffee we half-made, over a handful of sticks, was drunk scalding hot; cold rations were swallowed hurriedly, and everything was made ready for the battle, that, we were assured, was just before us. The brigade was moved a little forward, knapsacks were piled up and committed to a guard of [the] sick, and such other preparations made as indicated immediate conflict. At this time Jackson galloped along our line, from left to right. I cannot help dwelling on the circumstance, for it was the last time I ever saw him.

He rode in his usual unstudied manner, wearing a common oil-cloth over his shoulders, and with his hat drawn low upon his eyes. He looked forward more eagerly than I had ever seen him do, and there appeared to be a more than wonted contraction of the thin, firm lips. We rose, on the point, I felt, of breaking out into the old cheer, but reading battle in his haste and stern look, we contented ourselves with gazing at him and giving expression to our foolish speculations. He passed at once to the right, where soon after our artillery opened on the enemy. Our brigade was moved farther to the left and thus taken out of the reach of shells.

Early on May 2 Hooker's chief of staff, Daniel Butterfield, ordered aeronaut Thaddeus Lowe to make an aerial reconnaissance of the Rebel lines beyond Fredericksburg. In response to Butterfield's directive (left), Professor Lowe's balloon (right, #1) ascended from its camouflaged position near the ruined Phillips house on Falmouth Heights (#2). Lowe reported that most of the Rebel army had shifted west, to confront Hooker's forces at Chancellorsville.

One did fall on the right of the brigade, into a ditch where two prudent men had squeezed themselves, but it did not strike them. . . .

After lying still for an hour or more, we were marched by the left flank, back to and across the plank-road. . . .

We followed various devious country roads . . . first the plank-road, and then the unfinished railroad from Fredericksburg to Gordonsville, then moving through an almost unbroken wilderness of woods, until most of us became completely lost. The roads were, fortunately, just wet enough to be easy to the feet and free from dust. The weather was fine, but we suffered for water. We were concealed from the enemy, except for a little space just after we started. Here they threw some shells among us, but I doubt if a dozen persons were wounded in the brigade.

PRIVATE WYMAN S. WHITE

2D U.S. SHARPSHOOTERS, BERDAN'S BRIGADE

On the afternoon of May 2 Sickles lashed out at the rear of Jackson's column near Catharine Furnace. Using their breechloading Sharps rifles to good effect, White and his fellow sharpshooters trapped nearly 300 men of the 23d Georgia in the cut of an unfinished railroad and forced them to surrender.

Our regiment acted as pickets during the morning of May 2nd, but at about noon the bugle sounded forward and we advanced in skirmish line and were engaged with the enemy's skirmishers all afternoon. We forced them back over a mile. It was a contest of sharpshooting and, of course, we had the best of the game as we were better armed and possibly better qualified than the opposing Rebels.

During the afternoon several of our regiment were wounded, among them was Private Williams of our company. He was shot through the body owing to his own carelessness or foolhardiness. . . .

Williams, at the commencement of the fight, seemed very anxious to get in some good work and kept getting ahead of the line. He was cautioned several times not to get ahead as it gave the enemy a chance to get in a flank shot. It is just as necessary to keep a good line fighting in skirmish formation as when in line of battle. During the afternoon the fire was quite brisk from both sides and Williams, finally rushed from the line and took position up to a large pine tree some six or eight rods in advance of the line.

It happened that the right of the regiment was making their way through a swamp so they were not up with the left wing. This bend in the line gave the Rebels a good chance to see Williams, though he was as he thought, back of a big tree. So mister Johnny rebel put a ball through Williams' hips from right to left, the ball coming out opposite to where it entered. The shock and pain was terrible and in all my life in the army or out I have never heard such an outcry and yell as Williams gave when he was hit. He made the woods echo with his outcries. He

was carried to the rear as soon as the line came up with him. . . .

. . . soon after Williams was wounded, our line wheeled to the right and advanced firing on a Rebel wagon train we could see making its way to the south and west. We received a lively fire as we advanced from a spot near a large building. We got the bugle call "charge" and we made a quick run for the building and came down on a regiment covered in a large pit where the Rebels mined iron and the building was a foundry where they cast shot and shell for their artillery.

In the pit we found the 23rd Georgia Regiment who were glad to surrender and we corralled the whole regiment to a man. We got our captured regiment into column and sent them to the rear. We had advanced beyond the foundry but a short distance and stampeded the Rebels' wagon train when we heard sharp firing to our right and rear followed by the Rebel yell.

Berdan's Sharpshooters sported green uniforms, befitting their habitual role as woodland skirmishers. This frock coat was worn by Sergeant William F. Tilson, a young Vermont farmer who fought at Chancellorsville with the 2d Regiment.

JETER TALLEY
RESIDENT OF SPOTSYLVANIA COUNTY

Concerned that the Yankees might threaten the flank of his marching column, Jackson instructed Brigadier General Alfred H. Colquitt to detach the 23d Georgia to "guard . . . against a surprise." When the Federals struck, Colonel Emory Best managed to make his escape with the colors and a handful of men, but he was subsequently court-martialed. A youngster at the time of the battle, Jeter Talley later recounted the experiences of two ironworkers who found themselves caught in the fighting at Catharine Furnace.

A curious thing happened here, back in the war. It happened to Abner Chewning, who was boss blacksmith here at the time. They tell me Ab was the best blacksmith in the entire world in his day. . . .

Ab was not allowed to enlist in the Confederate Army, first because he was needed at the Furnace to help turn out iron; second, because he had such a bad rheumatism they had to carry him in some of his spells in a chair and hoist him to places in a sling so he could check up on jobs.

One of Ab's chief helpers was Sprig Dempsey, who was a good-hearted big fellow and a great friend of Ab's. Well, Sprig told me himself Ab got cured of his rheumatism in a way that seemed to everybody at the time nothing short of a miracle. They were fitting a ventilator, or something, on the roof of a low building connected with the foundry. Jackson's men went marching by, but everybody was used to seeing troops moving, so they kept right on with their work. But hardly had Jackson's soldiers gone and the wagons were passing at Welford when here came a Georgia regiment, left by Jackson to guard the road up

toward Hazel Grove, moving back to the foundry and moving fast. The woods were full of Yankees, they said, and they couldn't stand them off much longer. Well, that didn't phase anybody, because they were used to scares; and, anyhow, Ab and Sprig and the rest of the iron men had no doubt for a minute those Georgia boys could whip a woods full of Yankees anytime. So they just went on with their tinkering while the Georgians got into the foundry and spread out on both sides of it and fixed everything for a fight. A chance of them were on the bluff above the foundry, others were in these low-ground woods skirmishing like Indians.

All of a sudden up on the bluff there broke out such a racket of shooting and yelling that Sprig and Ab got uneasy and then—Whooee! Georgians began to pour over the bluff like a waterfall and the sky behind them clouded up and rained Yankees down into the Furnace hollow. Sprig and the rest of the iron men took out for Scott's run yonder, to'other side of which Posey's brigade was fortifying. The Georgians outside the foundry drifted back towards the railroad, jumping from tree to tree and shooting at the Yankees surrounding the soldiers in the foundry.

Sprig said he reached the bank of Scott's run in what seemed three bounds and was just about to plunge across when he remembered poor Ab Chewning back there on the roof. He stopped short and was studying what he could do to help Ab get away when a man shot by him like a bat out of a barn and made a leap that carried him clear across Scott's run, which was more than Sprig could do or had thought of doing.

It was Ab. . . .

Well, sir, Sprig Dempsey was so astonished he couldn't believe what he was looking at with his own eyes. He just couldn't, and as he stood gazing where Ab had vanished through the forest a parcel of Yankees that thought they were chasing Ab came running and captured Sprig.

Excavated on the Chancellorsville battlefield, a beveled iron bar, or "pig," bears the word Catharine, denoting its origin at the furnace of that name. Originally established in 1837 but abandoned 10 years later, the furnace was reactivated in 1862 in order to supply iron to the Confederate war effort.

"You may think you have done a big thing just now, but wait till Jackson gets round on your right."

PRIVATE JOHN L. COLLINS
8TH PENNSYLVANIA CAVALRY, DEVIN'S BRIGADE

At 4:00 p.m. on May 2, Major Pennock Huey's 8th Pennsylvania Cavalry was given the command to mount up and support General Sickles' foray at Catharine Furnace. Private John Collins, a Philadelphian who had served in a 90-day infantry unit before reenlisting in the cavalry, shared the general belief that the Confederates were retreating from the battlefield.

On the afternoon of May 2d, 1863, the 8th Pennsylvania Cavalry were ordered to dismount, slack saddle-girths, and rest in the vicinity of General Hooker's headquarters at Chancellorsville. Some of the men fell asleep holding their horses, some began talking of the battle, while a knot of officers, who always improved such occasions in this way, sat down to their favorite game of poker. Suddenly an order from headquarters made a complete change in the scene. At the word "Mount!" the sleepers as well as the talkers sprang to their saddles, the gamblers snatched up their stakes and their cards, and a regiment of cavalry took the place of a lounging crowd.

Passing to the left of the Chancellorsville House, we crossed our line of battle at the edge of a wood and came up with a reconnoitering party that had captured the 23d Georgia. We had heard that Lee was retreating, and supposed that this unfortunate regiment had been sacrificed to give the main body a chance to escape; but while we were commiserating the poor fellows, one of them defiantly said, "You may think you have done a big thing just now, but wait till Jackson gets round on your right."

We laughed at his harmless bravado, for we did not think he would betray Jackson's move had he known anything about it.

At the outbreak of war, brothers (from left) Daniel, John, and Pleasant Chitwood enlisted in the Bartow County Yankee Killers, which became Company A of the 23d Georgia Infantry. On October 31, 1862, Pleasant Chitwood died of chronic diarrhea in a Richmond hospital; Daniel and John were captured when their unit was overrun at Catharine Furnace on the second day of the battle at Chancellorsville. Both were exchanged three weeks later, rejoined the army, and came through the rest of the war unhurt.

Eight hours into his flank march, Stonewall Jackson paused to write out what would prove to be his last dispatch to General Lee, expressing his characteristic determination and abiding religious faith. After the war the message was widely reproduced as a memento of the great Confederate commander, and it was framed and hung in many Southern homes.

LIEUTENANT JAMES P. SMITH
STAFF, LIEUTENANT GENERAL THOMAS J. JACKSON

From early morning to late afternoon, the soldiers of Stonewall Jackson's corps wound their way through the Wilderness in a column 10 miles in length. The day was warm and water in short supply, and although the troops had to cover between nine and 14 miles before they would be in position to strike the Yankee flank, spirits were high, as Jackson's aide recalled.

Slow and tedious is the advance of a mounted officer who has to pass in narrow wood roads, through dense thickets, the packed column of marching infantry, to be recognized all along the line and good-naturedly chaffed by many a gay-spirited fellow: "Say, here's one of 'Old Jack's' little boys, let him by, boys!" in a most patronizing tone. "Have a good breakfast this morning, sonny?" "Better hurry up, or you'll catch it for getting behind." "Tell 'Old Jack' we're all a-comin'." "Don't let him begin the fuss till we get thar!" And so on, until about 3 P.M., after a ride of ten miles of tortuous road, I found the general, seated on a stump by the Brock road, writing this dispatch:

> Near 3 P.M.
> May 2d, 1863
> General,
>   The enemy has made a stand at Chancellor's, which is about 2 miles from Chancellorsville. I hope as soon as practicable to attack.
>   I trust that an ever kind Providence will bless us with great success.
>
>   Respectfully,
>   T. J. Jackson,
>   Lt. Genl.
> Genl. R. E. Lee
>
> The leading division is up, & the next two appear to be well closed.
>   T. J. J.

"All that May morning was marked by a strange quiet which settled down upon the corps as the soldiers rested in line, arms in hand, waiting the coming battle."

LIEUTENANT HARTWELL OSBORN
55TH OHIO INFANTRY, McLEAN'S BRIGADE

Osborn, a student from Norwalk, Ohio, enlisted in November 1861 and rose from private to 2d lieutenant in his first month of service. His apprehension on May 2 proved to be well founded; that evening he was severely wounded and captured. Soon exchanged and sent to a Federal hospital, Osborn finished the war in 1865 as a captain.

ened, sir," with another remark about western colonels being more scared than hurt. Colonel Richardson, of the Twenty-fifth Ohio, brought in four scouts who had been far to the front and reported that the enemy were massing on our right. General Devens directed General McLean to send him back to his regiment. Colonel Reilly, of the Seventy-fifth Ohio, sent his Lieutenant-Colonel, Friend, with an urgent message of like import; but General Devens said he had no such news from corps headquarters and did not believe it. Colonel Friend then went to corps headquarters, where he was laughed at and warned not to bring on a panic. But the most convincing evidence was from an artillery officer, a prominent character in the Eleventh, and afterwards in the Twentieth Corps, on account of his dare-devil gallantry in action, and also because he had a habit of wearing leather breeches. Captain

All that May morning was marked by a strange quiet which settled down upon the corps as the soldiers rested in line, arms in hand, waiting the coming battle. At noon guns were stacked for dinner, but were resumed when the meal was finished. The whole right wing was on tiptoe with suppressed excitement. Since 11 a.m. the picket line of the Fifty-fifth Ohio, under Captain Robbins, had been sending in every half-hour reports of a movement in our front to the right. Two or three shots were heard, first to our left, then in front, then to the right, and rumor spread about that pickets had heard artillery moving in our front. . . . As the afternoon wore away the reports from the pickets came in often and were so specific and imperative that Colonel Lee of the Fifty-fifth took the men to brigade headquarters, and then, with General McLean, to division headquarters, expressing his deep concern and anxiety and requesting some immediate action. General Devens received the information coldly, and upon the third visit grew impatient, and at last said to Colonel Lee, "You are fright-

Colonel John C. Lee, commanding the 55th Ohio, vainly tried to convince his division commander, Brigadier General Charles Devens, that a large Rebel force was working its way across the front and flank of the XI Corps. "A rifle-pit is useless," Lee later wrote, "when the enemy is on the same side and in rear of your line." Disgusted by the incompetence of his superior officers, Lee tendered his "immediate and unconditional" resignation five days after the battle. Following the war he served a term as Ohio's lieutenant governor.

Hubert Dilger, of Battery I, First Ohio Artillery, was a trained artilleryman holding a commission in the Baden Mounted Artillery, and on leave of absence to enable him to take part in our war. About 2 p.m. Captain Dilger determined to investigate the rumors of a large force on our right, and with an orderly rode west beyond our line after vigorous remonstrance from Colonel von Gilsa, who was very much disturbed and anxious over the situation. Captain Dilger soon ran into the enemy and had much difficulty in escaping capture, being chased several miles, but he at last eluded his pursuers, and about 4:30 p.m. reported, first at corps headquarters, and then, by direction of General Howard, to army headquarters, where he says a long-legged major of cavalry laughed at his story and refused to allow him to report. . . . Captain Dilger returned sadly to his battery, and made preparations for the fight, even refusing to allow his horses to go to water.

BRIGADIER GENERAL FITZHUGH LEE

BRIGADE COMMANDER, ARMY OF NORTHERN VIRGINIA

Marching north on the Brock road, Jackson's column was nearing the Orange Plank road—the proposed staging area for their attack—when Fitzhugh Lee's cavalry scouts reported that the position of Hooker's right wing was farther north than anticipated. Lee recalled how Jackson accompanied him on a personal reconnaissance of the unsuspecting Yankees before continuing northward to a new assembly point on the Orange Turnpike.

*U*pon reaching the Plank Road, some five miles west of Chancellorsville, my command was halted, and, while waiting for Jackson to come up, I made a personal reconnaissance to locate the right for Jackson's attack. With one staff officer, I rode across and beyond the Plank Road, in the direction of the old Turnpike, pursuing a path through the woods, momentarily expecting to find evidence of the enemy's presence.

Seeing a wooded hill in the distance, I determined, if possible, to get upon its top, as it promised a view of the adjacent country; cautiously I ascended its side, reaching a point upon its summit without molestation. What a sight presented itself to me! Below, and but a few hundred yards distant, ran the Federal line of battle. I was in rear of Howard's right. They were in line of defence, with abatis in front, and long lines of stacked arms in rear. Two cannon were visible in a part of

A veteran German artillery officer, Captain Hubert Dilger tendered his service to the Union and became renowned as a skilled and daring battery commander on the battlefields of Virginia and later Georgia. In 1893 he was awarded the Medal of Honor for distinguished gallantry in the Battle of Chancellorsville.

the line. The soldiers were in groups in the rear, laughing, chatting, smoking, probably engaged here and there in games of cards and other amusements, indulged in while feeling safe and comfortable, awaiting orders. In rear of them were other parties, driving up and slaughtering beeves. The remembrance of the scene is as clear as it was sixteen years ago.

So impressed was I with my discovery that I rode rapidly back to the point on the Plank Road where I had left my cavalry, and back down the road Jackson was moving, when I met Stonewall himself. "General," said I, "if you will ride with me, halting your column here out of sight, I will show you the enemy's right, and you will perceive the great advantage of attacking down the old Turnpike, instead of down the Plank Road, the enemy's line being taken in reverse. Bring only one courier, as you will be in view from the top of the hill." Jackson assented, and I rapidly conducted him to the point of observation. There had been no change in the picture. I watched him closely, as he gazed upon Howard's troops. It was then about 2 P.M. His eyes burned with a brilliant glow, lighting up a sad face; his expression was one of intense interest; his face was colored slightly with the sense of approaching battle, and radiant at the success of his flank movement.

To the remarks made to him while the unconscious line of blue was pointed out, he did not reply once during the five minutes he was on the hill; and yet his lips were moving. From what I have read and heard of Jackson since that day, I know now what he was doing then; while talking to the great God of Battles, how could he hear what a poor cavalry-man was saying?

"Tell General Rhodes," said he, suddenly whirling his horse toward the courier, "to move across the old Plank Road, halting when he gets to the old Turnpike, and I will join him there."

One more look upon the Federal lines, and then he rode rapidly down the hill, his arms flapping to the motions of his horse, over whose head it seemed, good rider as he was, he could certainly go.

An 1865 photograph taken from Dowdall's Tavern looks northwest across the Plank road to Wilderness Church (left of center) and the Hawkins farm (right), which served as headquarters for Federal general Carl Schurz. When A. P. Hill's troops advanced across his property, farmer Alexander Hawkins saw the men of his old regiment, the 47th Virginia. "This was too much for me," he recalled; "picking up a gun, I went off with them down the road, yelling with the rest of them."

LIEUTENANT JAMES P. SMITH
STAFF, LIEUTENANT GENERAL THOMAS J. JACKSON

Lieutenant Smith, Jackson's aide, recalled the dramatic culmination of the flank march as three divisions of Southern infantry prepared to launch a smashing blow against Howard's XI Corps. About 5:15 p.m. Major Eugene Blackford of the 5th Alabama ordered forward his detachment of sharpshooters 400 yards in advance, followed 15 minutes later by the battle lines of Rodes' division.

Rodes's division, at the head of the column, was thrown into line of battle, with Colston forming the second line and A. P. Hill the third, while the artillery under Colonel Stapleton Crutchfield moved in column on the road, or was parked in a field on

the right. The well-trained skirmishers of Rodes's division, under Major Eugene Blackford, were thrown to the front. It must have been between five and six o'clock in the evening, Saturday, May 2d, when these dispositions were completed. Upon his stout-built, long-paced little sorrel, Jackson sat, with visor low over his eyes and lips compressed, and with his watch in his hand. Upon his right sat Robert E. Rodes, the very picture of a soldier, and every inch all that he appeared. Upon his right sat Major Blackford.

"Are you ready, General Rodes?" said Jackson.

"Yes, sir!" replied Rodes, impatient for the advance.

"You can go forward then," said Jackson.

A nod from Rodes was order enough for Blackford, and then suddenly the woods rang with the bugle call, and back came the responses from bugles on the right and left, and the long line of skirmishers, through the wild thicket of undergrowth sprang eagerly to their work, followed promptly by the quick steps of the line of battle. For a moment all the troops seemed buried in the depths of the gloomy forest, and then suddenly the echoes waked and swept the country for miles, never failing until heard at the headquarters of Hooker at Chancellorsville—the wild "rebel yell" of the long Confederate lines.

A graduate of the Virginia Military Institute and a former railroad executive, 34-year-old Brigadier General Robert E. Rodes was considered one of the finest division commanders in Lee's army and was a stickler for detail. In battle "Rodes's eyes were everywhere," one soldier recalled, "humming to himself and catching the ends of his long, tawny moustache between his lips."

"I had always thought somehow that the Lord was not going to let me be killed in the war, and I remember thinking this was the test case."

SERGEANT LUTHER B. MESNARD
55TH OHIO INFANTRY, MCLEAN'S BRIGADE

With only two of nine regiments in his division facing to the west, General Devens was ill prepared to withstand the sudden Rebel onslaught, and within minutes both von Gilsa's and McLean's brigades were in shambles. Sergeant Mesnard, who had recently returned to Company D of the 55th Ohio following a stint as quartermaster clerk, described the chaotic scene.

Word had been passed along our line for the boys to eat supper and make themselves comfortable, our band was playing in the pine grove to our rear, when like a crash of thunder from the clear sky there came a volley of musketry from the right. As I looked down the road I could see the German officers trying to rally the men as everything seemed to be giving away, just then a couple of deer came out of the woods to our right, and Srgt. Major Lowe says, "See those deer," as a bullet struck the top of his cap and scorched his head. I then saw the rebs as they were coming out of the timber. A rebel battery had opened up in the road and began sending grape up the road by the hatful. I remember so well seeing a rebel color bearer as he jumped over the brush fence waving his flag. I fired five shots from this our first position when I watched my chance and jumped across the road between the charges of canister. I noticed several dead men in the road and that the grape as it swept up the road turned one over as I found myself running right into the rebs. They were all yelling as only rebels can, and it seemed to me ramming cartridges into their guns. I caromed off to my right, toward our left, and the 25th Ohio which had been in reserve was just deploying into line at right angles to our original front, and I fell into line. We stopped the rebs in our front for a moment, but there was a perfect hail storm of lead flying, a perfect mass of rebs not twenty feet away, the man on my right and left both fell, their heads toward the rebs, our right being overlaped [crumbled] away. The rebs surged ahead and I ran toward our left flank, and how I did run. Saw Col. Lee's cap on the ground, knew it [by] the letters, etc. on it. I soon saw Paul Jones, who by the way was regimental color bearer now. He had the colors on one arm and Gen'l Drevens on the other, the general having been wounded in the foot. I passed on but soon Paul overtook me. I said where is your general. He said, "Oh, d—— him he is drunk." About this time I saw Gen'l Howard, this was about twenty minutes after he had talked to the battery boys about starting for Richmond. I soon saw Col. Lee rallying men of all commands at a favorable place where some breast works deflected around the brow of a slight hill. We formed a good strong line with a battery to our right, a valley in front. The rebs seemed to stop a moment and form a line. I noticed that [as] they came down the slope opposite us that three lines of battle fired at once over each other heads, but as they came into the valley they became badly mixed up, and that the battery to our right plowed great gaps through their ranks. I felt that we were going to hold them this time sure, but in a moment I saw our battery was gone and the rebs

In Alfred Waud's sketch, panic-stricken fugitives from Devens' command (right) flee toward the lines of Schurz's division, along the Plank road near Dowdall's Tavern (middle distance). But this position, too, proved untenable. "Our rear was at the mercy of the enemy," Schurz reported; "the whole line deployed on the old turnpike, facing south, was rolled up and swept away in a moment."

through the smoke to my right. They had extended way beyond our right (although we had been firing toward our original right rear) I had my gun nearly loaded and wanted to give them one more shot. As I rose to fire over the low breast works the rebs were jumping over within a few feet of me and as I stuck my gun forward to fire they were very close in front, and as I turned to run, I saw their was not a Union Soldier to my left. I believe I was the very last man to leave this line. [I] started to run. I think it was the most dangerous place I was ever in. I had always thought somehow that the Lord was not going to let me be killed in the war, and I remember thinking this was the test case. "If the Lord was ever going to do anything for old Ira, now's the time," to quote from a well known negro story which came into my mind at the time, as I saw the dead and wounded so thick on the ground and heard the lead and cannon shot so filling the air. When I had passed an open field, some thirty rods, I had my gun loaded and turned behind the first tree and fired. As I passed into the woods I noticed a lot of ambulances, wagons and artillery which I think belonged to the 12th or 3rd corps. I thought

ther'll be a stampede, and I turned toward the left along a timbered side hill, while to my front, (as I was going to the south eastward along our general line of battle) there was a large space near a hundred acres of open or cleared ground, and I saw a sight which made my heart bleed. I saw a battery rushing down a hill and the lead horses fell or stumbled into a small creek and the other[s] right onto and over them. . . . while to the right or left or in front as far as I could see, everything was fleeing in panic. It seemed to me that the whole army had gone to pieces in a panic. All was lost—Oh my country, Can this be? There was no one near whom I knew. I look back to this as the darkest day in my experience.

CAPTAIN WILLIAM B. HAYGOOD
44TH GEORGIA INFANTRY, DOLES' BRIGADE

Advancing at the right-center of Rodes' division, four Georgia regiments commanded by Brigadier General George P. Doles quickly overran the enemy positions, capturing eight artillery pieces and hundreds of prisoners. Captain Haygood, whose letter described the running fight, was severely wounded two months later at the Battle of Gettysburg. His left arm amputated, Haygood was captured by the Yankees in a Hagerstown, Maryland, hospital.

Twenty-year-old Private Henry T. Davenport served in the 12th Georgia of Doles' command. Twice wounded in the fighting on May 2, Davenport recovered and returned to duty, only to be wounded two more times at the Wilderness, and yet again in the Battle of Spotsylvania in May 1864, where he was also captured.

We all then sprang forwards with such a shout, and yell, mingeled with a full round of minie balls, that they gave away at the first onset of our boys, thus their first works were carried, & when we once got them going, we pressed them back over and farther and farther, untill they got up a perfect stampede. leaving behind, in our hands, every thing that was cumberous, Such as knap sacks, blankets, hats, shoes, overcoats, all Sorts of clothing and all of their little viviets [too] tidious to mention, besides a large lot of fine Small arms, and several peaces of artilery. With quite a number of fine horses, as well as all of their killed & wounded, and a grate many firearms. by this time we were all mixed up. So bad that we could hardly tell which Reg. or Brig. we were in. that however made no difference. as we never stoped to learn who did this or that. but our watchword was onward. Onward we went untill long after dark. We then came to a halt, and began to look around to see after our several commands. When I came to a halt, I did not know but one man that was with me. though I new that I was with my friends and all was right with me. It took me about 2 hours to find my reg. When I came to it, my com. had given me up as lost or killed. Just hear let me say to you, that I never seen in all of my life. So much rejoicing, as we did over the different men, and parts of companies, as we came up to the reg. Some of the officers and men gave me a good old fashion hug. Which was reciprocated by me with all of my heart.

SERGEANT JAMES H. PEABODY
61ST OHIO INFANTRY, SCHIMMELFENNIG'S BRIGADE

Hastily changing front to meet the enemy threat, the brigade of Prussian-born Brigadier General Alexander Schimmelfennig could do little to stem the tide of Jackson's onslaught and was soon swept away in the rout. The brigade lost more than 400 men, half of them taken prisoner, although the wounded Sergeant Peabody was able to make his escape. His scornful opinion of General Howard was shared by many survivors of the XI Corps' debacle.

At this time our arms were stacked in the road, the boys still playing "draw poker"; but when they heard the whistle of bullets, concluded not to play longer.

That was the situation our brigade was in when the bullets began whistling over our heads along the flank. No one ever saw men hustle

Although undeniably brave—he had lost his right arm leading a charge at the Battle of Fair Oaks—Major General Oliver O. Howard was a dour New Englander whose religious fervor and abolitionist sentiments set him apart from most of his subordinates. "They looked at him with dubious curiosity," General Schurz recalled; "not a cheer could be started when he rode along the front."

on their traps and get into line any quicker than we did; each man picked up everything he had, not one of them leaving anything behind; and by the time we had gotten into line and taken arms, they had crowded us so much from the right as to turn me "right about." As I looked up along the line, I saw a piece of shell, or chunk of iron, coming with a ricochet along down the side hill—it was from the first gun fired—and the first thing I knew, it struck me on the ankle, knocking my foot out from under me. My first thought was that I had lost my heel, but, glancing down, couldn't see anything missing. By this time, the right had been driven back pell-mell; in fact, the whole line was broken. It would not have been good generalship on my part to have stopped and made a close examination, so I followed the rest. As we emerged from the woods into an open field, I saw a sight I shall never forget as long as I live. There were regiments, brigades and divisions completely disorganized and scattered; in the midst was General Howard and staff, or part of it; on the extreme right of that scattered line was a small body of men—which I afterward learned was McLean's brigade of the First Division—making a desperate attempt to check the advance of the enemy. I saw General Howard swinging his revolver in his hand—he had no right hand—and when I had gotten close to him, he was crying out, "Halt! Halt! I'm ruined, I'm ruined; I'll shoot if you don't stop; I'm ruined, I'm ruined," over and over again. I stopped, leaned on my musket, and looked at him in surprise and wonder, that a man who occupied the position he did should get so completely con-

fused and bewildered; in fact, he was "rattled." While I was standing there admiring the self-possession of the General, there was a Reb that got among us some way, no one knew how; he did not have any gun, only a knapsack, haversack and canteen. Some of the boys asked him how he got there, where he came from, and many other questions, but he wouldn't give any account of himself, and edged off; finally started to run toward our rear bearing to our left. He paid no attention to repeated calls to halt, and had not run more than one hundred and fifty feet or so, before two or three of our men drew up their guns and shot him dead; he fell headlong on his face and lay there. After the Reb was disposed of, I again looked over to our right and could see, coming out of the woods, a line, or rather mass, of Rebs, still on the flank of McLean's brigade, which compelled them to give way. There was no use fighting against such odds. I then turned again to General Howard, who was looking in the same direction, and when he comprehended the situation, he put "spurs" to his horse and rode to the rear of our right, or in that direction. I thought he was going there to impart the same information to them he had given us; that is, "I'm ruined." None of us knew or cared where he went.

Eyes peeled for plunder as he advanced through an abandoned Yankee camp in the second wave of Jackson's attack, Rebel private John O. Casler snatched up this snuffbox bearing the words "Help yourself" on its lid.

PRIVATE JOHN O. CASLER
PIONEER DETACHMENT, COLSTON'S DIVISION

Temporarily detached from the Stonewall Brigade—which saw no action on May 2—Private Casler advanced with Brigadier General Raleigh E. Colston's troops some 200 yards behind Rodes' division. Colston's units became intermingled with Rodes' men as the tide of battle swept down the Plank road and through the woods on either side. Casler described the chaotic but victorious charge in his classic postwar narrative "Four Years in the Stonewall Brigade."

Lt. Col. Chas. Walters

Killed at Chancellorsville

the 1st Lt. Col. of the 17th C.V.

Killed at Chancellorsville May 2—1863

It was a running fight for three miles. We took them completely by surprise, and our three divisions got merged into one line of battle, all going forward at full speed. Our artillery did not have time to unlimber and fire; they had to keep in a trot to keep up with the infantry. We ran through the enemy's camps where they were cooking supper. Tents were standing, and camp-kettles were on the fire full of meat. I saw a big Newfoundland dog lying in one tent as quietly as if nothing had happened. We had a nice chance to plunder their camps and search the dead; but the men were afraid to stop, as they had to keep with the artillery and were near a good many officers, who might whack them over the head with their swords if they saw them plundering but the temptation was too great, and sometimes they would run their hands in some dead men's pockets as they hurried along, but seldom procured anything of value.

I saw a wounded man lying beside the road and had got past him; but, noticing he was an officer, I ran back to him to get his sword and pistol. I asked him if he was wounded badly. He said he was not. He was shot through the foot, but thought he would lie there until the fight was over; that he was the Captain of some Ohio regiment. I took off his belt and sword, which was a very fine one, but I found no pistol in the scabbard. I asked him where the pistol was, and he said he supposed he must have lost it in the fight; that he did not know it was gone; but I thought he had it in his bosom, so I unbuttoned his coat and searched for it, but could not find it. He declared he did not have it, but he had a fine gold watch and chain. I was looking at it when he told me to take it along; but I would not do it. I told him that as he was wounded and a prisoner I would let him keep it. . . .

Our officers then commenced forming the men in line and getting them in some kind of order, but the men kept up a terrible noise and confusion, hallooing for this regiment and that regiment, until it seemed that there were no more than three or four of any regiment together. They were all mixed up in one confused mass. The enemy could hear us distinctly by the noise we made. They located us precisely, and immediately opened on us with twenty pieces of artillery, at short range, and swept the woods and road with the most terrific and destructive shelling that we were subjected to during the war.

Charlie Cross, Sam Nunnelly, Jake Fogle and myself were together when the shelling commenced. We stepped to one side and happened to find a sink, or low place, where a tree had blown down some time in the past, and laid down in it. We filled it up even with the ground, and

The officers of the 17th Connecticut strove valiantly to maintain order amid the disorganized retreat of McLean's brigade. Awed by the courage of Colonel William Noble (below), General McLean exclaimed, "He is by God the bravest man of us all!" Noble was wounded in the right arm, while Lieutenant Colonel Charles Walter (far left) was shot dead from his horse. Following the fight at Chancellorsville, Captain Douglas Fowler (left) was promoted to command of the 17th but was killed at Gettysburg two months later, when the XI Corps was again driven from the field on July 1.

Lt. Col. Douglas Fowler
Killed at Gettysburg Va.
The 2nd Lt. Col. of the 17th C.V.
Killed at Gettysburg July 1st 1863

it seemed as if the shells did not miss us more than six inches. Some would strike in front of us, scattering the dirt all over us. I believe if I had stuck my head up a few inches I would have been killed.

We could hear someone scream out every second in the agonies of death. Jake Fogle kept praying all the time. Every time a shell would pass directly over us Jake would say: "Lord, save us this time!" "Lord, save us this time!" Sam Nunnelly, a wild, reckless fellow, would laugh at him and say: "Pray on Jake! Pray on Jake!" and the two kept that up as long as the shelling lasted. Cross and I tried to get Sam to hush, but it was no use.

"As the men had been informed that Lee was running away, they had taken things easy."

LIEUTENANT FREDERICK OTTO VON FRITSCH
Staff, Brigadier General Alexander Schimmelfennig

One of many German-born volunteers in the XI Corps, von Fritsch was a graduate of the Dresden Military Academy. In 1856 he resigned his commission in the Saxon cavalry, immigrated to America, and in 1862 signed up with the 68th New York. During a reconnaissance on the afternoon of May 2, von Fritsch and artilleryman Hubert Dilger discovered large numbers of Confederates south and west of the XI Corps, but their warnings were ignored. In the bloody fight near Dowdall's Tavern, the Federals paid a heavy price for their commanders' indifference.

All at once I heard some noise. I listened, and down the Pike came a cannon ball, ricochetting; then I heard firing in the woods, and some queer sounds. I galloped to the ambulance, where my General was resting, loosened his horse and said:

"They are coming, General, and right through the woods on our flank." He mounted, rode to the Cross road, and excitedly gave the order to tell the commanders of his regiments on the Pike to change front and to form a line of battle north of the Plank road, a little east of the Cross road.

I delivered these orders safely and promptly, but as the men had been informed that Lee was running away, they had taken things easy, were lying about in groups and smoking pipes, or were looking for the best places to sleep in peace and comfort that night.

The command "Fall in," and the firing in the woods now naturally created the greatest commotion. Men began fighting for their guns, stacks of arms were upset everywhere, many trying to repack their knapsacks . . . pushing one another, trying to fix their accoutrements, while the excited shouts of the officers: "Fall in! fall in!" caused much disorder.

So it took some time before all the men fell in line and until the regiments were ready to march away to the new positions. General Devens's men already came running down the road, thoroughly demoralized and panic stricken.

General Devens had not done a thing to prevent the great disaster, and with no other excuse except that General Howard had approved his position in the morning. Now his poor men came running down the Pike, shouting such warnings as: "We are all surrounded!" "Keep off the road, boys; the Confederates have just placed a battery on it, and will fire away," etc. . . .

Our regiments on the Pike were blocked in and could not move, and already the bullets from the Confederates came whizzing into the ranks. General Schimmelpfennig shouted: "First Brigade, form here!"

"Form here, men of the First Brigade!" I sang out continually.

The officers of these regiments tried hard to lead the men there, fighting their way through Devens's panic-stricken men, but the confusion was too great. At that time General Howard arrived at a point about forty paces west of the Cross road, fell or jumped from his horse, and screamed: "Stand, boys, face about and fire!"

All very nice, but naturally without the slightest effect! I had caught his horse and called out to him to mount.

No, take that horse to the rear! he shouted.

Can't do that, General, I said, and you'd better mount, sir, as the Confederates are quite near!

Hundreds were killed near us that moment.

As he did not seem to be able to get on his horse I dismounted, grasped the back of his coat and helped him on. Then he rode towards Dowdall's.

I now worked my way to General Schimmelpfennig, and he sang out to me, "Bring the 82nd Illinois near this cross road and place it next to the 68th."

I brought the 82nd in double quick, down towards the General, when he gave the order:

"Too late, too late! Let Hecker front west at his old position, and I will collect the other men right behind him!"

"Verflugter Esel!" roared Colonel Hecker and then gave the command: "About face! Double quick! March!"

I rode along and waited till he commanded:

"Halt—Front—Fire!" The Confederates were already visible in the woods before him. Deer, rabbits and foxes came racing out of the woods. Just then Hecker's color bearer was killed, and the old Revolutionist seized the flag, and shouted: "Fix bayonets! Charge bayonets! Come on, boys! Charge!"

He was going to take the woods by storm, but that moment a bullet struck him, and he fell from his horse, screaming: "Fire away, 82nd!" and they did fire away nobly, and remained at their post. I now noticed my General right in the rear of this brave regiment, forming the men, and I assisted to get as many as I could in line. Devens's men had all passed up the Plank road, and were running toward Chancellor's. . . .

I galloped about, and was just going to tell the Commander of the 68th to fall back behind the 82nd also, in order to allow Captain Dilger to fire down the road—he was sending shells over their heads—when "Pfutt!" a bullet struck me in the belt plate, and nearly threw me off Caesar's back. Holding myself by his mane, I got into the saddle again, but thinking that I was mortally wounded, as I felt the pain in my back, and naturally thought that the bullet had pierced my stomach, I turned east, and chased toward Dowdall's to die away from the great tumult.

Just in front of Dowdall's I noticed General Howard holding a flag under his arm and shouting: "Rally round the flag; rally round the flag!" Mechanically I drew my sword and stopped some men coming up the road, but my voice gave out and I felt a new and fearful pain in my stomach. Thinking that my hour had come, I walked Caesar past Howard, and with my eyes directed toward heaven, said: "I am coming, Marie, make my sufferings short!"

At the outbreak of war cousins William H. Egerton (left) and William E. Johnson (right) enlisted as privates in the Warren Guards, Company F of the 12th North Carolina. Egerton was killed at Gaines' Mill in June 1862, while Johnson, promoted to lieutenant, survived to fight at Chancellorsville. During the charge of Brigadier General Alfred Iverson's brigade, advancing on the far left of Rodes' division, Johnson was shot in the head and died the next day.

CAPTAIN CHARLES I. WICKERSHAM
8TH PENNSYLVANIA CAVALRY, DEVIN'S BRIGADE

With Stoneman on a raid behind Rebel lines, most of the Federal cavalry was absent, and the remaining troopers had seen little rest since Hooker's offensive got under way. At 6:30 p.m. General Alfred Pleasonton ordered the 8th Pennsylvania Cavalry to support Howard's crumbling XI Corps. Only recently recovered from a bout of malaria, Wickersham described the disaster that unfolded when he and his comrades inadvertently rode into the midst of Jackson's advancing divisions.

In a few moments heavy firing was heard on our right, which up to this time had been quiet, and while we were listening, and wondering what it meant, an officer rode up to General Sickles, announced himself as an aide-de-camp to General Howard, and stated that General Howard's lines were giving way and he wanted a regiment of cavalry. General Sickles turned to General Pleasonton, who at once ordered Major Huey to report to General Howard. The aide was asked where General Howard could be found, and the reply was "about a mile out on the Plank Road." I then started to where the regiment was. Some of the men were asleep, some were talking of the battle in progress, while a knot of officers were playing a game of poker, Major Keenan, Captain Arrowsmith, Captain Daily, and Adjutant Haddock among them.

Major Huey rode up a moment later and ordered the regiment to mount. The sleepers, as well as the talkers, sprang to their saddles, and a regiment of cavalry was seen in place of a lounging crowd. Major Keenan looked up and said: "Well, Major Huey, you spoiled a d——d good game of poker."

The regiment was in good spirits when we left this point: the impression being that the enemy was retreating, and, although the firing was heavy on our left, where we were to find General Howard, we had no thought of what was impending. Sabres were in their scabbards; men were riding listlessly at a walk, in the road which led to the Plank Road, where we were told we would find General Howard. The firing which we heard had by this time increased very much, with some artillery fire added. We had gone not more than half a mile, when a solid mass of gray was seen on our left flank, moving rapidly toward us, firing as they came. . . . We could hear no orders on account of the firing, but we saw the battalion ahead of us draw sabres and take the trot. Spurs pricked the horses' sides and down the road plunged the column, the horses straining every muscle. The men, comprehending the great-

ness of the moment, lifted their sabres high in the air. Captain McCallom turned in his saddle as we trotted along, and, seeing the mass of the enemy in front, said to me: "I think this is the last of the 8th Pennsylvania Cavalry." I replied, "I think so too, but let us go down with our colors flying.". . .

At the command, "Gallop and charge," we rushed upon the astonished Confederates, who, suddenly confronted by what they thought was the head of our cavalry corps, stood motionless and irresolute for a moment, the horses trampling them. Sabre blows fell thick and fast: some threw down their guns and raised their hands beseechingly. Soon the lines behind them opened fire, and horses and riders tumbled headlong; for several hundred yards the cavalry column ploughed its way through more than one line of Confederate infantry before it lost its aggressive force. It was the work of but a few minutes, but in that short time three officers and more than eighty men, and twenty-six horses had gone down. . . .

. . . During this charge it seemed as though the enemy were firing almost in our faces, so close were their lines to us, and in one instance where our horses were checked a moment by those in our front, a rebel officer caught the bridle of one of our officers, and pointing a revolver at him, ordered him to surrender. The reply was what is known in the sabre exercise as "left cut against infantry." The rebel officer did not respond to roll call the next morning.

A former merchant, Major Pennock Huey commanded the 8th Pennsylvania Cavalry in its desperate charge down the Plank road. "We cut our way through," he recalled, "trampling down all who could not escape us." Rebel volleys felled most of those at the head of the column, including Major Peter Keenan and Adjutant John Haddock, while nearly a hundred of the Pennsylvanians were killed or captured during the charge into the enemy's ranks.

After nightfall on May 2, confusion abounded in the ranks of both armies, and one victim of the nocturnal chaos was Brigadier General Joseph F. Knipe's brigade (XII Corps). Earlier that day, three of Knipe's regiments were ordered to leave their entrenchments south of the Plank road to support Sickles' advance around Catharine Furnace. After the fury of Jackson's attack had subsided, they returned to reoccupy their old line—only to find it overrun by enemy troops of Rodes' division. When Knipe's 46th Pennsylvania ran unwittingly into the Rebels, more than 80 Federals were snagged, including the color bearer and the unit's state colors (above). Private J. S. Webber of the 12th North Carolina got credit for capturing the banner, later recovered in Richmond when the city fell in 1865.

SERGEANT LUCIUS B. SWIFT
28TH NEW YORK INFANTRY, KNIPE'S BRIGADE

With the departure of Knipe's other three regiments to back up Sickles' early afternoon foray, the understrength 28th New York was left behind and caught in the stampede of the XI Corps. The regiment tried to make a stand, but Howard's men, sheltering behind the 28th's barricades, bolted at the first sign of the enemy. More than 60 of the New Yorkers were captured, including Sergeant Swift.

Having nothing else to do, we had coffee early and had finished, when suddenly, about six o'clock, a tremendous battle opened to the west of us out where the 11th corps was. The musketry ran at once into a roll which comes only from rapid firing by a great number of troops. The artillery had a short spiteful sound such as it always seemed to me to have at short range. We listened intently and in half an hour a long line of prisoners were marched down the plank road toward Chancellorsville; from this we felt that the battle was in our favor. But, although we did not know it, this was in fact the Georgia regiment captured by Sickles which had been brought down from Hazel Grove to the plank road. . . .

. . . The battle lasted about an hour; the sound died away and silence followed. After a considerable wait, a second battle began lasting about twenty minutes and then silence fell again. Another period of waiting and then there appeared in front of us a Berdan sharpshooter dressed in dark green of his corps. He had no gun and no hat and had evidently run fast and far. Berdan's men were out south with Sickles and where this man came from is a mystery unless he was a skulker and was driven out of hiding by Jackson's advance. Seeing us, he came in and we asked him what the matter was. He said the troops out in front had been cut to pieces and then went on to the rear. We were at once ordered to fall in. Then came a dozen more soldiers, running and breathless, and beyond them we could see a multitude coming in great disorder. Colonel Cook at once deployed the battalion as skirmishers to stop the retreat. We went at it like beavers, first with orders and then with oaths and threats. The fugitives ignored us and kept on, and finally Colonel Cook gave the order to shoot and four or five were shot down. Colonel Cook was a dead shot and I saw him shoot one with a navy revolver at twenty rods; the man fell on his face. When they saw that we were in earnest, they stopped and went up to the works. Masses of soldiers all mixed up without formation of any kind came over our works and many still proposed to keep right on to the rear, but with persuasion and threats and more profanity than I ever heard before or since, the 28th, assisted by officers of the 11th corps, finally got them all up to the works for a long distance to the left and right of its own place. The plank road was now choked with retreating artillery and wagons and soldiers. Then heavy firing began again not far in front on the other side of the plank road, lasting perhaps twenty minutes. Our skirmish line did not reach to the plank road but after this last battle, the retreating men either of their own accord or by order stopped and manned the works clear up to the plank road, and now from the plank road to our place and for a good distance beyond the works were occupied by at least 2000 men and in some places three and four deep. But they were not soldiers in companies and regiments and under command; organizations were scattered to the four winds.

The enemy now came near our line and bullets went zipping past. Our skirmish line was called in and we took our place at the works. Many fugitives wanted a place with us, probably because they saw that we had a formation and officers, and we had a great deal of trouble in clearing them out. As we knelt behind the works, a strange soldier attempted to crowd in and I ordered him out roughly. He jumped up, threw back a common blue overcoat, displaying an officer's uniform and sword and said with a strong foreign accent in a protesting tone, "I am an officer!" I had unwittingly committed a breach of discipline and the captain said to me warningly "Steady, steady"; but I had steam up and in spite of the warning, I told the officer, not very mildly, to go down line where there were plenty of men without officers. He went and as he started off, he set up some kind of a foreign war cry. He was a harmless little fellow and I warrant he did no damage to friend or foe.

Some one came up and knelt quickly by my side. It was John, the drummer boy. He had thrown away his drum and had taken the belts, cartridges and gun from some dead soldier and equipped himself. The belts were much too big for him and the cartridge box hung below his hip; but there he was, alert and keen for the fight, and he never said a word, but began to look out steadily for the enemy. We waited for the expected asault and a few of our sharp-eyed boys, distinguishing Confederate skirmishers, fired, after careful aim over the works; but as a

body, we waited until we could see something more substantial to shoot at. We would be able to fire one destructive round and then the contest must be decided by bayonet; from this the 28th had no reason to shrink for we had been carefully drilled in bayonet exercise. Then a strange thing happened. Many general officers of the 11th corps were the last to leave the field and now several of them with their staffs forming group after group came down the plank road and turning into the woods on our side, went swiftly to the rear. Then the line behind our works up toward the road, for some reason, either by order, as some accounts state, or because their general officers did not stop, rose as one man and started for Chancellorsville. The example was contagious and in less than a minute every man, except the soldiers of the 28th, had left the works and was making his way to the rear as fast as his legs could carry him. It was useless to shoot into them and we all involuntarily stood up and looked after them with infinite disgust and profanity.

Corporal W. B. Yerger of the 128th Pennsylvania picked up this Confederate canteen during his regiment's ill-fated march on the night of May 2. Yerger and 200 others were captured when the regiment blundered into Rebel lines.

"A perfect storm of artillery lighted up with fitful flashes the forest openings."

LIEUTENANT PORTER FARLEY
140TH NEW YORK INFANTRY, O'RORKE'S BRIGADE

When Howard's lines gave way, Sykes' division of the V Corps was ordered to move to the threatened center of the Federal position. Shoving their way through demoralized fugitives, Sykes' troops—including the 140th New York—helped to shore up the embattled perimeter at Chancellorsville. Farley was serving as regimental adjutant.

The scene as we neared the Chancellor house was wild and exciting to the last degree. Darkness was coming upon us. The roads were crowded with the flying troops going in one direction and the reserves advancing rapidly and orderly to the rescue in the other. Hooker's headquarters were at the Chancellor house and the military band there stationed was energetically playing the national airs, having been ordered so to do as one means by which to check the disorder and encourage the Union troops. In front the fight was raging furiously. A perfect storm of artillery lighted up with fitful flashes the forest openings. The rattle of musketry was incessant. The shouts of the officers and the shrieks of the wounded filled the air, and the expectation of coming at any moment in the darkness face to face with an exultant enemy keyed us to a pitch of the highest excitement. It was one of the few great experiences of a life-time.

PRIVATE DAVID J. KYLE
9TH VIRGINIA CAVALRY, W. H. F. LEE'S BRIGADE

A 19-year-old farmer whose former home lay near Chancellorsville, Kyle was serving as a guide for Stonewall Jackson on the night of May 2 when the general and his escort rode beyond the Confederate lines and were fired on by soldiers of the 18th North Carolina. One of Jackson's couriers was killed, another wounded, and the general was hit by three bullets. Kyle and five others escaped the tragic volley and struggled to remove their stricken commander from the field.

Before I left General Stuart the fight had commenced; it was after 6 o'clock. I went towards Chancellorsville on the Easley road, then through the woods to the Lacy Mill; then I bore to my left, coming out on the turnpike in sight of Mr. James Talley's house, and on to the junction of the pike and plank road. Here I met some officers, who told me that General Jackson was certainly to the front, where the fighting was then going on. Putting spurs to my horse, I rode to the old Dowdall Tavern, where the Rev. Melzil Chancellor lived at that time. There I met Mr. Chancellor, who had just come back from General Jackson, having served him as a guide, and he directed me to him. I urged my horse on and was soon abreast with the General. I saluted, and said, "General Jackson, I have a dispatch for you from General Stuart," handing the envelope to him. He halted his horse, read the papers quickly, turned to me, and said, "Do you know all of this country?" I answered that I did, and he said, "Keep along with me."

We were then between Powell's old field and the schoolhouse. There were many dead horses in the road and by it. I learned that it was where the Eighth Pennsylvania Cavalry charged. From here General Jackson moved on until he got opposite the schoolhouse. There he halted for a few minutes and had a conversation with some officers. Then he started on, two of the officers riding by him. After leaving the schoolhouse and going about two hundred yards in the curved road, we came up on a line of Infantry standing obliquely across the road. General Jackson stopped a few minutes in conversation with the officers of this Command, then passed on through its front, going nearly a hundred yards further, and just behind a battery which was supported by a very thin line. As we passed I asked whose command it was, and they said it was Field's Brigade. I asked what Regiment, and one man said his was the Fifty-fifth Virginia, and another said his was the Twenty-second Virginia Battalion. We bore obliquely to the left and went to the left of the Battery, where there was an open space at the fork of the roads—to Bullock's and the Old Mountain roads—which intersected the plank and turnpike roads here. General Jackson asked for me. I went forward and he asked me where those roads led to. I told him that the left-hand one led to the Bullock farm behind Chancellorsville, and the other ran somewhat parallel with the plank road and came out on it a half mile below, towards Chancellorsville. He told me if I knew it to lead the way, which I did for about two hundred yards, when he rode abreast of me and kept so until we halted.

We went down the Old Mountain road some four hundred yards, when we came in hearing of the Federals, I suppose some two or three hundred yards distant. It seemed that the officers were trying to form their men in line. We stayed there a few minutes, when the General turned his horse around and started back the road we had come, a little in advance of me. When we were some fifty or seventy-five yards from where General Jackson turned back, four or five officers rode in between my horse and the General's. We were about half way back, and nearly

Stonewall Jackson's handkerchief—bearing the general's name written in his own hand—was in his pocket when he was wounded. Following the war Jackson's family presented the bloodstained relic to the Virginia Military Institute.

opposite the Van Wert house when General Jackson turned his horse's head towards the south, from a westerly course, and, facing the front of our own line of battle, he started to leave the Old Mountain road.

Just as he was crossing the road there was a single shot fired to the right of the Van Wert house in our line. In an instant it was taken up, and nearer there were five or six shots, like a platoon, and then suddenly a large volley, as if from a Regiment, was fired. General Jackson's horse wheeled to the right and started to run obliquely across the Old Mountain road, passing under the limb of an oak tree that extended across the road, which came near pulling him off his horse. The horse went to the opposite side of the road, some twenty-five yards from where the General was wounded, before he got control of him. He turned the horse and came back ten or twelve yards before he was taken down by some officers. After getting General Jackson off his horse, he was taken by four men and carried to the plank and pike road running here side by side, where he was laid down with his head resting on some officer's left leg as he knelt on his right knee—I think it was Gen. A. P. Hill—until a litter was brought from the Twenty-second (Va.) Battalion. It was unfolded and General Jackson put on it. Four men carried him across the pike and plank roads for the road that led to Stoney Ford. When in about twenty-five yards of that road the front left hand litter bearer, J. J. Johnson, Company H, Twenty-second Virginia Battalion, was struck in the left arm by a piece of shell from a Federal battery, which caused him to let loose the litter, causing General Jackson a very hard fall. The other three litter bearers ran to the cover of the woods on the south side of the plank road, but soon rallied and came back, and with the assistance of an officer, not very high in rank, wearing bars, they lifted General Jackson up and laid him on the litter just over the embankment of the road where it had been carried by one of the bearers in his flight. They raised the litter up on their shoulders with General Jackson on it, and started to the woods on the Stoney Ford road, and carried him back some distance before they met an ambulance. After getting him into the ambulance they took the Hazel Grove road to the plank road that comes out at the corner of the Dowdall field, and up the plank road to the old Dowdall house, where Rev. M. S. Chancellor supplied the doctors with some spirits for General Jackson. They halted there a very few minutes, then drove on up the pike to the Wilderness Old Tavern, where Mr. W. M. Simms lived at the time. They drove out on the right of the pike in the field to a hospital tent, where they took General Jackson out of the ambulance and carried him into the tent, which was the last I ever saw of him.

A photograph of the Plank road—with some of its wooden planking visible at right—was alleged to have been taken at the spot where Stonewall Jackson was shot. In fact, Jackson and his party were riding on the Mountain road, possibly the dark track visible to the right of the two men at center, leading from the Plank road.

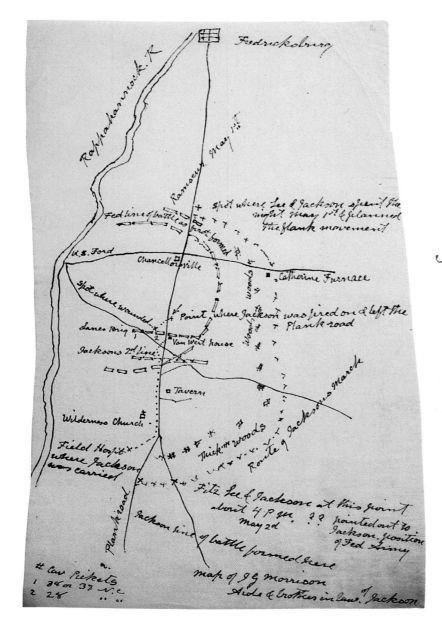

After the war, Jackson's brother-in-law and aide, Lieutenant Joseph G. Morrison, drew a map of the Chancellorsville battlefield tracing the circuitous flank march and Confederate positions on the night of May 2. The point where Jackson was wounded is visible at center, to the left (north) of the Plank road, in front of the line of Brigadier General James H. Lane's North Carolina brigade.

LIEUTENANT JOSEPH G. MORRISON
STAFF, LIEUTENANT GENERAL THOMAS J. JACKSON

The younger brother of Jackson's wife, Anna, Morrison had joined the general's staff after graduating from the Virginia Military Institute. He was most likely the anonymous author of this 1866 article detailing the circumstances of Jackson's wounding and his aide's efforts to quell the fire of the 18th North Carolina. The Yankee soldiers Morrison encountered were probably from the 128th Pennsylvania, one of Knipe's XII Corps units that had strayed beyond the main Federal line.

It was now near 9 o'clock, and General Jackson, who had been for some time near the front line, rode a little in advance of it to reconnoitre the enemy's position. A heavy skirmish line had been ordered to the front, and he supposed he was in the rear of this line. He was at this time accompanied by Captain J. K. Boswell, of the Engineers; Captain R. E. Wilbourn of the Signal Corps, Lieutenant J. G. Morrison, Aid-de-camp, and five or six couriers—and had ridden but a short distance down the pike, when a volley was fired at the party by the Federals in front and to the right of the road. To escape this fire, the party wheeled out of the road to the left, and galloped to the rear, when our own men, mistaking them for Federal cavalry making a charge, and supposing the firing in front to have been directed at the skirmish line, opened a galling fire, killing several men and horses, and causing the horses that were not struck to dash, panic-stricken, toward the Federal lines, which were but a short distance in front. The General was struck in three places, and dragged from his horse by the bough of a tree. Captain Boswell was killed instantly—Lieutenant Morrison leaping from his horse, that was dashing into the enemy's lines, ran to an interval in our line and exclaimed: "Cease firing! You are firing into our own men." A colonel commanding a North-Carolina regiment in Lane's brigade, cried out: "Who gave that order! It's a lie! Pour it into them, boys." Morrison then ran to the colonel, told him what he had done, and assisted him to arrest the firing as soon as possible. He then went to the front, in search of the General, and found him lying upon the ground, with Captain Wilbourn and Mr. Wynn of the Signal Corps, bending over him, examining his wounds. In a few moments General Hill, accompanied by Captain Leigh and a few couriers, rode up to where the General was lying, dismounted. On examining his wounds, they found his left arm broken, near the shoulder, and bleeding profusely. A handkerchief was tied around the arm so as partially to stop the bleeding. While this was being done, and while the party were bending over the General two Federal soldiers, with muskets cocked, stepped up to the party, from behind a cluster of bushes, and looked quietly on. General Hill turned to several of his couriers, and said in an under-tone, "Seize those men," and it was done so quickly that they made no resistance. Lieutenant Morrison, thinking that these were scouts in front of an advancing line, stepped to the pike, about twenty yards distant, to see if it were so, and distinctly saw cannoneers unlimbering two pieces of artillery in the road, not a hundred yards distant. Returning hastily, he announced this to the party, when General Hill, who was now in command of the army, immediately mounted and rode to the head of Pender's column (which was coming up by the flank) to throw it into line. He left Captain Leigh, of his staff, to assist in removing General Jackson. About this time, Lieutenant J. P. Smith, Aid-de-camp, who had been sent to deliver an order, rode up and dismounted. Captain Wilbourn had gone a few moments previous after a litter. The party thought it best not to await Wilbourn's return, and suggested that they bear the General off in their arms, when he replied: "No, I think I can walk." They assisted him to rise, and supported him as he walked from the woods to the pike, and toward the rear. Soon after reaching the road, they obtained a litter, and placed him on it, but had not gone over forty yards when the battery in the road opened with canister. The first discharge passed over their heads, but the second was more accurate, and struck down one of the litter-bearers, by which the General received a severe fall. The firing now increased in rapidity, and was so terrific that the road was soon deserted by the attendants of the General, with the exception of Captain Leigh and Lieutenants Smith and Morrison. These officers lay down in the road by the General during the firing, and could see on every side sparks flashing from the stones of the pike, caused by the iron canister shot. Once the General attempted to rise, but Lieutenant Smith threw his arms across his body, and urged him to lie quiet a few moments or he would certainly be killed. After the road had been swept by this battery—by a dozen or more discharges—they elevated their guns, and opened with shell. So the little party now had an opportunity of removing their precious burden from the road to the woods on their right, and continued their course to the rear, carrying the General most of the way in their arms. Once they stopped, that he might rest, but the fire was so heavy, they thought it best to go on. The whole atmosphere seemed filled with whistling canister and shrinking shell, tearing the trees on every side. After going three or four hundred yards an ambulance was reached, containing Colonel S. Crutchfield, General Jackson's Chief of Artillery,

"The General was struck in three places, and dragged from his horse by the bough of a tree."

Stonewall Jackson's raincoat still bears the marks of the fatal bullets. A musket ball entered the palm of his right hand, another round passed through his left forearm, while the third broke his left arm below the shoulder.

who had just been severely wounded—a canister shot breaking his left leg. The General was placed in this ambulance, and at his request, one of his aids got in to support his mangled arm. During all this time he had scarcely uttered a groan, and expressed great sympathy for Colonel Crutchfield, who was writhing under the agonies of his shattered limb. After proceeding over half a mile, the ambulance reached the house of Mr. Melzi Chancellor, where a temporary hospital had been established.

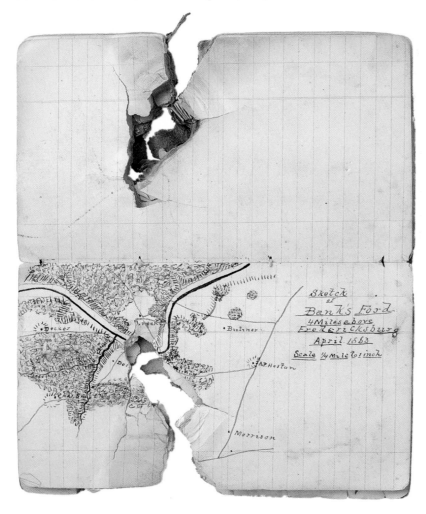

Sixty yards south of Jackson's party, General A. P. Hill and his nine-man escort also came under friendly fire that wounded or unhorsed all except the general himself. Captain James Boswell—Jackson's topographical engineer—was shot from the saddle and killed as he rode beside Hill. One bullet pierced the sketchbook (above) that Boswell carried in his breast pocket.

SURGEON HUNTER MCGUIRE
STAFF, LIEUTENANT GENERAL THOMAS J. JACKSON

Dr. McGuire, Jackson's chief medical officer, battled to save the life of his commander, who was in imminent danger of bleeding to death from an artery that had been severed by a jagged edge of broken bone when he fell from his stretcher. McGuire would later serve as president of the American Medical Association.

He was placed upon the litter again, and carried a few hundred yards, when I met him with an ambulance. I knelt down by him, and said, "I hope you are not badly hurt, General." He replied very calmly, but feebly, "I am badly injured, Doctor; I fear I am dying." After a pause, he continued, "I am glad you have come. I think the wound in my shoulder is still bleeding." His clothes were saturated with blood, and hemorrhage was still going on from the wound. Compression of the artery with the finger arrested it, until lights being procured from the ambulance, the handkerchief which had slipped a little, was readjusted. His calmness amid the dangers which surrounded him, and at the supposed presence of death, and his uniform politeness, which did not forsake him, even under these, the most trying circumstances, were remarkable. His complete control, too, over his mind, enfeebled as it was by loss of blood, pain, &c., was wonderful. His suffering at this time was intense; his hands were cold, his skin clammy, his face pale, and his lips compressed and bloodless; not a groan escaped him—not a sign of suffering, except the slight corrugation of his brow, the fixed, rigid face, and the thin lips so tightly compressed that the impression of the teeth could be seen through them. . . .

After reaching the hospital, he was placed in bed, covered with blankets, and another drink of whiskey and water given him. Two hours and a half elapsed before sufficient reaction took place to warrant an examination. At two o'clock Sunday morning Surgeons Black, Walls and Coleman being present, I informed him that chloroform would be given him, and his wounds examined. I told him that amputation would probably be required, and asked if it was found necessary, whether it should be done at once. He replied promptly, "Yes, certainly; Doctor McGuire, do for me whatever you think best." Chloroform was then administered, and as he began to feel its effects, and its relief to the pain he was suffering, he exclaimed, "What an infinite blessing,"

and continued to repeat the word "blessing," until he became insensible. The round ball (such as is used for the smooth-bore Springfield musket), which had lodged under the skin, upon the back of his right hand, was extracted first. It had entered the palm, about the middle of the hand, and fractured two of the bones. The left arm was then amputated, about two inches below the shoulder, very rapidly, and with slight loss of blood, the ordinary circular operation having been made. There were two wounds in this arm, the first and most serious was about three inches below the shoulder-joint, the ball dividing the main artery, and fracturing the bone. The second was several inches in length; a ball having entered the outside of the forearm, an inch below the elbow, came out upon the opposite side, just above the wrist. Throughout the whole of the operation, and until all the dressings were applied, he continued insensible. Two or three slight wounds of the skin on his face, received from the branches of trees, when his horse dashed through the woods, were dressed simply with isinglass plaster.

A year after the Battle of Chancellorsville, artist William De Hartburn Washington, a Virginia native specializing in portraits and historical scenes, made this sketch of Jackson being borne from the field as a study for a proposed painting of the incident. The composition was apparently never executed on canvas, although Washington did complete a painting of Jackson leading troops into Winchester during the 1862 Shenandoah Valley campaign.

Hooker on the Defensive: May 3

Despite the success of Jackson's attack on the evening of May 2, the Federals by all rights held the upper hand the next morning. Most of Major General John Reynolds' I Corps, summoned by General Hooker the day before, had crossed the Rappahannock, bringing the Federal total around Chancellorsville to 76,000 men, nearly double the number available to Lee.

In addition, the Confederate force was still divided into two wings separated by almost two miles of difficult terrain, Jeb Stuart to the west of Chancellorsville, Robert E. Lee to the south and east. The situation plainly called for hard, swinging Federal counterattacks to smash first one Confederate wing and then the other.

But Hooker, still unnerved, would not even consider an aggressive counterpunch. He was thinking only of a hedgehoglike defense—and he soon compromised even that when, in a spasm of extra caution, he ordered General Dan Sickles to abandon his forward position on Hazel Grove, the height southwest of Chancellorsville that jutted between the wings of the Rebel army and provided a matchless position for artillery to sweep the surrounding country. "There has rarely been a more gratuitous gift of a battlefield," wrote Confederate artilleryman Colonel E. Porter Alexander, who would soon take full advantage of it.

It was Stuart, of course, who did the attacking, as Lee had ordered. Working frantically through the night, Stuart reorganized Jackson's corps, moving A. P. Hill's division—now led by Brigadier General Henry Heth because Hill had been wounded—into the front line. Next came Raleigh Colston's

division and in a third line Robert Rodes' bone-tired troops, who had seen the worst of the fighting the evening before.

The Confederates, as usual hitting fast and hard, moved as dawn broke at 5:30 a.m. In half an hour Brigadier General James Archer's brigade on the right of Heth's line had advanced up the western slope of Hazel Grove where the forward skirmishers chased off the last of Sickles' withdrawing troops. In minutes Colonel Alexander, who had hidden 30 guns in a nearby woods overnight, had sped his batteries up the heights and was sending shells screaming into the Union artillery positions at Fairview Heights, near Hooker's headquarters at the Chancellor house, and into the brigades of Slocum's corps just to the east and northeast.

At the same time, the remaining five brigades of Heth's division attacked straight into the packed ranks of the II, III, and XII Corps manning the western margin of the defensive loop Hooker had put together around the Chancellor house. "The fighting here was the most desperate of the war," wrote one of Sickles' artillerymen. "It was dreadful, horrible, appalling." Dozens of regiments from both sides fought furiously until nearly half their numbers were dead or wounded. But by about 8:30 the headlong Confederate rush began to run out of steam. Heth's brigades had been hurriedly aligned and in the furious fighting began to lose touch with one another, exposing their flanks to counterattacks.

Seeing Heth's first line stalled, Stuart ordered Colston's division to advance and Rodes' as well. Unnerved by the horrifying carnage and with many of their officers killed,

some soldiers balked at the advance. But the pressure from the Confederates was relentless, and despite steadily mounting losses (one of Colston's brigades went through four commanders that morning) the Federals were driven back on the Chancellor house.

In the midst of the violence Hooker himself was put out of action when a round shot from a Confederate gun shattered a column he was leaning against on the Chancellor house porch. Hit by part of the column, Hooker was knocked senseless for a time, then rode about in a daze. But he did not notify General Couch, his senior subordinate, or turn over command.

At last, lying down in a tent to the rear, Hooker did tell Couch to take over—and immediately ordered him to start a general retreat to a new, shorter defensive line north of Chancellorsville. In utter disgust, Couch and the other Federal corps commanders—who still wanted to attack—began withdrawing their troops, moving them back into a semicircular line with both ends anchored on the Rappahannock.

In the meantime General Lee, seeing that Stuart's attack was almost spent, began his own assault, ordering R. H. Anderson's brigades led by Generals Carnot Posey, Ambrose Wright, and William Mahone to attack Hooker's southern perimeter, and sending Lafayette McLaws' troops charging up the Plank road and the Turnpike from the east. As the Federals withdrew, Lee ordered 40 guns moved from Hazel Grove to Fairview, where they blasted away at the retreating Union forces and finally set fire to the already half-demolished Chancellor house.

Lee observed the last attacks from Hazel Grove, calmly sitting astride his handsome horse, Traveller. Then in the late morning, while McLaws' and Anderson's brigades battled Hancock's troops forming the Federal rear guard, Lee rode down to the Chancellorsville clearing. There, one of his staff officers remembered, "the fierce soldiers with their faces blackened with the smoke of battle" all gave "one long, unbroken cheer," hailing "the presence of the victorious chief."

Lee basked in his triumph for a moment, then received a message from Stonewall Jackson confirming that he was wounded and congratulating Lee on the great victory. A look of anguish passed over Lee's face, a staff officer recalled, and his voice trembled as he dictated a reply: "Could I have directed events, I should have chosen for the good of the country to be disabled in your stead. I congratulate you on the victory, which is due to your skill and energy."

Faithful to Lee's orders to press the enemy "with the utmost vigor," Stuart hurled his new command at Hooker's line west of Chancellorsville beginning at dawn on May 3. Although the Rebels took heavy losses in repeated attacks on the Federals, the fury of the assaults was enough to persuade Hooker to begin falling back to the Rappahannock.

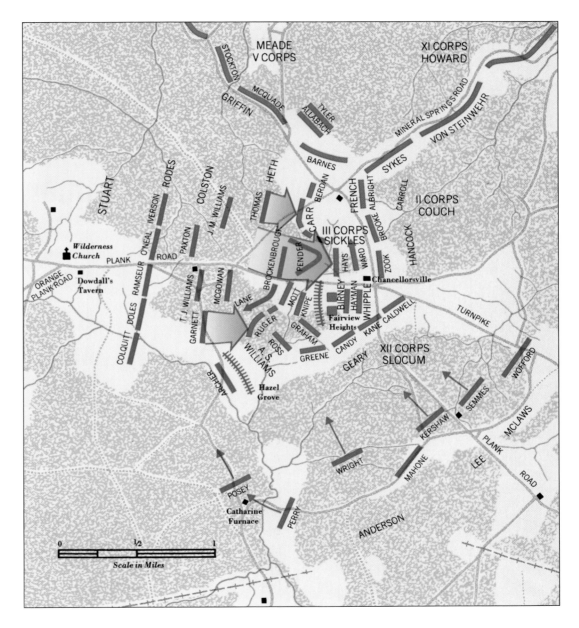

Crude by later war standards, field entrenchments such as these (left) were built by Federal troops on both sides of the Plank road to bolster the defenders against the attacks they knew would come on May 3. A Yankee soldier in Brigadier General John W. Geary's division who witnessed the furious assaults that day wrote, "Like the waves of the sea on a rock-bound coast, they dashed at the works, only to be broken and driven back in fragments." Largely because of these costly assaults, General Lee's army, in victory, lost nearly as many men killed as the Army of the Potomac at Chancellorsville.

LIEUTENANT J. F. J. CALDWELL
1ST SOUTH CAROLINA INFANTRY, McGOWAN'S BRIGADE

Among the first to charge the Federals on May 3, McGowan's South Carolinians reached the first line of Federal entrenchments, but there the attack stalled. As the Rebel line wavered, Ruger's XII Corps brigade stormed forward and threw the exhausted Carolinians back in fierce action, both sides loading and firing as fast as they could. Wrote Colonel Silas Colgrove of the 27th Indiana, "I can safely say that I never witnessed . . . so perfect a slaughter."

At dawn we were roused, the skirmishers were sent forward, and the line of battle moved close after them. The way was through a close, rough growth of pines, swamp trees and vines. . . . Soon the yell was raised and the pace accelerated—both mistakes, for the one discovered us to the enemy, when we might have

remained concealed, and the other disordered our line and, in the end, lost time. It was difficult, at common time, to keep the line dressed.

However, we cleared the woods, and came upon a formidable abatis of felled trees. Beyond this, at the distance of perhaps a hundred yards, were the enemy's breastworks of logs. We were agreeably surprised to see no fire open from it upon us. We passed it, with a shout, ascended to the crown of the eminence, and saw the enemy. Simultaneously a fire was opened by the two sides.

. . . We were on a pretty steep hill. Their main line was on the slope of the opposite hill. At the base of these hills, in a ravine, were a few men—skirmishers, I judge, who had fallen back before us. . . . We could not see much, for the morning was foggy, and the smoke of both lines soon became so dense that I could not even distinguish the colors of the enemy. The firing waxed furious. The advance was abandoned by us, the cheering was hushed. All on both sides addressed themselves to loading and firing as rapidly as possible. The two right regiments of the brigade were most hotly engaged. Indeed, the Thirteenth and Fourteenth had to fire to the right oblique. The slaughter of the Rifle and First regiments was immense. Gen. McGowan, just behind the colors of the First regiment, huzzahed lustily, seeming to be in the highest enthusiasm! . . .

. . . But now we were at a standstill. The enemy became emboldened, and advanced upon the unprotected right flank of our brigade. . . . At last the enemy swung forward, so as almost to enfilade the line. The Rifles gave way, the First regiment followed it slowly, and the movement extended gradually to the left of the brigade. . . .

. . . Gen. McGowan arranged us as well as possible . . . and the enemy continuing to advance, we resumed the battle. Gen. McGowan was wounded standing upon the works. The ball entered below the knee, inflicting such injury that he did not recover until the next winter. . . . Col. O. E. Edwards, of the Thirteenth regiment, now came into command, as senior colonel of the brigade. He behaved with great gallantry, moving up and down the line, encouraging the troops. The enemy now lined the crest of the hill above us. But they overshot us generally.

Brig. Gen. Colston brought in a fresh line during this time, himself and his staff riding up the works, conspicuous marks to the enemy. The Stonewall brigade passed over us, some of them saying, with not very pleasant levity, that they would show us how to clear away a Federal Line. But their reckoning was not accurate. They were forced back into the works with us. The firing continued, unintermitted, deadly. Col. Edwards was wounded in the shoulder and carried from the field. . . .

. . . Col. Abner Perrin, of the Fourteenth, assumed command. The onslaught of the enemy was daring and obstinate. They pushed upon the very works, and one color-bearer even planted his flag upon them. But it would not do. Our men were not accustomed to having things wrested out of their hands. They fired into the faces of the assailants tearing up their ranks, scattering them, and strewing the earth with dead and wounded. A regiment of zouaves were particularly impetuous; but even they were forced to give way, after frightful losses, and leave their disabled comrades behind them.

Col. Perrin now advanced the brigade across the works, following the retreat of the enemy towards the batteries and fortifications around Chancellor's house. . . . They advanced in splendid order, right against the stronghold of the enemy. The batteries of the latter, very active before, but inaudible to most of us, in the great roar of musketry, turned all their wrath upon the advancing line. The troops on the right of our brigade suffered most heavily, but the slaughter was great at every point. Still they pressed on at the hill of fire. But when victory seemed just in reach, a line of the enemy's infantry, on the unprotected left flank of our line, opened a withering fire upon it. To change front under such a fire was, of course, impossible. To attempt it was to murder one's own men. Advance was equally out of the question. The brigade had to be withdrawn a short distance. A better fortune favored the troops on the right of us. They there drove almost around the batteries on the hill-top, which were, in consequence, compelled to limber up with expedition, and retire. Some pieces were captured, after all. . . .

. . . We met Gen. Stuart coming from Chancellor's house, just after the Federals were driven from it. He rode full tilt, and as he passed up, raised his hat and shouted, "Go forward, boys! We have them running, and we'll keep them at it!"

CAPTAIN JAMES F. HUNTINGTON
BATTERY H, 1ST OHIO LIGHT ARTILLERY, WHIPPLE'S DIVISION

When Sickles' III Corps abandoned Hazel Grove, Battery H was ordered to remain as part of the rear guard. Supported by the 114th Pennsylvania, Captain Huntington prepared to defend his position with whatever ammunition was left in his limbers—his battery had fired every round of canister the previous day. After the battle, Huntington and his battery were transferred to the Artillery Reserve, and in October he resigned because of a hernia.

We made an early and frugal breakfast of crackers found in haversacks thrown away by the fugitives. I remember that on looking for a drop of commissary to wash them down, I found to my intense disgust that a bullet had struck my saddle pouch during the affair of Saturday evening, and smashed my flask into a thousand pieces.

It was nearly sunrise when I received orders to withdraw. The ground in rear being very difficult, I sent off the caissons in advance; as it turned out, it was fortunate I did so. The other batteries had gone, and mine was limbered ready to follow, when Captain Randolph, Corps Chief of Artillery, rode up and informed me that the arrangement was changed, and that my battery was to remain. In reply to my inquiry, he said there were no other orders. This was a serious omission, leaving me as it did in doubt whether we ought to hold the position even at the sacrifice of the battery, or if we were at liberty to retire when a longer stay would

"It was plain that an attempt to hold the position longer would result in a useless sacrifice of men and material."

Shown here is one of the gun crews of Battery H, 1st Ohio Light Artillery, in the spring of 1863. The last unit to retreat from Hazel Grove, the battery left three of its six 3-inch Ordnance rifles in a ravine as the men withdrew under heavy musketry fire. Lieutenant George Norton (right, and sixth from left in the above photograph), took over the battery after Captain Huntington assumed command of an artillery brigade before Gettysburg. Since his enlistment in the fall of 1861, Norton had risen quickly through the ranks, but owing to "mental depression" he resigned in March 1864.

render such a result probable. In fact, I have never ascertained to this day what good we were expected to do there.

I now carefully examined the ground about us for the best defensive position and the exact nature of the line of retreat. The ground in our front was level or with a gentle roll, but not far in the rear of where the guns then stood, it descended by an easy slope into marshy ground intersected by a small stream. It was found that by putting the guns just behind the crest, their recoil would throw them under cover, where they could be loaded and pushed to the front till the muzzles just looked over the ground. The battery was presently established in this position. . . .

. . . In support of the battle a regiment known as the Collis Zouaves

were in line in our rear beyond the stream, and the 110th Pennsylvania Infantry prolonged our left. I was confident that we could repel a front attack, unless made in overwhelming numbers, as long as the ammunition lasted. It was a question what sort of ammunition we should use, as we had expended all our canister on the previous evening, and the work was likely to be too close to admit of cutting fuses, and percussion shell are of little value against a line of infantry. I therefore determined to use fuse shrapnel with the fuse hole left open, allowing them to burst in the gun. It speaks well for the toughness of the metal that this rough treatment did not perceptibly injure the rifling.

All being in readiness and every man at his post, we awaited the attack. The suspense was short, for soon a strong force broke from the woods in our front and advanced with their customary yell. Our bugles, sounding the sharp notes of "commence firing," promptly made response. It is probable that the enemy, aware of the contraction of our lines, did not anticipate resistance at this point. They halted and opened a smart fire. For some time we did nicely, thanks to our cover. Though the bullets came thick and fast, stripping the little trees about us of leaves and bark, our loss was slight; while the close and rapid fire of our guns evidently inflicted serious damage on our opponents. I was engrossed with matters in front, when my attention was called to the proceeding of the Zouaves, who were making off in some haste. I remarked that their departure was of no consequence, as they could have been of no use to us in the position they had occupied, and that the regiment on our left still stood firm.

I had hardly done speaking, when that regiment broke, passing our rear in great confusion, doing us the favor to fire a scattering volley through our lines as they did so. I then realized that the right of Archer's brigade had overlapped our flank and was now swinging round on our left and rear. The safety of the guns was already seriously compromised. It was plain that an attempt to hold the position longer would result in a useless sacrifice of men and material. I therefore determined

to retire piece by piece from the left, keeping up the fire of each gun till the instant before it was limbered, to avoid fatal crowding and confusion at the narrow rail bridge. Five guns crossed it in safety; the last of these, however, the drivers being unable to guide the wounded horses, got entangled with a tree on the further bank and was abandoned.

By this time the enemy had closed in on us, firing rapidly. The drivers and horses of the last gun were killed or wounded, and the piece

Private George F. Murray (above) of the 114th Pennsylvania Infantry, or Collis' Zouaves, was wounded in the right shoulder at Hazel Grove. The rout of the Zouaves resulted in a misconduct charge against their leader, Colonel Charles H. T. Collis, who was later acquitted. Murray survived the war and continued to wear his repaired Zouave jacket (left). He also carried the devotional book pictured at far left.

The Bessent family of Davie County, North Carolina, included (clockwise from upper left) Baptist minister Calton W. Bessent; his wife, Rebecca; daughter and son Sarah and Thomas; and son Daniel, a member of Company F, 13th North Carolina, a regiment of William D. Pender's brigade. On the morning of May 3 Pender's Tarheels charged into the Union line north of the Plank road; the 13th North Carolina captured the II Corps' brigade commander, General William Hays, during the confused fighting. But Yankee troops counterattacked and repelled Pender's Carolinians, who suffered heavy losses: 693 casualties with 116 killed, among them Daniel Bessent.

went over into the water. I dismounted to assist in a hurried attempt to extricate it, when my horse, thinking he was at the wrong end of the battery, started off at a furious gallop, and amid all the noise and confusion kept straight on till he overtook it, when he fell into his accustomed place at its head of his own accord. Our infantry in the rifle pits near by had opened fire, which crossing that of the enemy, made ours a decidedly warm place. Telling the few men near me to save themselves if they could, I retired in a most undignified manner,—by crawling as close to the ground as possible,—and gained the shelter of a rifle pit, the only man with the last piece who was lucky enough to do so. We lost five killed and nine wounded (two of the latter mortally), most of them in the retreat.

CORPORAL NICHOLAS WEEKS

3D ALABAMA INFANTRY, O'NEAL'S BRIGADE

Having enlisted in April 1861, Nick Weeks had made it through the war safely thus far. Now, as O'Neal's five regiments moved forward to the attack on May 3, Weeks could see that they were heading into a maelstrom of artillery fire. His description of the devastation by the Yankee artillery at Fairview, written 40 years after the war, contains nothing of the glory of war. Corporal Weeks would be wounded and captured at Gettysburg. Exchanged a month later, he was given light duty for the remainder of the war and never rejoined his regiment.

As we advanced, solid shot and shell greeted us, and when we got nearer, grape accompaniment was added. There must have been fifty guns at play in front and flank. The biggest tree afforded no protection. One might as well have been in front as behind it. Limbs and the tops were falling about us as if torn by a cyclone. Then from the rear shells came shrieking over our heads from Carter's battalion of artillery. We were enveloped, as it were, in dense fog, the flashing of guns could be seen only a few feet away. A fellow can't see very far in a fight, but he sees a plenty when he is scared. At every breath we were inhaling sulphurous vapor fresh and hot from cannon mouth and bursting shell. What a din. What a variety of hideous noises. The ping of the minnie ball, the splutter of cannister, the whistling of grape, the "where are you" "where are you" of screaming shells and the cannon's roar from a hundred mouths went to make up the music for the great opera of death.

I saw the arm and shoulder fly from the man just in front exposing his throbbing heart. Another's foot flew up and kicked him in the face

as a shell struck his leg. Another disemboweled crawled along on his fours, his entrails trailing behind, and still another held up his tongue with his hand, a piece of shell having carried away his lower jaw. Others sank to earth as if to rest, and some plunged forward, as though tripped by a snare, never to rise again. I had just about made up my mind that "this is hell sure enough" when one, two, three, and the fourth shell dropped almost in the same spot as fast as one could count, exploding as they struck the ground—and all was darkness around me. I could say blackness, so black and thick I could feel it, and my feet seemed to rest on a sheet of flame. It could have been only a few seconds when I recovered to find myself standing alone and fourteen lying in the space of about ten feet around me. . . . At this juncture General Rodes dashed up to Captain Bonham who commanded our regiment, and ordered him to charge regardless of those in our front. We were near the colors and Captain Bonham in the lead, other regimental commanders, not having received the command, thinking Bonham had gone wild endeavored to stop him. . . . He replied only by shouting out the command "Forward, Third Alabama!" "the order is forward—follow me!" The other regiments quickly responded. . . . When we reached the lines in our front they had lain down on the brink of a ravine, on the opposite side of which was the enemy's artillery, and half way down the slope their infantry line behind breastworks. The very air seemed black with shot.

A 32-year-old Bladen County farmer, Colonel Thomas J. Purdie, led his 18th North Carolina forward just south of the Plank road with the other regiments of Lane's brigade. The Carolinians stormed over the Federal breastworks and cracked the enemy line, only to face "terrific and galling" artillery fire. As the 18th began to retreat, Purdie was struck in the forehead by a bullet and killed. Purdie's uniform coat (left) bears his blood on the front and down the left sleeve.

Colonel George A. Cobham of the 111th Pennsylvania captured the colors of the 5th Alabama (above) on May 3, wresting the flag from Captain Elijah B. Moseley and taking him prisoner. The flag was returned to the state of Alabama in 1905.

Over and down we went and our line melted away as if swallowed up by the earth. It was here that Cecil Carter fell, the noblest and bravest of all. I halted an instant, and with the help of Jim Harrison, the old wheel-horse of the company, dragged him to a tree. He opened his eyes and asked, "What are you fellows doing?" "Nothing, Cecil, you are wounded; don't try to get up." "No, I am not. Where?" "In the breast," we said. He stuck his finger in the wound. "The bullet must have bounced out," he said. "I can't feel it." The blood gushed forth, and he sank back. I thought, dead, and his dream verified. We reached the bottom of the ravine and started up the other side in the face of artillery on top of the hill and infantry just below—and both busy. Here we encountered their abatis, which destroyed everything like order in our ranks and every man went on his own hook, crawling over and under the felled trees, not stopping to fire a shot till we struck the infantry and drove it back to their guns. The whole earth seemed to be ablaze

before us, and other than gunpowder smoke was stifling us now. The woods were afire, and the leaves a foot thick on the ground with the wind blowing direct in our faces. There was a rush for the clearings and road, and then we stood huddled together under the pitiless rain of cannester and shell till the flames swept by. As soon as the fire had passed we rushed back through still hot and burning leaves to our places. If you remember we recovered none of our wounded alive on this part of the field. Their charred bodies dotted the ground and we could see by the ashes where they had scratched the leaves away in a vain attempt to save themselves from the more awful fate of burning alive.

CORPORAL RICE C. BULL
123D NEW YORK INFANTRY, ROSS' BRIGADE

On the morning of May 3, the 123d New York, never tested in battle before, lined up behind an "imperfectly completed" log breastwork and faced the attacks of Lane's North Carolinians south of the Plank road. For 21-year-old Rice Bull, a farmer from Hartford, New York, the thrill of combat was soon erased by a painful neck wound during the Carolinians' second charge. Bull, one of the regiment's 114 wounded, then had to worry about staying alive.

Looking down the line of our Company as the yelling of the enemy came nearer and nearer to us, I judged that everyone felt about as I did; there was no levity now, the usual joking had ceased and a great quiet prevailed. I could see pallor on every face as we brought the hammers to a full cock. I believe every arm trembled as we raised our guns to our shoulders to fire but all eyes were to the front, not one looked back. This was a testing time and there was not one of our Company that did not pass the test.

Fortunately for us, the enemy began firing before they reached the top of the hill so their first volley was over our heads. We were warned not to fire before ordered to do so but as soon as the Johnnies opened on us some of the men commenced. Most of us, however, held our fire until we saw the line of smoke that showed that they were on the ridge; then every gun was fired. It was then load and fire at will as fast as we could. Soon the nervousness and fear we had when we began to fight passed away and a feeling of fearlessness and rage took its place.

The enemy continued to advance, firing as they came nearly to the fallen trees. Finding our fire too heavy to face they wavered and fell back over the ridge and we gave a "Yankee shout and hurrah." We had

"Soon the nervousness and fear we had when we began to fight passed away and a feeling of fearlessness and rage took its place."

a short breathing spell for perhaps five minutes, the musketry fire near-ly ceased on our front; but the artillery kept pounding away. After we all loaded our guns we took a long breath and waited, but not for long. We again heard their yell and they were coming on, this time not mak-ing the mistake of firing before they reached the top of the hill. There they gave us a volley and advanced on the run. When they reached the fallen trees they had trouble in making headway and their first line fal-tered and fell back but their troops were massed and their second line continued the attack. We loaded and fired as fast as possible but still they came on. The smoke was so dense we could seldom see them but we could see the flash of their guns as they advanced yelling. The crash of the musketry was deafening. Climbing over and pushing aside the fallen timber in their front they were soon not more than twenty feet from our barricade.

I had just fired my gun and was lowering it from my shoulder when I felt a sharp sting in my face as though I had been struck with something that caused no pain. Blood began to flow down my face and neck and I knew that I had been wounded. Ransom Fisher standing next to me saw the blood streaming down my face, and said, "You are hit. Can't I help you off?" I said, "No, Ransom, I think I can get to the Surgeon without help." I took my knapsack that lay on the works in front of me and started to go to the left of our Regiment where our Surgeons were located. I passed in the rear of several Companies, all were firing rapidly, and when back of Company K felt another stinging pain, this time in my left side just above the hip. Everything went black. My knapsack and gun dropped from my hands and I went down in a heap on the ground.

I do not know how long it was before I became conscious but the battle was raging furiously; two dead men who were not there when I fell were lying close to me, one across my feet. Captain Wiley of Com-pany K was standing near by. I attempted to rise and when he saw my effort stooped over me and said, "I thought you were dead. Who are you?" The Captain was an old friend of our family but I was so covered with blood he did not recognize me. I told him who I was and asked if he could get someone to help me go to the Surgeon. He had two

Colonel Amor A. McKnight of the 105th Pennsylvania was a 30-year-old lawyer from Blairsville. As McKnight led his Wildcats, part of Graham's III Corps bri-gade, forward in support of Ruger, a bullet passed through his upraised sword arm and crashed into his brain, killing him instantly. His body was never recovered.

stretcher-bearers come; they did not take me to the Surgeon but car-ried me back about fifty yards to a small stream that ran parallel to our battle line. Here was a depression some three or four feet below the general level of the ground where the wounded would be protected from musketry fire. When I reached the stream its banks were already well lined with many dead and wounded. Some had been carried there, others had dragged themselves to the place to die. Many were need-lessly bleeding to death. . . .

This sketch by Alfred R. Waud for Harper's Weekly shows Federal artillery (left) and infantry (right) at Fairview firing into oncoming Rebel troops in the woods to the west. Fresh Union troops of the III Corps (foreground) stand ready to support the guns. Visible in this sketch is a penciled grid super-imposed by a Harper's engraver; each square was engraved—in reverse—on a wood block, then the entire woodcut was assembled and printed. Harper's published 344 of Waud's military sketches.

. . . I was not suffering much pain but was very weak as both my wounds had bled profusely. My face was coated with blood and it had run down my back and breast and saturated my clothes which were soaked from head to foot, as my wound in the side had also bled freely. After a time my bleeding nearly stopped. As far as I could discover no bones were broken.

My mind was clear so I reasoned as I lay on the ground that if it was possible it would be better for me to get farther to the rear where there would be more chance to have my wounds cared for. I raised myself to a sitting position but found I was so dizzy and faint from loss of blood that I had to lie down. My effort had opened my wounds and they started to bleed again. I knew I could not get to the rear without help, so made no further attempt. Fortunately my canteen had been filled; my thirst had become great and I had some water to wash the blood from my face. During this time the battle on our front continued with un-lessened fury; the Minié balls sung over our heads, cutting off leaves and branches from the laurel bushes that lined the stream. These bushes were ten feet high, and the tops were in range of the musket fire.

The artillery on the ridge were pouring shot and shell over our heads into the Rebel line. Musketry made a continuous roar, the shouts of our men could be heard, and often the shrill yell of the enemy. It seemed to us wounded men that the battle went on for a long time. . . .

As near as I can estimate it was about an hour after I was taken to the gully that the musketry firing gradually lessened, and shortly after-wards almost ceased. From the place where I lay, when no smoke filled the air, I could see back to our line. Shortly after the firing of musketry ended, the smoke cleared away and I saw that our men had disap-peared; not an able-bodied man was to be seen. . . .

After the artillery ceased firing, there was for a time comparative quiet; but soon there was a great commotion with men shouting and officers giving orders. Looking back in the direction of our abandoned line, which I could barely see as the smoke still hung low, was a scat-tered line of men coming toward us on the double-quick. They ad-vanced to near where we wounded men were lying, as that in some measure put them out of range of our artillery which then seemed to be again working with redoubled energy. Coming to a halt they dressed

their line, which was much broken, and lay down. They were not dressed in Union Blue but in Confederate Gray. They made a soldierly though not a handsome appearance, as no two uniforms were exactly alike in style or color or material. The officers were much better dressed than the men; they had light gray uniforms, well fitted. Many of them presented a handsome and soldierly authority over their command. The men looked to be well armed and equipped and so far as I could observe under rigid discipline. As a whole they seemed to be older than our men but a few were very young. Their first line was followed by a second that also dressed and lay down. The officers, who were all on foot, held a brief council near us, after which the men were ordered to cross the stream. They had to cross around or over the wounded and were cautioned by their officers to be careful not to disturb them more than was necessary. They passed over us carefully, without any unkind actions or words. A few asked questions as: "Well, Yanks, how do you like it?" or "Haven't you fellows got about enough of this?" Most of them seemed and acted as though they had troubles of their own and had no desire to annoy us.

LIEUTENANT WILLIAM M. NORMAN
2D North Carolina Infantry, Ramseur's Brigade

The four regiments of Ramseur's brigade charged forward just south of the Plank road and pierced the Federal line, but they became separated in the confused fighting and finally were shattered by artillery barrages and an infantry counterattack. So disastrous was the fight that afterward Lieutenant Norman could find only one private in his company who survived.

Early on Sunday morning, the 3rd of May, we received orders to move forward, which seemed to suit General Ramseur. We advanced in line of battle through the dense forest and thicket. The artillery and musketry were roaring to such a degree as almost to deafen anyone. We charged through the wilderness about half a mile and halted behind the breastworks built by the enemy on the night before. We lay here only a few moments. While we were lying here a brigade was ordered to charge the next line of the enemy's breastworks, but they seemed to refuse, or at least were somewhat backward.

Brigadier General Stephen D. Ramseur was just shy of 25 years old when he led his four regiments into the May 3 fighting. An 1860 graduate of West Point, Ramseur started the war as an artillery captain and was promoted to general in November 1862. At Chancellorsville his brigade suffered 52 percent casualties, and he was wounded as well. On October 19, 1864, Ramseur was mortally wounded at Cedar Creek.

General Ramseur sprang upon a log and gave the command to "forward and charge them boys, charge them!". . .

. . . As soon as we passed the first line of breastworks, which the enemy had built and had been driven from, the men on my right and left and front were falling rapidly. As I was advancing, one of my company was shot right in front of me. I passed over him but saw that he was dead by the time he struck the ground. Some of the company would holler out to me that they were wounded, what must they do, etc. I would tell them to get to the rear. I could not stop to take care of these poor fellows.

When we arrived behind the breastworks where we had routed the enemy just in front of their batteries, forty-odd pieces of artillery were pouring out the grape and canister by the bushel on us. We halted and began to pour volleys of musket and Minié balls into their ranks. I seized hold of one of my company's guns and was shooting while he handed me cartridges. I could see men shot through—some in the head and some torn all in pieces by the belching cannon in our front. Colonel Cox's (my colonel was wounded and Lieutenant Stallings also) orders came down the line for us to fall back, which I learned afterwards was a false alarm. However, this was a fortunate thing for me, for if I remained there only a few minutes longer, I would have been captured by the enemy on my right, who were falling back towards us in our rear and captured most all that remained at the breastworks. I came very near being captured, but by a flank movement I avoided it.

I have never in my life heard the missiles of death whistle so fast and thick around me. I was very nearly covered in the earth many times by

bombshells. The bark from the trees often made my face sting, and splinters knocked from the neighboring trees or saplings were stuck in my clothes. Even when I went to the rear I was very much exposed, for I did not go but a short distance before I joined Major Hurt's command of sharpshooters and was again soon among the front line.

After we joined the regiment, which was about one o'clock, I went down the short line to go to my company, but alas, not one could I find. I felt very much mortified indeed. I knew that most of them were killed or wounded. I asked permission of General Ramseur to go over a portion of the ground where we had fought to look for Captain Waugh and the balance of the company. He gave me the authority. General Ramseur had cried like a child when he saw that his brigade was cut up so bad.

LIEUTENANT CLAY MACCAULEY
126TH PENNSYLVANIA INFANTRY, TYLER'S BRIGADE

Later on the morning of May 3, General Erastus B. Tyler's V Corps brigade was sent to help General William G. French's II Corps troops hold the line. Tyler's four regiments, the only V Corps units to be actively engaged that day, advanced against the Confederate far left and held until flanked by some of Rodes' troops, then fell back in confusion. Lieutenant Clay MacCauley, 19 years old, found himself face to face with an Alabamian who demanded his surrender.

By the right flank, we advanced in line of battle. What an advance! Leaving the open field we entered the wilderness. Our progress was, for the most part, a mere scramble over logs, through dense underbrush, briers, and in mud. We were scratched and bruised, and our clothing was torn. We pushed on, for perhaps a hundred yards, into the thicket. There in a somewhat thinner woods we halted, and, when in line, lay down and began to load and fire at will. It was an ugly give and take. We could not see the enemy, but the whizz and ting of bullets proved that they were not far away. How long this aimless firing continued I do not know. . . .

. . . So continuous had been the firing, that the underbrush at our front was literally cut down at about waist height. Gradually I saw one after another of our men cease firing. Ammunition was exhausted. We called for supplies. None were to be had. Something had gone wrong. The men began to feel it. As our firing slackened I noticed a foreboding disorder on our right. Then a feeling of suspense and doubt seemed to thrill along the line. About that time I felt a blow on my right side, as

"Probably you understand just what it is to look into a loaded gun, whose hammer is up and whose trigger is under the finger of a man who would just as soon pull as not."

if I had been struck by a heavy hammer. A spent ball had hit me, the effects of which I felt for a year thereafter. The disorder, changing into tumult, came near and nearer. At last it swept in upon the company next to mine. Then it struck my own company's right. The companies, rising in successive ranks from the ground, the men with questioning looks at one another, started at first slowly and then rapidly backward. It was not a panic. It was a rather disorderly falling back of almost help-less men, from a coming danger they felt themselves powerless to resist. They were good soldiers. They had led in the boldest and far-thest charge made by the Union forces up Marye's Heights at Freder-icksburg, the preceding December. . . . But what can men do when without ammunition they see the line of which they form part steadily backing away from some oncoming force? A wave rolling backward on a curving beach does not more steadily sweep broken on its way than did the retreat of our battle line from right to left that Sunday morning. The rebels, discovering that our ammunition was exhausted, had charged upon us, striking our extreme right. . . .

. . . Soon I found myself alone. I saw that I must run or be killed. I started to run, but after a few steps my scabbard caught between my legs and threw me down upon my face. Up again, I tried to break through the bushes, but the bullets were whizzing around at a terrible rate. I fell again and was so exhausted that I could go no farther. I crawled alongside one of the wounded. In a moment the rebels were on me. I remember well, now, that poor mangled fellow, at whose side I was. Seeing me he had begged for water. I was about to give him my canteen, when, looking up, I discovered the rebels rapidly coming through the brush. Those moments are now more like the memory of some dreadful dream. Instinctively I started to rise. But, as I rose, I saw a rebel skirmisher take a sudden and not very agreeable interest in me. With a jerk he brought his musket to a direct aim. I was his mark. Prob-ably you understand just what it is to look into a loaded gun, whose hammer is up and whose trigger is under the finger of a man who would just as soon pull as not. Under the circumstances, naturally, I remained

Sergeant William A. Hightower (shown here as a private in 1861) left his studies to enlist in the 23d Virginia. At Antietam he was captured and later exchanged. On May 3, as Warren's brigade attacked south of the Plank road, he was hit in the left leg. The leg was amputated, but Hightower died on May 21. Shown here are his frock coat and trousers.

just where I was, in a half-risen posture. For several seconds I looked into the muzzle of that advancing musket. I saw, as in a mist, many moving men, and heard the noise of their rush. But my brain was concentrated on that one advancing figure. He came upon me swifter than I can write of him. When within a few paces, down came the gun to a charge, and with the bayonet at my breast he yelled out, "You —— —— —— of a ——, give me that sword." While he spoke the rebel line came up. It passed with a rush. Two regiments deep they were. I afterwards learned that the Sixth and Fifth Alabamas were at our immediate front. My captor, a big, tawny-bearded fellow, noticing that I was but a boy, changed his manner at once as I gave him my sword. Seeing that I did not rise, he asked me if I was hurt. "I do not know," I replied. I added, "Get me out of this as quick as you can." I suddenly remembered that

Taken in camp near Fredricksburg Va Feby 23d '63 129 P Vols

just beyond where we had entered the tangle, in the open space, were batteries, about forty guns, planted in a crescent and bearing on the woods. I thought that our line would fall back to those batteries and rally there. I was sure, too, that, as soon as the rebels should appear at the edge of the woods, something would happen. I had no desire to be killed by grape, canister, shell, or anything else from our own guns. I therefore urged our retreat into the rebel lines as quickly as possible. My new acquaintance from Alabama agreed with me. He put a strong arm under my shoulders and, half carrying me, started for the rear. I cannot tell how far we had gone—perhaps it was a hundred yards— when the expected something happened. It seemed as if a tornado out of a clear sky had, all at once, burst upon that forest. We had just reached a breastwork and where there was quite a deep hole. With the first crash, into that hole we fell. For about ten minutes a roaring torrent of iron plunged through the air above us. We were almost covered by fallen tree-limbs and branches. The noise was horrible. Gradually the devastating stream ceased, but as it slackened back came the rebel crowd all in disorder. . . . Back with the retreating rebels we two scrambled towards the farther rear. Soon the rebels halted under the shouts of their officer. I was carried on to where I at length met General Rhodes, to whom I surrendered and by whom I was sent still farther back. Our way lay over one of the plank roads so much spoken of in connection with the fight. On this the struggle of the day and night before had been severest. Our own and the rebel dead by the score lay side by side there. Twice batteries plunged by us, the hoofs of the horses and the carriage-wheels crushing and mutilating the dead bodies of friend and foe. Along the roadside were gathered hundreds of wounded of both armies. Their only shelter from the blazing sun was blankets stretched over them and held in place by the closed hammers of four muskets, the muskets reversed and stuck upright by their bayonets into the ground. It was a sickening march.

Private Charles H. Rhoads (left) was serving in Company K, 129th Pennsylvania, at midmorning on May 3 when the regiment, part of Tyler's brigade, was flanked by Colquitt's Georgians and lost its two flags in hand-to-hand combat. The 129th's commander, Colonel Jacob G. Frick, rallied some of the soldiers and succeeded in saving the colors before the Pennsylvanians were forced to retreat. After the end of his nine-month term, Rhoads enlisted in a militia battalion, then served in the 214th Pennsylvania Infantry in 1865.

The 37th New York Infantry, an Irish regiment from New York City, was fighting in support of Federal artillery south of the Plank road when the New Yorkers were hit hard and driven back to the Chancellor house clearing. Sergeant Michael Lloyd, who was carrying a national flag, tore the silk banner from its staff and wrapped it under his uniform to prevent its capture. When Lloyd was killed and buried in an unmarked grave, the flag went with him. The regimental colors (left) survived the battle and went home when the unit mustered out in June. The 37th, of Hayman's brigade in the III Corps, suffered 222 casualties during the battle, most of them on May 3.

PRIVATE JOHN W. HALEY
17TH MAINE INFANTRY, HAYMAN'S BRIGADE

The 17th Maine, one of David Birney's III Corps regiments, found itself in action on May 3 as the Union perimeter around the Chancellor house began to crumble. In his journal John Haley wrote of losses among the Federal commanders—Joe Hooker was knocked unconscious for a time, and Hiram G. Berry and Amiel W. Whipple, two of the III Corps division commanders, were killed.

When we reached the clearing a few rods west of the house we made another stand, and the battery we had saved was soon working as pertly as ever. In moving one of the heavy siege guns, it became mired. General Hooker dismounted, put his shoulder to the wheel (literally), and helped push it out. The effect was electric, and plenty of hands rushed to extricate it. . . .

General Hooker was everywhere, in the thickest of the fray, a conspicuous mark for sharpshooters, of course, because he was mounted.

A few moments after freeing the siege gun he galloped down to the house now being used as headquarters and while there met with an accident that deprived us of a commander for some time. He was leaning his head against a post of the piazza when a shell whizzed through the house and struck the opposite end. The heavy concussion knocked General Hooker senseless.

It has been asserted that Hooker was unconscious from a too generous patronage of the canteen. He doubtless is a close observer of canteens, as are most of the other generals, but no one could have been so soon overpowered by drink who only a few minutes before had shown such agility on the field. A man accustomed to his potations is not so easily overthrown.

A few minutes before the accident, we had heard General Sickles say to him, "They're whipping us badly."

Hooker replied, "Well, Dan, the boot will be on the other foot directly."

Whatever his plans, they were now locked in his own bosom, and they remained so just long enough to upset our apple cart.

Hooker was carried to a tent and laid for some time in a stupor. He

Major General Hiram G. Berry, a bank president, a member of the Maine legislature, and the mayor of Rockland, rose from colonel of the 4th Maine to command the 2d Division of the III Corps. On May 3 a bullet struck Berry near the heart. Carried from the line of fire, he died within minutes in the arms of his assistant adjutant general, Captain Le Grand Benedict. Berry's last words were "Take me from the field, Benedict."

was aroused by nausea and got up to vomit. He had just left his bed when a shell came right down through the center of it.

This was certainly a hairbreadth escape for General Hooker. Such escapes are very common, and some people even counterfeit them. One of these latter cases came to my attention today. General Ward took a pickaxe and, after making an incision in a tree above his head, called General Sickles's attention to it, saying, "See how near the d——d Rebel came to hitting me." No doubt he has had narrower escapes this day, as has General Sickles, who is said to have remarked as his aides kept falling around him, "I guess they mean *me*, Birney."

This morning our army suffered an almost irreparable loss in the death of General H. G. Berry, our first brigade commander. When I say that General Berry was loved by this brigade, I use no idle phrase. He was shot by a sharpshooter, who must have been up in a tree, while rallying troops to fill a breach in our lines. The bullet passed down through his shoulder and heart, killing him almost instantly. He was carried off the field on his horse, supported by two of his aides, a sad sight to us who fairly idolized him. He was our general, from our own state, and we were justly proud. When his body was set down in front of Hooker's headquarters, he wept for a dear friend, exclaiming, "O my God, Berry, why wasn't I taken and you left?" He kissed his dead friend over and over again, and seemed utterly overwhelmed and broken.

General Hooker felt very keenly the unfavorable turn the battle had taken and was heard to exclaim in the anguish of his spirit, "I wish to

God someone would put a bullet through my head." This was after his injury received at the Chancellor House. . . .

General A. W. Whipple of our 2nd Division was the next to fall after Berry. He was also shot in the heart and carried from the field mortally wounded. How any bullet ever pierced General Whipple's armor of dirt is a mystery of mysteries. I considered him perfectly safe from any missile weighing less than a ton, having a casing of dirt of unknown thickness supposed to be invulnerable.

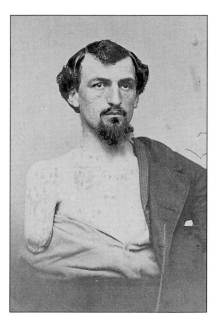

PRIVATE JOHN F. CHASE
5TH MAINE BATTERY, ROBINSON'S DIVISION

Chase, a farmer from Augusta, earned a Medal of Honor for his bravery on the morning of May 3, as he fought with the 5th Maine at the Chancellor house. On July 2 at Gettysburg, a shell exploded next to Chase, lacerating his body with 48 wounds, breaking two ribs, blinding his left eye, and causing the amputation of his right arm. He survived and lived until 1914.

On Sunday morning, May 3rd . . . my battery, the Fifth Maine, was ordered to take position in an apple orchard between the Chancellor House and the woods. The sight which presented itself to our eyes as we came through the woods to our designated position was enough to make the heart of the bravest man falter. Limbs and twigs of trees were falling struck by a storm of iron hail; the very air was laden with these flying missiles of death and it seemed impossible to be in that hell of shot and shell and survive. Into that position of death and annihilation we were ordered, and obeyed. Our battery was ordered to strip for action, a short prayer was offered and the command given: "Mount battery, forward, gallop," and as fast as the horses could go, we galloped forward.

The boys were singing: "I am going home, to die no more," and in

On May 3 General Hancock sent Lieutenant Edmund Kirby (left) to take command of the 5th Maine Battery after all its officers had been shot down. Though badly wounded in the leg, Kirby stayed on the field until the guns were withdrawn. After his leg was amputated, blood poisoning set in, and he died on May 28. That day he was commissioned a brigadier general, a promotion sponsored by his fellow officers in order to provide a more generous pension to his mother.

less than thirty minutes half of our number had gone "home." Even before we could get into position our horses and men went down like grass before the scythe. We had to place our guns by hand, and open fire on the enemy's batteries, which were masked on a wooded ridge about 200 yards in our front, and on several regiments of Confederate infantry to the right and left. Our orders were: "Fight your guns to the death." Our beloved Captain, George F. Leppien, had his leg shattered, the other officers were soon killed or wounded, and within a short time only two guns out of the six could be worked.

General Hancock sent Lieutenant Kirby, of the First U.S. Battery, to take charge of us. He had just reached my gun, when a shell exploded, shattering his hip and breaking his horse's leg. I shot the horse to keep him from tramping on the wounded officer, whom I asked whether I should take him from the field. Lieutenant Kirby answered: "No, not as long as a gun can be fired." He was lying on the ground near the gun, bleeding from his wound, and liable to be hit again at any moment.

Only one gun going now, and that short handed! I was number one cannoneer—my duty was to sponge the gun and ram the cartridge home. Beside myself, there was now left only Corporal Lebrooke. We could have gone to the rear and carried honors with us, but we had made up our minds to lie there on the battle field with our dead comrades, and fight the last gun to the death. We loaded several times with canister, and fired at the column of infantry that was charging up to capture our guns. Oh! how we hated to see the guns that we had served

through many a hard fought battle, go into the hands of the enemy. At last a rebel shell struck our piece, exploding in the muzzle, and battering it so that we could not get another charge into it. I stepped to the rear of the gun, and reported to Lieutenant Kirby that our last gun was disabled and only two of us left. I also asked him if I could take him off the field. He replied: "No, not until the guns are taken off." What a display of courage in that young officer, lying there with his life's blood slowly ebbing away and putting duty before life.

At this moment the Irish Brigade came charging in to our support. Corporal Lebrooke and I held up the trail of our gun, while the men of the One hundred and sixteenth Pennsylvania, belonging to the Irish Brigade, and led by Colonel St. Claire A. Mulholland, hitched on with the prolong rope and helped us draw it off the field. As soon as I saw that the guns were safe, I returned to Lieutenant Kirby, took him up in my arms and carried him to the rear, where I put him into an ambulance and started him back across the river.

SUE CHANCELLOR

Fourteen-year-old Sue Chancellor, her mother, and five sisters were among those sheltering in the Chancellor house as the battle started. Although the house had passed out of family hands before the war, Sue's mother was renting the place at the time General Hooker took it over as his headquarters. The family was at first allowed the use of a back room, but as fighting erupted nearby, they and a number of wounded soldiers were sent to the basement. When the house caught fire, everyone was evacuated and led to safety.

Early in the morning they came for us to go into the cellar, and in passing through the upper porch I saw how the chairs were riddled with bullets and the shattered columns which had fallen and injured General Hooker. O the horror of that day! The piles of legs and arms outside the sitting room window and the rows and rows of dead bodies covered with canvas! The fighting was awful, and the frightened men crowded into the basement for protection from the deadly fire of the Confederates, but an officer came and ordered them out, commanding them not to intrude upon the terror-stricken women. Presently down the steps the same officer came precipitously and bade us get out at once, "For, madam, the house is on fire, but I will see that you are protected and taken to a place of safety." This was Gen. Joseph Dickinson, but we did not know it at the time. Cannon were booming

"Cannon were booming and missiles of death were flying in every direction as this terrified band of women and children came stumbling out of the cellar."

Ohio artist George Leo Frankenstein, who served in the Army of the Potomac's commissary department, returned to Chancellorsville in the late 1860s to paint scenes of the battlefield, including this view of the ruined Chancellor house. Later, a smaller house was built on the old foundation, but it burned in 1927.

and missiles of death were flying in every direction as this terrified band of women and children came stumbling out of the cellar. If anybody thinks that a battle is an orderly attack of rows of men, I can tell them differently, for I have been there.

The sight that met our eyes as we came out of the dim light of that basement beggars description. The woods around the house were a sheet of fire, the air was filled with shot and shell, horses were running, rearing, and screaming, the men, a mass of confusion, moaning, cursing, and praying. They were bringing the wounded out of the house, as it was on fire in several places. Mammy Nancy had old Mr. F——'s basket of papers, and she and the little negro girl were separated from us and bidden to stay behind. A Yankee snatched the basket from the old woman and was making off with it when Aunt Nancy gave a shriek: "Miss Kate, for the Lord's sake git your pa's basket!" An officer turned and, sternly reproving the miscreant, gave the basket into Miss Kate's hands. Slowly we picked our way over the bleeding bodies of the dead and wounded, General Dickinson riding ahead, my mother walking alongside with her hand on his knee, I clinging close to her, and the others following behind. At the last look our old home was completely enveloped in flames. Mother with six dependent daughters, and her all destroyed!

We took the road up toward United States Ford, which was held by the enemy, and after a while got out of sight of the battle. After walking about half a mile one of my sisters, who had been sick, had a hemor-

Lieutenant Colonel Joseph Dickinson, an assistant adjutant general on Hooker's staff, had tried to help stem the rout of the XI Corps on May 2 by standing his ground with some of Howard's staff. On May 3, out of genuine concern for the Chancellor family huddled in the basement, Lieutenant Dickinson got them safely out of the house, escorted them to the rear, and sent an ambulance for a sick daughter. Dickinson kept in touch with the family and visited the Chancellors after the war.

rhage from her lungs. General Dickinson stopped a soldier on horse-back, made him get down, put my sister on his horse, and then walked behind her to hold her on. After a while Miss Kate stopped, completely exhausted, and said she could go no farther. General Dickinson asked her if she could ride, adding: "If so, you can take my horse and I will walk at his head." She said she was too much exhausted to attempt that, but she could ride, pillion, behind him. "That is impossible," he said sternly. "I fear I cannot provide for you." After a few minutes pause, we went on. Presently we met an officer, who wheeled on his horse on recognizing our leader and demanded with an oath: "General Dickinson, why are you not at your post of duty?" I will never forget General Dickinson's reply. He drew himself up proudly and said: "If here is not the post of duty, looking after the safety of these helpless women and children, then I don't know what you call duty."

After walking three miles we reached the ford, where the Yankees had crossed on a pontoon bridge four days before. Here at the old La Roque house General Dickinson left us in the care of a New Jersey chaplain and went to see about getting us across the river. We saw here the corpse of an old negro woman who, they said, had been frightened to death. We all sat on the porch waiting, not knowing what would happen next. Presently General Dickinson returned, went with us to the bridge, and bade us good-by. A nobler, braver, kindlier gentleman never lived.

PRIVATE HENRY MEYER
148TH PENNSYLVANIA INFANTRY, CALDWELL'S BRIGADE

A millwright from Rebersburg, Meyer and his regiment spent the early morning of May 3 east of the fighting, listening to the sound of battle coming closer. As Union troops withdrew from the Chancellor house area, Caldwell's brigade and the rest of Hancock's division were left as rear guard, fighting the enemy in two directions. Finally, it came time for the division to get away as best it could. Meyer survived but was later wounded at Spotsylvania and discharged from service.

We held this position until near noon, and all this time were ignorant about the result of the conflict on the right of our Army which we heard the evening before, or what had taken place in the same locality up to that moment. Were our troops success-ful or did they suffer defeat? These were anxious thoughts. But we were not to be left in doubt much longer. Shells began to drop in rapid succession into our line, coming from the direction of Chancellorsville. At first it was supposed that our own batteries were trying to send shell across our men into the lines of the enemy, and that the guns were not properly elevated. A Lieutenant went back to notify our batteries of their mistake. He brought the intelligence that they were rebel guns. Huge volumes of smoke arose to our rear, caused, as we learned later, by the burning of Chancellor House. Captain Forster having been wounded during the morning, May 3d, was obliged to go to the rear and Lieut. S. S. Wolf assumed command of the company.

It now became plainly and painfully evident that we were being

Among the items found in the burned-out shell of the Chancellor house were a prewar blue glass bottle for liniment or medicine, distorted by the heat; an iron toy horse; and the remnant of a cart once attached to the horse.

Colonel Nelson A. Miles of the 61st New York (left) commanded Hancock's skirmish line on May 2 and 3, fending off every Confederate attack against his position straddling the Turnpike. He was shot in the abdomen on May 3—his third wound of the war—but survived and won the Medal of Honor for his performance. Hancock, observing Miles' heroics, told a staff officer to "ride down and tell Colonel Miles he is worth his weight in gold." Miles, a store clerk with no military background, later fought in the Indian wars and in 1898 was named general in chief.

LIEUTENANT D. AUGUSTUS DICKERT
3D SOUTH CAROLINA INFANTRY, KERSHAW'S BRIGADE

Lieutenant Dickert's brigade, part of McLaws' division, had been engaged in skirmishing with Union II and XII Corps troops southeast of the Chancellor house through the early morning of May 3. Finally, when Stuart's assaults began to falter, Lee ordered McLaws' and Anderson's troops forward. Dickert's account describes the confusion of the final minutes of active battle at the clearing, when the two wings of the Army of Northern Virginia were united and a Confederate victory was all but sealed.

As our brigade was moving through the thicket in the interval between our main line and the skirmishers, and under a heavy fire, we came upon a lone stranger sitting quietly upon a log. At first he was thought an enemy, who in the denseness of the undergrowth had passed our lines on a tour of observation. He was closely questioned, and it turned out to be Rev. Boushell, a methodist minister belonging to one of McGowan's South Carolina regiments, who became lost from his command in the great flank movement of Jackson (McGowan's Brigade belonged to Jackson's Corps), and said he came down "to see how the battle was going and to lend aid and comfort to any wounded soldier should he chance to find one in need of his services."

The batteries in our front were now raking the matted brush all around and overhead, and their infantry soon became aware of our presence, and they, too, began pouring volleys into our advancing column. The ranks became confused, for in this wilderness we could not see twenty paces in front. Still we moved forward with such order as was under the conditions permissible. When near the turn-pike road General Kershaw gave the command to "charge." The Fifteenth raised the yell; then the Third dashed forward; the Seventh was somewhat late on account of the almost impassable condition of the ground, but still it and the Third Battalion, with the Second on the left, made a mad rush for the public road, and entered it soon after the Fifteenth and Third. A perfect sea of fire was in our faces from the many cannon parked around the Chancellor House and graping in all directions but the rear. Lee on the one side and Stuart on the other had closed upon the enemy, their wings joining just in front of the house. Some of the pieces of the enemy's artillery were not more than fifty yards in our front, and the discharges seemed to blaze fire in our very ranks. Infantry, too, was there massed all over the yard, and in rear of this one vast, min-

hemmed in on all sides by the enemy. We beat a hasty retreat, every man for himself, and by taking advantage of several deep ravines, and by an acceleration of speed, we succeeded in extricating ourselves out of the trap. Our picket line to the right of us was captured. As we emerged from the woods and entered a small field, we saw the entrenchments of a new line on the opposite side. In this field were a mass of retiring troops, leisurely and without formulation, moving in the direction of the new line of works, just mentioned. Looking back across the field in the direction of Chancellorsville, I noticed coming up at a gallop, a Confederate battery and taking position in the woods on the other side of the clearing. In less time than it takes to tell it, they were in position and opened a terrific storm of shot and shell into our retreating troops, and it accelerated their retreat wonderfully. The sickening, dull thud of the cannon balls tearing through their mass was distinctly heard from my point of observation, two hundred yards away from the scene. When the field was clear our batteries opened on those of the rebels and silenced them in a moment. After I got inside our new line, a piece of shell grazed my right leg above the knee. I dropped my gun and clapped both hands to the spot and thinking that half the limb was cut off, I dreaded to look down. The injury was not very serious, however, simply a black spot as large as a hand, and my leg stiff for a day.

gling, moving body of humanity, dead horses lay in all directions, while the dead and wounded soldiers lay heaped and strewn with the living. But a few volleys from our troops in the road soon silenced all opposition from the infantry, while cannoneers were hitching up their horses to fly away. Some were trying to drag away their caissons and light pieces by hand, while thousands of "blue coats," with and without arms, were running for cover to the rear. In less than twenty minutes the firing ceased in our front, and men were ordered to prepare breastworks.

> ## "It must have been from such a scene that men in ancient days rose to the dignity of gods."

MAJOR CHARLES MARSHALL
Staff, General Robert E. Lee

Major Charles Marshall, an aide-de-camp on General Lee's staff, was on the scene as Confederate infantry and artillery swarmed into the open fields around the Chancellor house and drove Hooker's men back. General Lee, riding his favorite horse, Traveller, followed his troops to the burning house. In spite of heavy losses, the flames, the cries of wounded men, and the din of battle, soldiers stopped to cheer their beloved general at perhaps his greatest moment.

General Lee accompanied the troops in person, and as they emerged from the fierce combat they had waged in the depths of that tangled wilderness, driving the superior forces of the enemy before them across the open ground, he rode into their midst. The scene is one that can never be effaced from the minds of those who witnessed it. The troops were pressing forward with all the ardour and enthusiasm of combat. The white smoke of musketry fringed the front of the line of battle, while the artillery on the hills in the rear of the infantry shook the earth with its thunder, and filled the air with the wild shrieks of the shells that plunged into the masses of the retreating foe. To add greater horror and sublimity to the scene, Chancellor House and the woods surrounding it were wrapped in flames. In the midst of this awful scene, General Lee, mounted upon that horse which we all remember so well, rode to the front of his advancing battalions. His presence was the signal for one of those outbursts of enthusiasm which none can appreciate who have not witnessed them.

The fierce soldiers with their faces blackened with the smoke of battle, the wounded crawling with feeble limbs from the fury of the devouring flames, all seemed possessed with a common impulse. One long, unbroken cheer, in which the feeble cry of those who lay helpless on the earth blended with the strong voices of those who still fought, rose high above the roar of battle, and hailed the presence of the victorious chief. He sat in the full realization of all that soldiers dream of—triumph; and as I looked upon him in the complete fruition of the success which his genius, courage, and confidence in his army had won, I thought that it must have been from such a scene that men in ancient days rose to the dignity of gods.

Salem Church and Federal Retreat: May 3-5

As the cheering for his victory died down, General Lee immediately gave orders for yet another assault on Hooker's defenses. But then a courier galloped into the Chancellorsville clearing and blurted out alarming news. Sedgwick and his Federal VI Corps had attacked at Fredericksburg and were marching west from there to join up with Hooker.

Sedgwick had, in fact, received an urgent series of messages from Hooker on the night of May 2, after darkness had halted Jackson's flank attack. Sedgwick was to move immediately from his positions along the Rappahannock south of Fredericksburg, push through what Hooker imagined to be the negligible enemy force still in the area and, marching fast, fall upon Lee's rear at dawn on May 3.

The careful Sedgwick had no intention of risking a night attack. Besides, he knew he faced a dangerous obstacle—about 9,000 men of General Jubal Early's division backed by 56 guns entrenched in the formidable earthworks on the heights overlooking the river south of Fredericksburg.

Sedgwick set out nevertheless to obey orders. He formed battle lines during the night of May 2-3, and the next morning he ordered the advance. He first attempted to outflank Marye's Heights with converging attacks from north and south of Fredericksburg. When those probes were turned back, there was nothing left but the frontal route, and about 10:30 a.m. Sedgwick sent Brigadier General John Newton's division charging toward the infamous stone wall at the foot of the heights.

Newton's columns were hurled back three times by Rebel guns, but finally in a fourth charge, the Federals cleared the stone wall and dashed on up Marye's Heights, forcing Barksdale into a hasty retreat. With the Federals pushing west, Early ordered his division to fall back south to avoid being outflanked, leaving Brigadier General Cadmus M. Wilcox's brigade to fall back west and delay Sedgwick's advance.

Absorbing the news of Sedgwick's move with his usual calm, Lee coolly divided his battered army yet again, sending Lafayette McLaws with four brigades marching east along the Turnpike to join up with Wilcox and meet the new threat. This left Lee only about 25,000 able-bodied men to face the 75,000 Federals in their new positions north of Chancellorsville.

Sedgwick did attack, hitting Wilcox's soldiers, who were drawn up on a rise near Salem Church, with McLaws' brigades deployed to the north and south. In a first assault the Federals drove the Confederates back, capturing the church and a nearby schoolhouse that Wilcox's men had turned into strongholds. But the Rebels swiftly countered with a furious rush that beat back the Federals. Sedgwick replied by moving up two fresh divisions, but night was coming on and it was too late for a full-scale assault.

Lee, seeing a chance to annihilate Sedgwick's force, ordered Jubal Early to advance from the south at daybreak on May 4 and take Sedgwick in the rear, while R. H. Anderson's division maneuvered to hit Sedgwick's flank from the south and McLaws attacked from the west.

But coordinating the complex maneuver took time, and Lee was not ready for a full-scale attack until almost 6:00 p.m. Then, unaccountably for such veteran units, the assaults went awry. Jubal Early attacked as planned, throwing back Brigadier General Albion P. Howe's division, but Anderson's men veered off course, heading eastward toward the sound of Early's fight. McLaws' brigades became tangled in dense woods and failed to reach the enemy lines.

Well before that, Sedgwick, sensing the danger, had shifted many of his 19,000 men into a defensive horseshoe to the north. During the night he slipped out of the trap, falling back to get his corps across the Rappahannock at Scott's Ford by 5:00 a.m. on May 5.

Lee swiftly turned his troops around once more and prepared to attack Hooker. But Hooker did not wait, ordering his entire force to recross the Rappahannock at United States Ford. By 9:00 a.m. on May 6 virtually all the 75,000 Federals were on the north side of the Rappahannock, marching in disgust to their old camps around Falmouth.

His dazzling victory complete, Lee was anything but satisfied. He was angry that he had failed to trap and destroy any large body of enemy troops, and although the Federals had lost 17,000 men, his own army had suffered proportionately worse damage with 13,000 casualties. Almost worse, Lee had lost a staggering number of invaluable officers killed or wounded, including two division leaders, 11 brigadiers, and 40 regimental commanders. And then there was Jackson's wound. On May 5 Jackson was taken to a small house on a plantation near Guiney Station, south of Fredericksburg, where Lee sent the message "Tell him to make haste and get well. . . . He has lost his left arm, but I have lost my right."

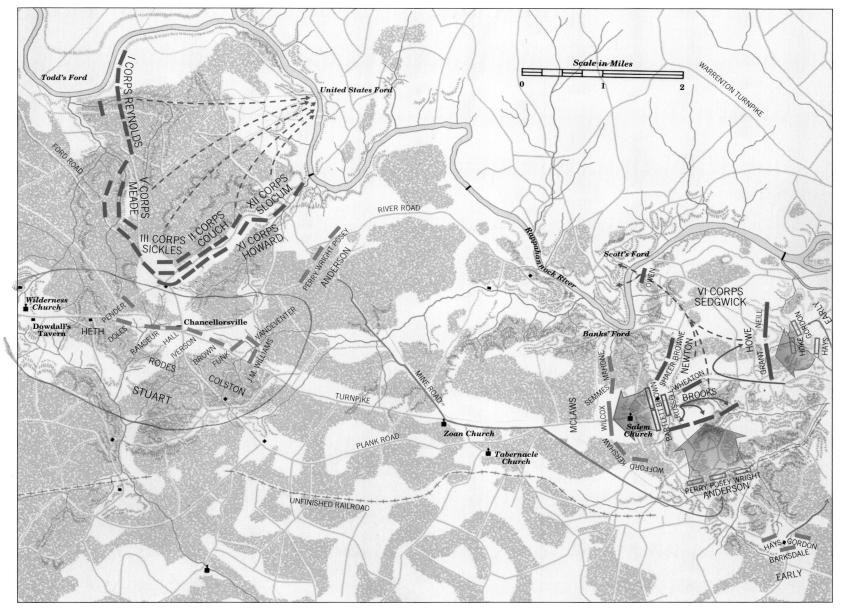

Pressured by frantic appeals from Hooker, Sedgwick finally got his VI Corps moving from Fredericksburg on the morning of May 3. After a brief but furious struggle, the Yankees cleared Barksdale's Mississippians off Marye's Heights and continued their westward march, but they were stopped cold at Salem Church. With Hooker reeling, Lee shifted troops back to the east in an attempt to trap Sedgwick. But despite Early's recapture of Marye's Heights on May 4 and the near encirclement of his corps, Sedgwick managed to escape across the Rappahannock. By the morning of May 6 all of the Federals had crossed the river and the campaign was over.

"They had perfect range of us and there was no shelter for us, but the boys never faltered or wavered a particle but marched along as though at a Dress parade or drill amid that shower of Iron and lead."

LIEUTENANT CHARLES H. BREWSTER
10TH MASSACHUSETTS INFANTRY, BROWNE'S BRIGADE

Held back during their brigade's assault on Marye's Heights, Lieutenant Brewster and his regiment were still close enough to get a good view of the action and to take casualties from Rebel artillery. Just returned from a long medical leave for chronic diarrhea, Brewster served as adjutant and chief recruiter for the 10th Massachusetts.

We arrived at a hill which we could not see over, in front nor on either side as the road was cut deeply into the hill. here we halted near a house and found it contained a lot of wounded and were told that Col Shaler's Brigade which preceeded us had had a fight here and lost [their] Major of 1st Chasseurs of NY. Very soon we made to the side of the road and two Batteries 6 guns each passed on to the front and directly we heard dropping shot of musketry from the flankers close to us, and then the roar of Artillery, and then came the word "Forward, double quick" and up the hill we went and lo! we were in the midst of the city of Fredericksburg, round the corner we went up a long street to the Rail Road, turned up the track and into the Depot where we halted in plain sight of the terrible heights rifle pits and fortifications behind the city which the whole of the centre Grand Division

could not take last December. this was about 5 o'clock Sunday morning May 3rd amid the roar of Artillery as our Battery poured [their] fire at the force on top and rifle pits and stone walls on the side of the roads. never was a calm waked up so fearfully on a quiet Sabboth morn before. it was little while before every street was full of blue jackets we staid here until about 9 o'clock Col Eustis having been sent for twice by Gen Newton to see to the planting of some Batteries finally orders came to fall in and we moved up the river to a long street with rifle pits on both sides connecting the houses and every little ways crossing the streets as (we) moved out of the town on the other side onto a long plain the enemy commenced shelling us from the top of the hills and following along the crest of the hills and in the rifle pits keeping even with the head of our column. they had perfect range of us and there was no shelter for us, but the boys never faltered or wavered a particle but marched along as though at a Dress parade or drill amid that shower of Iron and lead the kind of shell they fired were what is called Spherical Case and is a hollow iron ball filled with Musket bullets and when it bursts it throws a perfect shower of fragments of iron [and] these balls it is just like taking a handful of beans or shot and throwing them all at once only the effect is much more serious if they hit you.

Confederate batteries on Marye's Heights, their positions marked by trailing clouds of smoke, open fire on advancing Federals on the late morning of May 3. A. J. Russell exposed this view from a safe vantage point across the Rappahannock from Fredericksburg, just south of the destroyed railroad bridge. Rebel guns kept up a steady fire on the attacking Federal ranks as they pushed up the heights.

SERGEANT W. R. JOHNSON
15TH MASSACHUSETTS INFANTRY, SULLY'S BRIGADE

When the II Corps marched off to join Hooker, Gibbon's division remained behind opposite Fredericksburg. On the morning of May 3 Sergeant Johnson's brigade crossed the river to support the VI Corps attacks, although the brigade commander, Brigadier General Alfred Sully, had just been relieved for failing to take "extreme measures" against some two-year men who refused to fight.

At the time of the Chancellorsville fight we did not go with the rest of the corps, but the division, under command of General Gibbon, was ordered to support Sedgwick, and cross the Rappahannock at the city, the Sixth crossing below. After getting up into the city we passed the charging party, who had thrown off knapsacks and were ready for business. Filing off to the right we marched up a street running parallel with the river, and were ordered to make a [point] on our extreme right against the enemy's left, to draw their attention from the actual point of attack.

As soon as we reached the outskirts of the city the rebel artillery [fired] on us, but marching in column of [pairs], we opened out so as to give their shells more room, and started on the double-quick, never stopping till we reached the end of the plain, a mile and a half away. The move had the desired effect, as the rebels double-quicked a column opposite us, and kept even with us all the way up, finally dropping into the rifle pits in front of us, under the crest of the hill. Here we were ordered to lie down and take all cover possible from their artillery.

After lying there quite awhile we heard heavy firing down on the left, on the plank road running from the city up over the heights. From

the nature of the ground the charging party could not be seen distinctly, but by the enemy's rapid fire I know that our friends had got well to work, and very soon the firing ceased at that point, and a line of battle appeared in sight, coming toward us on the crest of the heights, and marching at right angles with the rebel works, but, as we could see no colors, there was quite a discussion as to whether they were our men or rebels. The question was soon settled by the line obliging to the right, and, as if rising out of the ground, the colors came slowly into sight. What a picture—the old Stars and Stripes rippling in the breeze of that beautiful May day! The sun was just right to bring out every color and give the best effect. It thrills me to day as I think of that sight. Every man stood up, (no thought of rebel shells then!) and for an instant

silently gazed on the scene, and then, as if by common impulse, there broke such a yell from our line as I never heard before. Men went wild, and caps were flung so high in the air I thought they'd be out of style when they came down. For a few minutes one would have thought an insane asylum had broke loose. The rebels could not understand it, not seeing what we saw, but began to drop out of the pits by twos and threes, and finally they all went with a rush out and over the hill. We could not reach them on account of a canal between us, so we took up our line of march for the city, struck the plank road over the heights, and followed the Sixth Corps two or three miles, when we were ordered back to guard the pontoon bridges in front of the Lacey house, where we lay till the whole army had recrossed the Rappahannock.

Shortly after his resignation in late 1863 because of illness and the lingering effects of a wound, Colonel John Ely of the 23d Pennsylvania Infantry (left) commemorated the actions of his command during the assault on Marye's Heights by issuing a private award. Known as the Ely Medal, it bears on the front (below, right) clasped hands with a legend giving the unit and the place and date of battle, and on the reverse, a figure of Liberty with patriotic mottoes. The example illustrated here was bestowed on Private Robert Elliot (right).

PRIVATE ALVIN H. DIBBLE

33D NEW YORK INFANTRY, NEILL'S BRIGADE

Just as Newton's Federals crested the stone wall, Albion Howe's division on the left with Brigadier General Thomas H. Neill's brigade in the lead joined in the rush up the heights. The 18-year-old Dibble was wounded during the attack, and his right arm was amputated at the shoulder. After a lengthy convalescence he was discharged.

etween ten and eleven o'clock A.M. the order came for the assault on the enemy's works . . . and at precisely eleven we arose from the ground where we had been lying. In front of us was the now historical "Stonewall" and back of that again Marys Heights bristling with cannon and swarming with exultant rebels who thought that nothing that bore the semblance of man could wrest it from them. . . . The order came. Into the tempest of shot and shell we dashed, our dead and wounded falling in heaps, as a ball tore through our ranks, but we closed up and onward we pressed regardless of everything but the business at hand. The 7th Maine of our Brigade carried the "Stonewall"—we, more to the left, drove the afrighted rebels from their rifle pits at the point of the bayonet, up the crest we made our way, the four remaining gunners are either bayonetted or made prisoners, and Maryes Heights was ours. We had no time for rest but hastily reforming—tho with thinned ranks—and giving one awakening cheer for our success, we charged on a heavy battery to the left of those we had just captured and which had opened a heavy cross fire on us. The ground was rough in the extreme and rendered more [so] by natural obstructions and such artificial ones as rebels against [us] could invent, but nothing could damp the ardor of the boys of the "Empire State" whose motto is *Excelsior;* the battery was captured. Here I had the fortune to capture a huge specimen genus "Johnnie," but not having time to attend to him in person I threw away his gun and ordered him to the rear—as famous old John Bunyon wrote long ago, "I saw him no more.". . .

Having again reformed, we pushed for the rear of the works and found the rebel regiments which had supported the battery drawn up in line of battle under partial shelter of some bush and low trees. Here we had a sharp musketry fight, but the 7th Maine and 21st New Jersey coming to our support, we at last drove them with heavy loss. It was near the end of this part of the action that I, in company with a few others, being considerably in advance of the regiment, was wounded severely in the right wrist and shoulder, besides receiving a slight bayonet wound in the knee. Being no longer able to carry arms I was obliged to go to the rear for medical attention.

Brigadier General William Barksdale (left) served as a fiery proponent of states' rights in Congress for eight years before the war. He was no less enthusiastic in battle; one superior described his "wild radiant joy" as he led his brigade of Mississippians into the attack. Although he was badly outnumbered on May 3, his reputation remained untarnished. Two months later at Gettysburg, Barksdale fell mortally wounded leading his command.

Posted behind the infamous stone wall, the 18th Mississippi fended off successive assaults before finally giving way, losing its colors and numerous men. Private William Blake (right) escaped but was later wounded and captured at Gettysburg. His left leg amputated, Private Blake was eventually exchanged and detailed to commissary duty.

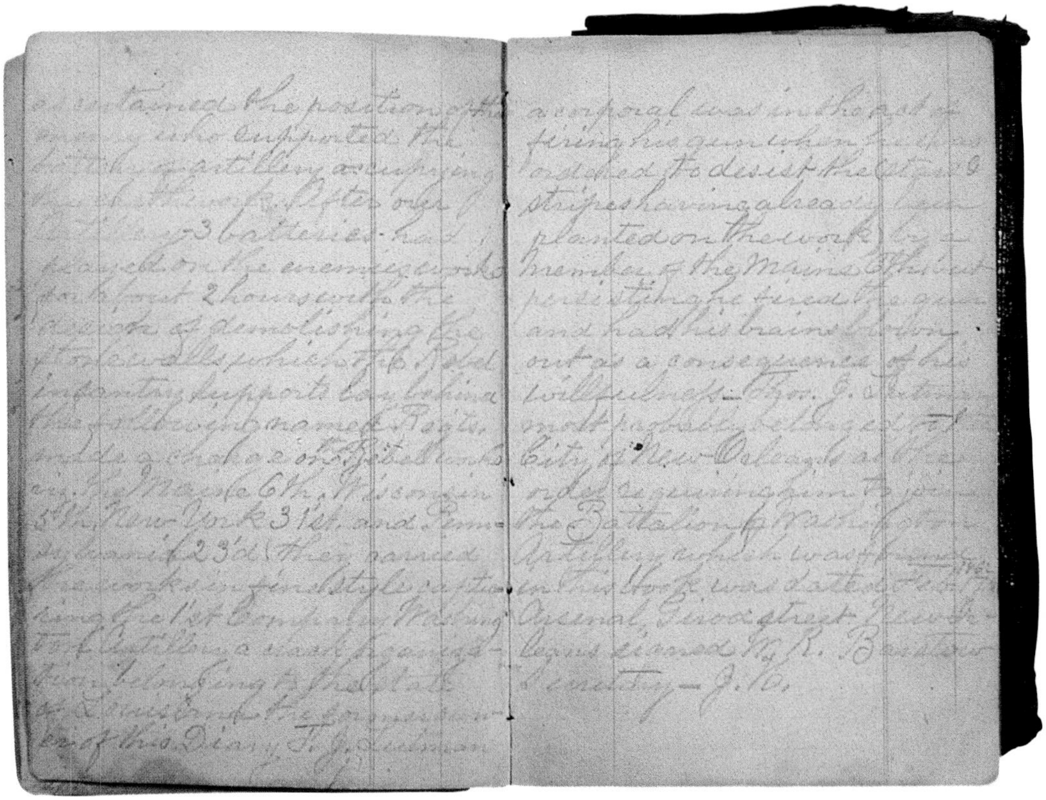

Standing in a narrow lane overlooking Hazel Run on the west slope of Marye's Heights, General Herman Haupt (at left) and one of his assistants, William W. Wright, examine a wrecked caisson and dead team belonging to the Washington Artillery of New Orleans. In the fighting of May 3, the Washington Artillery lost six guns and 29 horses. Haupt and Wright, in the company of photographer A. J. Russell, explored the battlefield on the following day and barely escaped capture when Jubal Early's Confederates reentered Fredericksburg. At right is the diary of Corporal Thomas J. Lutman of the Washington Artillery, killed during the fight. A Federal soldier recovered the diary, wrote in it his account of the battle (shown here), and added that Lutman "had his brains blown out as a consequence of his wilfulness."

CAPTAIN PETER A. S. MCGLASHAN

50TH GEORGIA INFANTRY, SEMMES' BRIGADE

Lee barely had time to savor his triumph in the clearing at Chancellorsville when word arrived of Sedgwick's successful breakthrough. Lee quickly ordered McLaws' division east to shore up the units trying to slow the Federal advance. McGlashan, who by war's end would be colonel of his regiment, remembered the tributes paid to Lee at the time—not only by Rebel troops but even by Yankee prisoners.

It was near mid-day on May 3, 1863, when our brigade, consisting of the 10th, 50th, 51st and 53rd Georgia regiments, under command of the gallant Gen. Paul J. Semmes, were lying in the woods near the plank road leading to Fredericksburg. The men, kept at attention by the occasional dropping of a shell from the enemy's works, when Gen. Lee and staff rode slowly from the woods and approached Gen. McLaws' men where we lay. The air was full of rumors. Troops were rapidly shifting position, prisoners pouring in from the front, and the

men watched the conference of the two generals with keen interest.

As Gen. Lee concluded he nodded pleasantly to Gen. McLaws and said in a louder tone: "Now, General, there is a chance for your young men to distinguish themselves."

The brigade was called to attention, a rapid inspection made, cartridge boxes filled and we filed out into the road which was filled with prisoners, who rapidly fell to one side as we passed.

Here an incident occurred which I shall never forget. As the prisoners fell to one side an exciting murmur ran through them of: "That's him! that's Lee! Hats off, boy's!" I looked back. Gen. Lee was following us with his staff, I thought never looking before so grand and noble. As he came up the prisoners, to a man, faced him and uncovered, and he looking, as I thought, sadly at them, raised his hat and bowing his head acknowledged their salute. It was a picturesque scene. The prisoners represented all branches of the service, red and blue zouaves, infantry, artillery and cavalry. Lee was then at the zenith of his fame, and their recognition of his greatness seemed so fitting and graceful it called forth cheers from our troops.

"Although we had been running until our tongues were hanging out still we saw no escape from capture or death unless we could reach that church before the Yankees did."

LIEUTENANT EDMUND D. PATTERSON
9TH ALABAMA INFANTRY, WILCOX'S BRIGADE

Born and raised in Ohio, Patterson ventured south as a book salesman in 1860 and decided to take up residence in Alabama just months before the war began. In May 1861, at the age of 19, he entered Confederate service, feeling he would be labeled a spy if he returned to Ohio. Severely wounded at Frayser's Farm in June 1862, he saw his next major action the following year on May 3 when his brigade sought to delay Sedgwick's advance.

While we were all lying there we could hear fighting both above and below, and it was not long before a courier reached us from Gen'l. Barksdale, asking our immediate assistance. We double quicked as rapidly as possible down towards Fredericksburg and reached the top of the hill just above Stanbury house, in time to see the Yankees come over the breastworks. By overwhelming numbers, they had succeeded, after several attempts, in running over his troops, and as we came down the slope of the hill we were met by rapid fire from their sharp shooters. Old Wilcox immediately threw us into line, but we soon saw that we were not strong enough to check them for before we could get a battery in position the shells and shot were pouring into us in such a style as to become murderous. Quickly the order was passed to each regimental commander to make his way to the Brick Church. Although we had been running until our tongues were hanging out still we saw no escape from capture or death unless we could reach that church before the Yankees did; and not only so—for if they arrived there first there would be nothing between them and the main army under Gen'l. Lee, who were fighting at Chancellorsville, with their backs to us.

A mediocre West Point cadet but a reliable commander, Brigadier General Cadmus M. Wilcox marched his Alabama brigade from its position near Banks' Ford to the sound of the guns on May 3. Wilcox conducted a masterly delaying action, resisting Sedgwick at every ridge and tree line until reinforcements arrived.

The Yankees had secured the plank road and had us cut off between them and the river, and we had the dirt road to travel on to reach Salem Church. It gave them the shortest cut, but they were afraid to advance up rapidly. The fire of their sharp shooters was so severe that we were compelled to throw the brigade into column of companies, so as to bring the rear of the column far enough forward to be out of reach of the fire until we could throw out a line of sharp shooters to keep them back. In this way we double quicked back to the church.

LIEUTENANT LEWIS VAN BLARCOM

15TH NEW JERSEY INFANTRY, BROWN'S BRIGADE

*In the van of Sedgwick's push down the Turnpike, Colonel Henry W. Brown's
New Jersey brigade and the rest of Brooks' division were repeatedly stalled by
Wilcox's skillful tactics. Finally, with four brigades from Lee just coming up, the
Rebels deployed across the road on either side of Salem Church and the Federals
attacked. The 15th New Jersey lost nearly 150 men. Van Blarcom was untouched
until the following May when he was wounded and captured at Spotsylvania.*

Moving rapidly along the plank road toward Salem church we
saw no signs of the enemy, but an occasional dead soldier
lying along the line of march was proof that sharp skirmishing
had been going on. Suddenly we encountered soldiers lying at rest along
the road, and soon after marching by the flank, in four ranks, we filed to
the right from the road into a field, and marching a short distance, we
heard the order "left face, forward march," and we were marching in the
line of battle toward a woods. Probably, scarcely a member of the Regiment except the Colonel commanding knew that the 15th was about to
engage in its first pitched battle, until some men of the 3d N.J. who were
lying along the fence sang out, "throw off your knapsacks." The Regiment approached the woods and entered it, not a shot having been fired,
as I recollect. After having gone into the woods about a hundred yards,
we were met by a scattering skirmish fire, followed a few seconds after by
a crash of musketry from a line of battle probably not more than fifty
yards ahead. The Regiment halted, and without any general order to fire,
the four hundred and fifty rifles of the 15th responded with a deafening
roar to the rebel volley. After the smoke cleared away I saw two men of
the 15th lying dead, Joshua D. Banker and James Hendershot, both shot
through the head, and two others, whose names I care not to mention,
lying on the ground nearly frightened to death. In a little time, however,
they recovered from their scare, and upon a suggestion how to load and

fire, both these men went to work and fought bravely through the entire
action. The situation was terrific with our own fire that of the rebels' in
front, the thunder of our batteries in the rear and the crashing of solid
shot and shell through the tree tops, it was quite impossible to hear a
voice. The men kept well in line and loaded and fired with great rapidity.
I saw men, their pieces having become fouled, trying to drive the bullet
home by pressing the rammer against a tree, and, failing in that, throw
down the useless gun and pick up the rifle of a dead or wounded soldier
and resume their places in the ranks. The fire of the rebels was incessant.

DOG "JACK,"
*Attached to the 102d Regiment Pennsylvania Vols.,
was in the following Battles:*
Siege of Yorktown; Battle of Williamsburg; Fair Oaks;
Battle of the Pickets; Malvern Hill, (wounded;) First and
Second Fredericksburg; Captured at Salem Church, was
exchanged and returned.

*Jack, a stray dog adopted as the mascot of a Pittsburgh fire company, went to
war when the firemen enlisted as a company in the 102d Pennsylvania Infantry.
Jack marched with his two-legged comrades from Yorktown in 1862 until his
disappearance in 1864, even taking a bullet through his shoulder and neck at
Malvern Hill. On May 3 Jack was captured at Salem Church and held prisoner
for six months until he was exchanged for a Confederate soldier.*

As the fighting escalated, both sides called in more units to shore up their hard-pressed lines at Salem Church. Captain John Large (above) and the rest of the 102d Pennsylvania moved to the right to support a flagging New Jersey regiment. Within minutes the 102d took more than 50 casualties, among them Captain Large, who was killed leading the color company into the fray.

CAPTAIN PETER A. S. MCGLASHAN
50TH GEORGIA INFANTRY, SEMMES' BRIGADE

First on the scene to reinforce Wilcox was Semmes' Georgia brigade. During the desperate struggle to drive back the Yankees, a line of woods obscured McGlashan's regiment from the view of its brigade commander. After the battle, Semmes confronted the 50th's commander, insinuating his unit had dodged the fight. The indignant colonel responded by handing the general a just-completed report showing that of the 316 men who had gone into action only 125 now answered the roll.

The news that Sedgwick was rapidly approaching, driving Wilcox's Alabama brigade before them, cast an air of defiant cheerfulness over the men. Ranks were closed up, the pace increased, and between 3 and 4 P.M. we arrived in sight of Salem Church, a little country church by the side of the road, where a stirring sight awaited us.

The enemy in magnificent force, and three lines deep, at right angles to and crossing the road, with flying colors and glancing bayonets, were driving Wilcox's Alabamians, who were gallantly struggling to delay them, before them. As we looked, Wilcox, pressed and outflanked by the enemy, left their position and rapidly falling back took up a fresh position on the right and left of the church across the road.

There was not a moment to lose. The enemy was almost in possession of the rising ground in front that would have commanded our position. But McLaws was equal to the emergency. Rapidly disposing of his troops to the right and left of Wilcox, our brigade was ordered to the front, and left Mahone's brigade in reserve.

The moment was critical; we could scarcely reach our line before the enemy. There was no time for brigade movements. Each regiment commander rapidly noted the position his regiment would occupy and rushed for it by the nearest route at the double-quick. . . .

The 50th Georgia on reaching their ground found the formation obstructed by a ditch and cedar wattled fence at the edge of the field. Leaping over that, like so many deer, the men formed like lightning on the right by file into line. Receiving a terrible fire from the enemy at 60 yards range, and then, with a wild yell, we charged and drove the enemy over and beyond the line in confusion and ranged up along side the 53d Georgia to receive their next assault. We had lost about 15 or 20 men, but a more gallant deed I never witnessed.

The enemy reformed quickly, and cheered by their officers

"I shall have no regiment left . . . if this lasts a half hour longer. Oh, that the sun would set; is there no supports?"

advanced again and again to the assault, only to be repulsed with terrible slaughter.

Meanwhile we were suffering terribly, three color bearers shot down in succession. Gaps were seen along the line strewn with dead and wounded, the men steadily closing up the gaps, and kneeling, were firing with deliberation. The roar of musketry was incessant and terrific. Still the men cheered and loaded and fired, not a break or waver in the line, although nearly two-thirds of their number lay dead and wounded around them. Rush after rush was made by the enemy and as often vigorously repulsed. Our rifles were leading up so they were useless, the men throwing them away would pick up the rifle of some dead or wounded comrade and resume the fight.

We had used up sixty rounds of ammunition, the litter-bearers were dispatched for more, the wounded left uncared for. "I shall have no regiment left," shouted Kearse to me, "if this lasts a half hour longer. Oh, that the sun would set; is there no supports?" Mahone's brigade lay a short distance in our rear, but gave no sign of their presence.

While he was speaking the men began shouting: "They are giving way; let us charge them." It was true. Appalled by the stubborn resistance and fearful punishment inflicted by our troops, the enemy were at last giving way; with a wild yell, the regiment charged and in an instant the enemy were in full retreat. Some of the men made a dash at the colors of the Forty-sixth New York Regiment, but the gallant color-bearer tore off the colors and escaped, leaving the staff in our hands.

LIEUTENANT WILLIAM C. MATHEWS
38TH GEORGIA INFANTRY, GORDON'S BRIGADE

With the bulk of his division out of position to block Sedgwick's advance on May 3, Jubal Early pulled back to the south to regroup. The next day, as part of Lee's counterstroke, Early backtracked to retake Marye's Heights and cut the Federals off from Fredericksburg. Here, in an excerpt from a letter to his father dated May 8, Mathews tells of the opening Rebel attack of the day. Lieutenant Mathews, who served as regimental adjutant, was captured two months later on the retreat from Pennsylvania and spent the rest of the war in prison.

We lay on our arms and after a most refreshing sleep were awakened about sunrise and skirmishers immediately advanced in the direction of the heights. It was not certain that we were going to take them by storm. Gen. Gordon rode in front of our brigade and said if there was a sick man or a man that was afraid to follow him that he might fall out and leave. Who would have left then? I am proud to say that none did. We commenced the advance then and for two miles we saw not a Yankee, but on ascending a hill near the old plank road we got a sight of them in line of battle behind the road that afforded some protection to them. I thought that the tug of war had come, for we had to charge down the hill and across a deep mill pond and then up a long slant to dislodge them. They had commenced shelling us also. After a little halt, during which time bayonets were fixed, we commenced the charge. We went down the hill like an avalanche and into that mill pond where the water on the right of the regiment reached to our waist. We were soon across and under the brow of the hill. Re-formed and started again. When the bullets commenced their music but before we could get near the road the Yankees were going like a parcel of sheep through the woods, having wounded but 3 of our regiment, while we had killed several and took some prisoners, that were so scared they could not move and also took a portable Black Smith shop, a number of ambulance and several horses. Being on foot I made for one of the wagons and soon cut a great big sorrel horse from the harness and mounted him. I had hardly secured my prize before we made for the hill where the Washington Artilery had been taken the day before, and there we run another force into the city, without a scratch. These heights we occupied until late in the evening, the Yankee Sharpshooters popping

From his vista at Falmouth Heights just north of the Rappahannock River, special artist Edwin Forbes produced this panoramic sketch showing the battlefield as it appeared at about 6:00 p.m. on May 4, with General Sedgwick already falling back to Scott's Ford and the Rebels pressing hard on three sides. A Federal battery (#9) fires from a bluff over the Rappahannock (#1) at columns of Early's Confederates (#2, #5) marching across their front. In the distance, Confederate battle lines (#4) engage VI Corps troops (#3) positioned along the edge of the woods used by Sedgwick to shield his movements back to the river. In the left part of the sketch, Union artillery (#6) duels with the massed batteries of McLaws' and Anderson's divisions (#7).

at us from the town the whole time. We had to keep ourselves in a ditch all the time and when one would put his head out there would be a dozen bullets whizzing all around him. . . .

. . . By daybreak the next morning, we commenced bringing in prisoners, and plundering their knapsacks that were thrown all over the field. I got about a peck of coffee mixed with sugar, a nice portfolio with paper and pens. . . . I was never so bothered in my life. A fortune in my grasp and no way to carry it off. I was vexed but contented myself with a few small trinkets, and my coffee and sugar and canteens.

I have got my horse yet, and am going to keep him, though I will have to buy him from the Government who claims all captured property in that line.

CAPTAIN
H. SEYMOUR HALL
STAFF, BRIGADIER GENERAL
JOSEPH J. BARTLETT

Lee's bid to bag Sedgwick failed not only because of a late start by most of his forces, but also because of a ferocious Federal defense. Hall, who received the Medal of Honor for gallantry at Gaines' Mill, described the murderous fire dealt out by a Massachusetts battery and from the rifles of the 27th New York, the captain's former regiment.

One of General Gordon's officers in action on May 4 was Lieutenant George W. Wood (above) of the 60th Georgia. Like the rest of the regiments in Gordon's brigade, the 60th took only light casualties on May 4 but was harder hit two months later. On the third day of Gettysburg, Wood was wounded in the lungs and liver and died 20 days later in a Yankee hospital.

Our brigade being on a ridge on the left of Captain McCartney's battery (A, First Massachusetts), was fully exposed to this fire, from which we would have been sheltered by moving down the slope a few paces to the rear. General Bartlett sent me to General Brooks to request his permission. As I rode off a regiment on the right of the battery, not of our brigade, retired behind the hill, and the movement was seen by General Sedgwick. As I neared the piazza on which he was standing with General Brooks, Sedgwick, without looking at my face, my uniform being covered by a poncho, took me for the commander of that regiment and said: "Colonel, why did you move your regiment without orders, sir?"

Before I could reply, he recognized me and asked: "What is it, captain?" I replied: "General Bartlett sends his compliments, sir, and requests permission to retire his brigade a few yards, behind the shelter of the ridge." He responded: "Give my compliments to General Bartlett, and say that his brigade must remain in position and not move a foot now." As I rode to the front Generals Sedgwick and Brooks rode to the brigade after me, reaching our position by Captain McCartney's battery just as General Lee in person was directing his infantry to the attack on us. The 27th New York Volunteers . . . was on the skirmish-line in front of our brigade and McCartney's battery. The particular force to which our brigade was opposed at this time, 6 p.m., was Hoke's and Wright's brigades, and as they came within range our skirmishers and McCartney's battery absolutely stopped their progress and threw them into confusion.

The boys of the 27th took advantage of every place of shelter on the skirmish-line from which to deliver an accurate and rapid fire, while the artillery smashed and scattered the advancing columns. At the enemy's hesitation and confusion, our skirmishers cried out: *"Come on Johnnie; do come over and see us."* Falling back in the shelter of the timber, out of the range of our guns, the formation of the enemy was changed from column to line of battle, and again advanced to attack us, but our skirmishers redoubled their former efforts to repel the attack, repeated their derisive cries, yielded not one foot of ground, and as the artillery-

men warmed to their work, McCartney formed his guns by battery, sent home the case-shot, and as the contest warmed his blood, raised in his stirrups, shouted to his eager men: *"Aim,* right section to the right oblique, left section to the left oblique, *fire!* and *shell the whole —— country."* The men, blackened by powder smoke, worked like demons, the guns belched forth a flood of fiery death, and the hill seemed to rock under the terrific thunder of the battery; great gaps were opened in the enemy's lines by the tornado of shot and shell; they retired into the friendly shelter of the woods, and night, darkness, and silence drew a curtain of mercy over the fearful scene.

LIEUTENANT HENRY E. HANDERSON

9TH LOUISIANA INFANTRY, HAYS' BRIGADE

After severing the Federals' line of retreat, the men of Hays' brigade regrouped, and then, after a long wait, joined in the general attack. Scrambling over a line of low hills, Handerson, who was slightly wounded, and his comrades were soon slowed by the terrain and stiffening enemy resistance.

Finally about 5 P.M. my brigade was conducted by a circuitous route through a deep ravine to the foot of an enormous hill, which I now believe to have been the same Taylor's Hill from which we had retreated the day before. Here we were drawn up in line of battle and ordered to await the signal of three guns upon our left. The men spent the interval in snatching a hasty supper (for many of them their last) of crackers and bacon, chatting, smoking and jesting as if danger were the last thing in their minds.

Before us rose the hill to a height which shut out any prospect of the summit, while its sides were covered with brush and fallen timber to such a degree that an orderly ascent was utterly impossible. An occasional head was seen peering down upon us from the crest, and was presumably that of an enemy, but not a shot disturbed the security of the quiet valley in which we stood watching the lengthening shadows cast by the declining sun. At last the signal guns boomed forth upon the quiet air, and with a shout of "Charge" Gen. Harry Hays launched us up the hill

on a full run. Of course military order was out of the question. Each man made a route for himself and rushed for the summit. My long legs and good wind enabled me to keep a place among the foremost, and when our advance reached the crest of the hill we halted for a moment to await the approach of our less speedy comrades. But our appearance was the signal for a cross-fire of artillery and musketry which seemed to make the very air boil. Men fell on every side, and, without further delay and with another shout of "Charge," Gen. Hays again led us forward against an enemy as yet unseen but manifestly not far off.

On we rushed across an open plateau, along the further border of which a high brush fence opposed a formidable obstacle to our advance. As I approached the fence, which in front of me was fully breast-high, I hesitated for a moment what course to pursue; whether to tear open a passage through it, or to try to jump it. Short time, however, was afforded for reflection, and, as a shell shrieked by my ear, I rose with a tremendous leap and, as I cleared the brush, saw before me with dismay a sunken road about eight or ten feet deep, into which I fell in a heap upon the heads and backs of a number of Federals, who from this natural defense had been furnishing us with a hot reception. It is hard to say which of us was most surprised, and for a moment I thought my time had come. But numbers of my comrades, after a somewhat similar experience, poured into the cut, and the enemy at once surrendered. Leaving them to take care of themselves, however, we clambered out of the other side of the roadway and rushed forward once more to complete our victory. By this time, of course, all semblance of military order had been totally lost. Captains lost their companies, and companies and regiments were so intermingled that the brigade formed simply a howling, rushing and firing mob, without pretense of organization or authority. Somewhat blown by my exertions, and badly shaken by my unexpected jump into the roadway, I gradually drifted behind the mass of my comrades, and in spite of my utmost exertions, soon found myself almost alone, save a few stragglers, who, like myself, had been unable to keep up the headlong rush of the advance.

In this painting by Union veteran Julian Scott, a regiment of Lewis Grant's Vermont brigade moves up into line, passing behind another regiment furiously matching volleys with Early's Confederates during the retreat to Scott's Ford. William Stowe of the 2d Vermont remembered that so many Rebels were knocked down that "their dead covered the ground as grey as a badger in front of us."

SURGEON DANIEL HOLT
121ST NEW YORK INFANTRY, BARTLETT'S BRIGADE

Busily attending to casualties while the battle raged around him, Holt and his medical staff failed to pull out in time to avoid capture. The doctor's regiment suffered the highest number of casualties in the entire VI Corps. During his brief captivity Holt was a dinner guest of General Wilcox and was visited by General Lee, who offered the doctor all available resources for the care of the wounded.

It was upon the evening of the 4th, next day after the sanguinary engagement at Salem Church, where we were almost totally annihilated, as the enemy was pressing upon our retreating [columns], there I left my position a few rods in rear of our brigade, taking a stand a short distance to the left when I established our field hospital, and went to work dressing the wound[s] of those brought to the rear, when I was ordered to change quarters as the rebels were pressing and very close upon us. I did not immediately obey, but continued to dress such wounds as came to me. . . . I was delayed beyond the time I ought to have been; but gathered together my squad and addressed them upon the importance of keeping together and under no circum-

stances to straggle, remarking, as I mounted my horse for them to follow Silver tail (the name given to my cream colored, white mane and tail horse) and that if we went to the d——l we would all go together. Let me tell you I feared that all was not exactly right, because I had seen the rebels "singing around the circle" and enclosing us in a net, and our forces going for sweet life to the only outlet for them—"Banks Ford" on the Rappahannock, four or five miles above Fredericksburgh. It was now after dark, so that I could not distinguish between our own men and those of the enemy; but proceeded in the direction of the cheers close at hand. Not feeling quite so secure, I sent out scouts, who came back reporting that nothing could be seen but behind that cheering came from our own men, as they were occupying the ground but a very short time previously. Having no alternative, I rode along where I saw just ahead of me, not more than three rods distant, a moving line of battle, up to which I rode and asked an officer—a captain who was leading his company, "What Brigade is this?" to which the answer came, "Kershaw's!" Well, thought I, "this *is* rather queer:" but as Brigadiers were as plenty as blackberries in the army, I did not know but our own side had many such names in it, but of that fact, I knew nothing. After imparting to me this cheering piece of news, the officer to whom I addressed the inquiry, asked me: "To what regiment do you belong?" "The 121st" says I, at the same time halting my men who were close upon my heels. "Halt! Halt!! Halt!!!" ran all along the line in answer to mine for my men. It took but a moment to ascertain that the "Kershaw" in question was Rebel General Kershaw of the South Carolina forces instead of ours. "The 121st what?" says my interrigator. "The 121st N. York" says I. "What rank do you hold," says Johnny Reb, for so he was. "Surgeon!" says I. "Well, I think you will have to dismount. I am very sorry to say that you have fallen into the hands of the rebels this time, and there is no help for you!" Imagine my disgust at such information. Surely in following Silver tail, we had all gone to the d——l together. As I have said before, I commanded my men to "halt!" in the most approved style—loud and clear—and this order was given all along the rebel line, bringing to a stand still the entire rebel army—two lines being in motion at the time of my moving, like a fool, into their very mouths. While still upon my horse, an officer rode up in [a] great rage, inquiring as he advanced "Who had the audacity to command a halt at that time?" In the simplicity of my heart I answered that "I" had been guilty of the offence. "By what authority did you do so?" "No authority, only I could not well run over you, and gave my men orders to halt!" "Who are you, sir?" "Surgeon Holt of the 121st Reg. N.Y. Vols. of the federal Army!"—"Federal army

"A tired, disappointed, disgusted army had nothing for the present to do but to wend its way back to its old camping grounds."

be damned! and you too!! Captain place a guard over him and his men and keep them safe until morning!"—It is necessary to say that it was done in "due and ancient form," and you[r] beloved husband from henceforth rode his own national horse "Silver tail," accountenements, blankets, etc. etc. etc. jostling quietly and gently into the hands of others.

LIEUTENANT PORTER FARLEY
140TH NEW YORK INFANTRY, O'RORKE'S BRIGADE

Beginning late on the afternoon of May 5, heavy rain fell for hours, denying Lee the chance to advance on Hooker one last time. The Federal retreat slowed to a crawl, but the three pontoon bridges at United States Ford held, and the columns trudged back across the river to safety. As Farley relates, many in the V Corps rear guard began to worry, but by midmorning on May 6 the last units got across.

The retreat across pontoon bridges laid at United States ford, at the point where the first, second and third corps had crossed the Rappahannock to join that portion of the army which had made the long detour.

. . . Our position had been not more than two or three miles from it, yet so slow and tedious was our progress that it was broad daylight when we came to the bridges, and even then we were not to cross, for the eleventh corps was just going over, and it was evident that it would be a long time before our turn could come. Prudence dictated but one course, and it was adopted. Lines of battle were formed, facing toward the enemy, and we marched back some way to occupy higher ground and make the best disposition possible to resist an attack should one be made. . . .

Whatever might have been done, we felt pretty certain that in case we were attacked no help would be sent back to us and that our only dependance was our own exertions and the batteries planted on the northern bank.

It was a repetition of our experience at Fredericksburg: better, per-

haps, as regards the position we were in, which was not a bad one for defense, but worse as regards time, for it was broad daylight, and we were kept waiting and waiting till it seemed a wonder that the enemy did not come. . . .

To us, as we watched the eleventh corps filing over the two bridges, it seemed as if they moved at but a snail's pace.

At last they were over and our corps began to make the crossing. We breathed easier when our feet at last struck the planking of the bridge. As we toiled up the steep northern bank we looked back and saw the regulars coming safely in from their perilous picket line.

When we reached the top of the bank we halted, formed column by divisions and rested. The Chancellorville campaign was over, and a tired, disappointed, disgusted army had nothing for the present to do but to wend its way back to its old camping grounds.

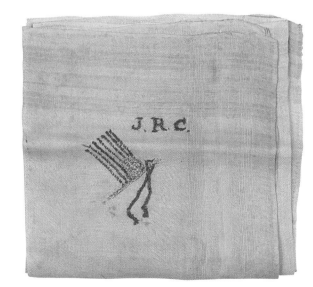

This handkerchief, embroidered with initials and a flag, belonged to Lieutenant John R. Clemm of the 3d Maryland, who was wounded in the head on May 3. Despite a surgeon's description of his wound as slight, Clemm died on May 22.

"What Will the Country Say?"

In the days following the Federal retreat, General Hooker tried to shift the blame for his ignominious failure and put the best face possible on what had happened. "The Cavalry have failed in executing their orders," Hooker's chief of staff, Dan Butterfield, informed Washington, and "General Sedgwick failed in the execution of his orders." Hooker himself proclaimed that his forces had "inflicted heavier blows than we have received," adding that the Army of the Potomac had "added new luster to its former renown."

The troops were not fooled. "The wonder of the private soldiers was great," one Massachusetts volunteer, Warren Goss, later wrote. "How had one half of the army been defeated while the other half had not fought? The muttered curses were long and deep as they plodded back in the mud to their own camps." Many of the troops, another soldier summed up, were "dejected, demoralized and disgusted."

President Lincoln was not fooled either. He realized with horror that the Army of the Potomac had been defeated again when, about 1:00 p.m. on May 6, he received a wire from Butterfield announcing that Hooker's entire force had recrossed the Rappahannock. "Had a thunderbolt fallen upon the President he could not have been more overwhelmed," remembered Noah Brooks, a California newspaperman who had become a close friend of the Lincolns. "Never, as long as I knew him, did he seem to be so broken, so dispirited, and so ghostlike. Clasping his hands behind his back, he walked up and down the room, saying: 'My God! My God! What will the country say?' "

The country was in fact deeply shocked and dispirited. The defeat also gave new impetus to the North's several antiwar factions, especially the Republican president's most virulent and vocal political enemies, the Peace Democrats, who wanted to arrive at a negotiated settlement even at the cost of offering the South some sort of provisional independence.

Lincoln, shaking all this off as best he

Confederate dead from Barksdale's Mississippi brigade lie in the sunken road on Marye's Heights, where they fell during a spirited but doomed attempt to hold off Sedgwick's Yankees. A. J. Russell took this picture on May 4, just before Early's recapture of the heights.

could, shortly traveled to Falmouth to confer with Hooker at his headquarters. There Lincoln refrained from blaming Hooker and left him in command, asking only about the condition of the army.

Many of the army's officers were not so charitable. One found Hooker's behavior "inexcusable" and recommended he be fired. General Couch refused to serve under Hooker any longer and asked to be relieved. General Reynolds urged Hooker's removal. One of the more acid comments came from a rising young cavalry captain named George Armstrong Custer, who pronounced that "Hooker's career is well exemplified by that of a rocket, he went up like one and came down like a stick." Military engineer Washington A. Roebling, who would one day build the Brooklyn Bridge, was even more stinging: "Hooker was simply a moral fraud. He has always posed. When it came to the supreme test, he failed utterly."

While Hooker's men glumly settled into their old camps, Lee's dog-tired troops dragged themselves back down the Rappahannock to their fortifications near Fredericksburg, to be ready if Hooker or some other Union general decided to try to storm across

the river once more. At Chancellorsville, Lee left two brigades to do the dismal work of cleaning up the battlefield. In all, the Confederates recovered no fewer than 19,500 muskets and other small arms, as well as cannon and a mountain of ammunition. They also found themselves guarding thousands of Federal prisoners.

The Confederate troops treated the Federal prisoners kindly, sharing rations and doing what they could for the wounded. But as the captives were marched south in long columns toward Richmond, the trek became an increasingly dreadful ordeal. "There was no food, no nursing, no medicine to dull the pain of those who were in torture," recalled a New York soldier named Rice C. Bull. In Richmond, many were shoved into the city's infamously overcrowded and unsanitary Belle Isle and Libby prison camps, where they suffered from festering wounds and diseases before being exchanged within the next few weeks.

Soldiers assigned to burial parties back at Chancellorsville did their best to inter the dead of both sides decently. Most of the graves, however, were hastily dug and shallow. When another great battle took place

in the Wilderness a year later, the combatants discovered ghastly relics everywhere in the form of bones and skulls that had worked their way to the surface.

The most famous of the wounded, Stonewall Jackson, seemed to be recovering well after reaching the little house at Guiney Station on May 5. Jackson himself was confident of recovery. "I do not believe I shall die at this time," he said. "I am persuaded the Almighty has yet a work for me to perform." But on May 7 he took a turn for the worse, and Dr. Hunter McGuire, his surgeon, diagnosed pneumonia, a disease for which there was then no effective treatment.

Jackson died in the afternoon of May 10, shortly after saying in a quiet voice, "Let us cross over the river, and rest under the shade of the trees."

Confederate president Jefferson Davis declared a day of national mourning. Jackson's body, taken to Richmond, lay in state in the capitol as thousands of mourners filed by. His remains were then taken to Lexington, Virginia, in the Shenandoah Valley, and he was buried on the grounds of the Virginia Military Institute, where he had taught before the war. "His fame will be grand and enduring," the Richmond *Dispatch* said, "as the mountains at whose feet he was cradled."

Deeply mourning Jackson's death, General Lee quietly turned to business, reorganizing his army. A plan was forming in his mind. It would not be wise, he told President Davis, to sit still waiting for the Federals to move. Instead he would march his always ill supplied and hungry army west into the Shenandoah, then north up the valley into the rich farmlands of eastern Pennsylvania.

It would essentially be a defensive maneuver, Lee said, forcing Hooker to follow him and derailing any plans the Federals had to advance again toward Richmond. Besides, by ranging into enemy country and posing a threat to Washington, Lee and his army might convince the people of the North that the war was hopeless. This would give the Peace Democrats and other anti-Lincoln forces extra leverage and force the president to make peace. Just possibly, Lee thought, he would be able to surprise part of the Army of the Potomac on the march and destroy it, but a general engagement was probably to be avoided. What Lee did not foresee was that he would be heading toward the most violent and fateful battle of the entire war, at Gettysburg.

CHANCELLORSVILLE CASUALTIES

FEDERAL		CONFEDERATE	
Killed	1,606	Killed	1,581
Wounded	9,762	Wounded	8,700
Captured or missing	5,919	Captured or missing (estimated)	2,545
Total	17,287	Total	12,826

CORPORAL RICE C. BULL
123D New York Infantry, Ross' Brigade

Wounded and captured during the morning of May 3, Bull could not have imagined the privation he would suffer at the hands of his benevolent but ill-equipped captors. Exchanged after spending nine days within Rebel lines, the future bank cashier and railroad official would, a year later, see heavy action in the Atlanta campaign and the march to the sea.

Lieutenant Colonel Thomas Clark (above) of the 29th Ohio suffered from intestinal problems and resigned a month after the battle. "Great God," he wrote, "if this is one of Joe Hooker's reconnaissance—deliver me from going into one of his battles."

The Federal debacle at Chancellorsville was the Army of the Potomac's second failure in less than six months and took a staggering toll in casualties, including 9,762 wounded. In the photograph at right, convalescents pose for the camera in Armory Square Hospital in Washington, D.C.

By May 8th our wounds had all festered and were hot with fever; our clothing which came in contact with them was so filthy and stiff from the dried blood that it gravely aggravated our condition. Many wounds developed gangrene and blood poisoning; lockjaw caused suffering and death. While the stench from nearby dead horses and men was sickening it was not worse than that from the living who lay in their own filth. Finally, not the least of our troubles were the millions of flies that filled the air and covered blood-saturated clothing when they could not reach and sting the unbandaged wounds. As days went by none of these conditions improved, except the cries of the mortally wounded gradually lessened as they, one by one, were carried away and laid by the side of those who had gone before them. . . .

. . . many citizens of the surrounding country came to see the battlefield and get a view of the wounded "Yanks." They were mostly old men and women and children. These elderly people did not have the kindly feeling for us shown by the soldiers that had fought a few days before. The battle had, it would seem, created a feeling of respect on the part of soldiers. Usually when these people came they were on horseback. They would ride up close to the wounded seemingly filled with hatred. They would give no words of sympathy or cheer and no word of kindly help. Some of them seemed to rather enjoy seeing us so badly off and would make sport of our wretched condition to the women and children who were with them. One fat old fellow on horseback rode up close to our tent and said in a loud voice: "What are you'ens doin down here fightin we'uns in our bush for?" Our Johnnie friend, who was with us at the time, turned on the old man and said, "You just keep quiet old man, don't you see these are wounded men. You have no right or business to insult them." The old fellow rode away without finding out why we were in his bush. . . .

Early Tuesday morning, May 12th, we were told that a Federal ambulance train was on its way to Chancellorsville to take us back to our Army and friends. We had been nine days wounded prisoners, a fearful experience. When the news came there was a faint cheer, for help was at hand. . . . It was nearly three in the afternoon when the ambulances came in sight over the road from United States Ford. All were excited and hope revived in even the weakest and most despondent. The placing of the wounded in the ambulances was slow and tedious, half of them could not help themselves in any way. Four badly wounded were placed on the floor of each wagon side by side; those who could sit up were closely packed on the seats. It was nearly five o'clock when we were ready to move. . . .

As soon as the ambulances were loaded, they started on their journey to the Union lines. We of the 12th Corps were to go to Aquia Creek, twenty-five miles from our prison camp. As we rejoiced at our deliverance we little realized what was before us in making that awful

It took at least two hours to reach the Ford. The river was high, so pontoons had been laid for the ambulances to cross. We were met by quite a large force of cavalry, all on the north side of the river except a few who were waiting for us to cross.

When we reached the little valley bordering the river, we found an eager crowd of civilians waiting our arrival. They had come from the North in search of, or to get information about, their friends or relations who had been in the battle and who were missing and probably killed or wounded. When each ambulance crossed the bridge they would visit it, anxiously looking at the wounded. They would not, however, remain long as they could not stand the stench of those they saw. Many turned away quickly, their stomachs could not stand the pressure. We remained at the river only long enough to complete the search for the missing. When this was over most of the enquirers looked depressed and downcast for they had looked in vain. I wondered as I saw these prosperous men, for none but those who had means and influence could come so far to the front, what manner of story they would have to tell when they returned to their peaceful homes in the North. They would probably think they knew something of the horrors of war; yet how little they did know.

journey. The storm that had caused us so much suffering had brought havoc to the roads. Our Army had found them next to impassable and had been forced to corduroy them to move the artillery and trains. The ambulances had to use these roads to get us to the hospitals.

There could be no rougher surface than that of a corduroy road as made by soldiers in the Civil War. All kinds of available material was used in their building but they were chiefly constructed of logs, rails, and poles. These were laid across the road without regard to size; a log a foot through might be placed next a pole only three inches thick. . . .

. . . After we started we found it was no pleasure trip for as our wounds were commencing to heal the least jar seemed to be tearing them apart. It would have been painful enough had we been traveling over good roads; this primitive Virginia road was far from that and we soon found that the journey would test our endurance. . . .

One of the physicians who worked tirelessly in the aftermath of the battle was Assistant Surgeon Henry Reissberg of the 68th New York Infantry. A recent German immigrant who had anglicized his name—Heinrich Reissberger—upon making America his new home, the doctor served with Alexander Schimmelfennig's brigade, badly cut up in the rout of the XI Corps on May 2. The unfortunate Reissberg was plagued by carbuncles and chronic diarrhea; he resigned in February 1865 citing medical reasons.

In this sketch by Edwin Forbes, Federal cavalry guards proudly fly captured Confederate colors as they lead a contingent of Rebel prisoners to the rear on May 3. Trudging along the United States Ford road past a party of Yankees taking their ease, infantry guards keep the line of diversely attired Confederates moving. The artist was apparently fascinated with the variety and often striking features of Confederate dress. He produced on several occasions during the war superb sketches like this one, meticulously recording the appearance of Rebel soldiers. The prisoners shown here were some of the 2,500 Southerners who fell into Federal hands, nearly all of whom were exchanged a week later.

"Union or Rebel, lay him down tenderly. Spread his bloody blanket lightly over him, it is all the shroud he has."

LIEUTENANT CLAY MACCAULEY
126TH PENNSYLVANIA INFANTRY, TYLER'S BRIGADE

Captured on May 3, MacCauley experienced firsthand the stringent conditions under which his Confederate counterparts were forced to operate. On the way to Richmond's Libby Prison he also got a taste of civilian hostility when a local woman along the route screamed out to the Rebel guards, "Kill 'em all, colonel! Kill 'em all right here for me!" After being exchanged, MacCauley mustered out with his regiment on May 20 and later became a Presbyterian minister.

After a short rest I began to take observations of my new situation and surroundings. One of the things most to attract attention was the generally miserable appearance of the soldiers of Jackson's corps. Dirt and tatters seemed to be the rule in their clothing, and a used-up, emaciated look in their physique. They were what one would call a hard-looking crowd. Nor could one style them wearers of the gray. Dusty brown, rather, were they, from their rusty slouch hats, sandy beards, sallow skins, butternut coats, and pantaloons down to their mud-stained shoes. I thought them emaciated I said, but perhaps I would better say that they were lank and lean. Certainly they had shown remarkable endurance, and they were yet able to do exhausting and desperate work. I suppose the facts were that already the Confederacy was beginning to suffer from poverty in its quartermaster's department, and that, accustomed to the round, well-fed look of the soldiers of the North, I could not judge correctly of men who had become chiefly sinew and bone by such work as Stonewall Jackson demanded of them. Nevertheless, as we soon found out, the rebel commissariat was neither well filled nor luxurious. One of our guards gave me a small piece of his hard-tack for luncheon. He said that they were all on short rations. We officers, as it proved, were unfortunate in having put our haversacks on pack-mules that morning before going into action. Consequently we had become in every sense of the word dependents on our captors' bounty. How generous that was the sequel will show.

Towards noon the prisoners were formed into a sort of column, the members of numerous Union regiments ranked side by side as chance ordered, and were started off southward on a road towards Spottsylvania Court-House. We were guarded by a South Carolina regiment. As we marched, it was about fifteen miles to the court-house, which, at nightfall, we reached. The officers were driven into the court-house yard, where we spent the night on the grass under the shelter of the overspreading trees. As I lay there, looking up at the quiet stars and sky, I realized fully for the first time what the events of the day meant. I was a prisoner and doomed to—I could not tell what. I dreaded the fate of the unknown future, but, worse than all, I suffered from thinking of the suspense of the father and mother at home, who would not know what had become of the boy they had expected so soon to see. At last I went to sleep under a miserable depression of brain and heart.

THE REVEREND J. W. MCFARLAND

Serving as chaplain with a unit on provost duty in Washington, McFarland, eager to go where he was most needed, joined Humphreys' V Corps division at the front on April 30. Eventually hooking up with the 123d Pennsylvania of Colonel Peter H. Allabach's brigade, the cleric got more than he bargained for. He volunteered his services first to the surgeon, mostly treating the wounded of the XI Corps, whom McFarland notes were "nearly every one of them shot in the rear." This was followed on May 4 with the grisly burial of the dead.

The burial of the dead is a very common-place business affair. For this battle we buried only those who were brought off the field. Of these, I with three or four to assist me buried thirteen in one day in one place—eleven of our own and two of the enemy. There their bodies rest together in peace. Their weapons of war have perished. Death has established a bond of union, at least between their bodies. Do their spirits still strive with each other? Do they go off quarreling into the unseen land? Union or Rebel, lay him down tenderly. Spread his bloody blanket lightly over him, it is all the shroud he has. Bring some small cedar twigs and lay on those dirty rags that are to be his last pillow. There are no attendants but those who carried him here from the place a few rods distant where he died. No tears are shed here; but away in that home where loved ones dwell there will in a little be bitter weeping. For them and for ourselves we offer a brief prayer. The workmen take off their hats but keep on smoking while the prayer is said, now they cover them with their two feet of clay and the ceremony is over. In this work some things occur that at home would be considered extremely barbarous. For example—on Monday we were burying some of the dead. The hole was dug for five to be laid side by side. One of the dead was very tall and could not be got in. The grave diggers were told to make the grave longer for him. One of them, a Catholic Irishman, swore he would not spend all day burying a d——d heretic; and at once raised an axe and struck one of the limbs a blow to cut them off, to shorten him. The officiating chaplain without thinking what he was doing at once drew his fist and knocked the heathenish fellow in the head and sent him reeling over into the hole he had just dug. All this was only a momentary interruption of the burial ceremony.

PRIVATE EDWARD H. C. TAYLOR
4TH MICHIGAN INFANTRY, McQUADE'S BRIGADE

As the Army of the Potomac retreated across the Rappahannock, dejected and demoralized soldiers of the Federal army contemplated the ignominious defeat that Fighting Joe Hooker had engineered. Along with many of his comrades, Taylor was still smarting from General McClellan's dismissal the previous November. In a letter to his sister, Taylor did not mince words when he expressed his opinion of his commander, sentiments undoubtedly shared by many.

The great movement has ended and contrary to my hopes no great success has followed. Splendid fighting has been done and at one time the city was in our possession, but some blundering was committed and the result is that we are now in our old camp. In fact, we had to retreat. They say the "Rebs" also retreated, so much the more shame to us. . . .

Is Hooker only "getting his hand" in? And are men to be sacrificed for his practicing? Is he capable of the position? I can't answer the questions, but I know that fearful blunders were made and many lives thrown away—for what? People at home will never know the extent of these blunders nor the extent of this failure, for means are taken to prevent such a result. You are perhaps told it is a victory! I can't say who is to blame only I know there is blame.

I enclose Gen. Hooker's order previous to the final attack. How different the result from his anticipations! Instead of the Enemy retreating we retreated! Our men didn't wish to fall back and were unwilling to obey the order. What a howl would have been raised north had McClellan delayed his moving until the last of April and then retreated from a retreating enemy! A year ago they howled when they could not make Gen. McClellan move before the 10th of March. I don't wish to condemn Hooker until we know all the facts, all I know now is that we failed in our ends—and were compelled to retreat and that from an enemy who we had every reason to think was also falling back. If I judged at all I should say that the error was in dividing our forces as was done and thereby putting it in the power of the enemy to crash one portion before aid could be given. If that be the error Hooker is to blame. Time will settle the question, and Hooker will be sure to get justice. . . . He confesses his failure in the accompanying order: "If it has not accomplished all that was expected, etc." He places the reason "unforeseen obstacles." The only obstacles I know of were that the enemy outflanked us by superior maneuvering and of course it was full time to recross the river. What business had he in letting them out maneuver him? I can't trust Hooker. Most of the winter I have lived within ten rods of his quarters and know him to be a *whiskey* "bloat"—one of the most profane men I ever knew and a terrible braggadocio. Still when he took command and particularly just as this move began I was willing to give him all support in word and deed, for I thought there must be something beneath the exterior—something of a great General, to win such praise from the papers and public and such powerful support from the administration.

The sketch at left, drawn on May 6, portrays a young Union straggler leading a tired mule loaded up with a blanket, tent, canteens, a rifle, and cartridge boxes. As with many Federals who had served their two years, this soldier was ready to muster out; Edwin Forbes titled his drawing "I've got enough of Chancellorsville."

"People at home will never know the extent of these blunders nor the extent of this failure."

"Genl. Orders No. 49" in part tells the truth but would leave the impression that a *substantial* gain had been obtained. Not so. Everything here is now in "status quo" and the real bravery was wasted for naught. The design of this order is to make the world believe Hooker a great General as the gainer of a substantial victory. Now no papers are permitted to be sold within the lines unless they contain laudations of Hooker and the Administration. All others are prohibited. Is he afraid the soldiers will see their own opinion in print?

MAJOR GENERAL JOSEPH HOOKER
COMMANDER, ARMY OF THE POTOMAC

The official line regarding Chancellorsville treated Hooker gently, a courtesy he did not extend to his subordinates. Years later, the San Francisco Chronicle published an interview with Howard in which he accepted some blame. For Hooker, the admission was long overdue, and he was quick to respond with his own outspoken views.

And now as to Howard. You know our army took its position, the other corps having crossed at United States Ford, at Chancellorsville, on the 30th of April, 1863, Lee's army being three or four miles in advance of our position, between us and Fredericksburg, nearly east. On the 2d of May Jackson moved north and west. At 1 o'clock p.m., on Saturday, I sent Howard a telegram informing him of Jackson's movement toward his right and directing him to keep his

"Howard was always a woman among troops. If he was not born in petticoats, he ought to have been, and ought to wear them."

pickets out, keep himself thoroughly informed as to the enemy's movements, and keep me informed of the same at headquarters. Carl Shurz was with Howard when my telegram was received. Howard was lying on his bed. He never communicated the order to his division commanders, and made no disposition of his forces. He pocketed the telegram without reading it, said he was tired, and went to sleep. He seems to have been under the impression that Jackson was retreating. I knew of Jackson's movements, and was not taken by surprise a single moment, and supposed, of course, that my telegram had made Howard fully alive to the situation. But, instead of obeying my orders, he went to sleep, and a portion of Jackson's forces came up in rear of his right. Howard's troops were away from their arms, which were stacked along the line of defense, and did not know of the enemy's presence until fire was opened on them. They left guns, knapsacks, and everything, and the whole corps ran back like a herd of buffaloes. . . .

. . . Howard was always a woman among troops. If he was not born in petticoats, he ought to have been, and ought to wear them. He was always taken up with Sunday Schools and the temperance cause. Those things are all very good, you know, but have very little to do with commanding army corps.

Two years of war and the blockade had made some common necessities scarce in the South, especially in the army. Captain Edward Armstrong (opposite) helped himself to some patriotic writing paper probably abandoned by a Federal soldier in the rout of the XI Corps on May 2. In letters to his family composed just after the battle (right), written while he was "seated on a yankee oil cloth, dressed in yankee britches, writing on yankee paper, with yankee pen and ink," Armstrong described his part in the fighting and the terrible casualties in the Confederate ranks.

In trenches
May 4th 1863

Dear Pa

We have been marching and fighting since Wednesday last. We left Camp Wednesday about 11 oclock my company numbering about 50 at the time. We came to Fredericksburg [...] a line and [...] Thursday morning We were aroused about 5 oclock and by daylight were on march for this place, we marched until we came to the first line of battle and halted there until nearly night.

CAPTAIN EDWARD H. ARMSTRONG
3D NORTH CAROLINA INFANTRY, WARREN'S BRIGADE

When he enlisted in February 1862, Armstrong was in his third year at the University of North Carolina. That September he was one of only three officers of his regiment to emerge unscathed from the Battle of Antietam. After Chancellorsville, he wrote in a letter to his father of a sense of despair and foreboding. A year later, Armstrong would be mortally wounded at the Battle of Spotsylvania.

We are now in camp. evry thing is quiet and may remain so for some time yet: though I must say that I anticipate active operations very soon.

Hookers army is said to be reinforcing and ours has increased enough probably to cover our loss in the late fight, so that we now have about as many men as we took into the fight at Chancellorsville.

The news from Vicksburg of day before yesterday is somewhat cheering, but I believe the place will be taken ultimately. I see no prospects whatever for a cessation of Hostilities. Richmond is yet ours, but it is impossible to tell how long it will remain so. Suppose the Yankees advance an army by way of the Peninsula, another by way of Suffolk, and another by way of Orang C. H. or Fredericksburg. How will we meet them? They have immense numbers of men, and certainly numbered two to our one in the last fight. They have men enough scattered about to make another army of 50,000 men, and if they advance in the way I spoke of, we will most certainly fall back to Richmond. That place will be defended stubbornly but still it may fall. If it falls, it will be a misfortune to us, but we can still fight on. We must be successful in the end, but when will the end be? The south will be as I believe a desert: from one end to the other, all property will be destroyed, and the whole country a wilderness, before this thing ceases. The Yankees have set their heads on our destruction, and are resolved to subdue us, though they perish themselves in the attempt. . . . We may yet be reduced to an unorganized body of bushwhackers, but that will not occur in many years yet. We can hold out for several years, with our present army, though we may be driven back in evry engagement: yet we will inflict on them a loss greater than ours, and finally after they get tired of fighting the affair will be peacably settled. Verry few of us will witness the settlement; but some that come after us will. The country will be about where it was when the old revolution ceased: children will be brought up in ignorance, and evry thing will be again in a rude state. perhaps some other nation may take charge of both parties, and reduce us again to the position of colonies. Time will show. I am not at all discouraged, though you might think so from reading the above. I would not accept a discharge from the army, now if it was given me. I shall share in its victories and defeats; until perhaps I am called to go with many better men who have preceeded me. I am as firmly resolved now as at first; to go forward in the path of duty regardless of consequences.

If I fall I should prefer to be buried at home, but if circumstances prevent, I can rest with others on the battle field.

LIEUTENANT COLONEL DAVID R. E. WINN
4TH GEORGIA INFANTRY, DOLES' BRIGADE

Winn, a physician from South Carolina who had been practicing in Americus, Georgia, when the war broke out, took command of his regiment when Colonel Philip Cook was wounded. Winn wrote to his wife of the horrors of the battlefield and his yearning for hearth and home; two months later he was killed at Gettysburg.

*I*n camp near Fredericksburg Va
May 9, 1863
My Darling Wife

As everybody knows—it is easy to make promises—it is sometimes hard to keep them. So it has proven with me. On writing to you a day or two ago—I told you I would write again next day. I have been so utterly worn out that I could not arouse myself to sufficient energy to undertake such a task. Now—at last—I am rested, but without an idea, so completely have I been occupied with battle reports and reorganizing our terribly messed up regiment. . . . No description of what we have endured or what we have seen could give the slightest idea of the horrible truth. Hundreds of wounded died because not moved in time Thousands of Yankee wounded & hundreds of Confederates were *burned* by the Yankees setting fire to the woods in which they were lying for the purpose of destroying the ammunition left by them in the woods. And this will not give you even a faint idea of the horrible reality. My heart sickens at the thought of our terrible loss Doles' Brigade lost 437 officers and men. Our reg. lost twice as many as any other regiment 150 killed & disabled by wound. to say nothing of 25 or 30 slightly wounded but not incapacitated. This regiment has "covered itself with glory"—dearly bought. It is distressing and I could scarcely refrain from weeping this evening.—at our first occasion of the kind since the battles, to see the attenuated ranks of Companies of "dress parade."

"No description of what we have endured or what we have seen could give the slightest idea of the horrible truth."

Where ten days ago we had 500 on parade, to day we had 130 men. A great many of our absentees were exhausted or sick—But you are sick of this . . . I'll tell you no more of it. Suffice it to say—that I received not a scratch & your husband lost no credit, having stuck to his colors & carried in & brought out his flag, while three of the color bearers were killed and two wounded. By the way it has occured to me that about two weeks ago I received a letter from you telling me you would write to me the next day—This promised letter I have never received. Did you [know] I wore your picture in my left breast coat pocket & for fear that the Yankees might get it folded in its case this note "To be sent to Mrs. F. M. Winn, Americus, Ga., if I am so unfortunate as to lose it or be killed in the battle, with the information that it was worn upon the person . . . as the image of the Guardian Angel of her devoted Husband" I still have the picture safe as myself. How has my dear little wife decided in regard to having the pattern of those spring dresses changed? Is it now a fixed necessity or were your apprehensions premature? Is it to be little Anna Maria? Oh for a brief visit to my dear home . . . never have I felt so anxious for it. . . . Sad thought and yet how grateful should I be that I have still an opportunity; that I am even still alive. Dear Fannie—I have not written half I would or expressed half I feel in this very hasty note but my paper is filled & I now want to hear from you. Write to father how wonderfully I have been protected. Give my love to sissy & my dear boys & believe me

Yours devoting
D. R. E. Winn

Mortally wounded at Chancellorsville, James F. Toms (above) of the 34th North Carolina spent his last hours in the company of his uncle, Adolphus B. Carson, one of three brothers in the ranks. Carson wrote to the boy's father: "He was shot in the bowels. He suffered very much while he lived. I was with him when he died and buried him the best that I could under the circumstances."

SURGEON HUNTER MCGUIRE

STAFF, LIEUTENANT GENERAL THOMAS J. JACKSON

The black mourning band worn by Dr. McGuire places this image about the time of Stonewall Jackson's funeral in mid-May. The doctor's gaunt appearance bears testimony to the tireless efforts he undertook to save his commander. From the moment the general was borne off the field, the physician rarely left his side, attending to his patient and friend until the end.

About one o'clock Thursday morning, while I was asleep upon a lounge in his room, he directed his servant, Jim, to apply a wet towel to his stomach, to relieve an attack of nausea, with which he was again troubled. The servant asked permission to first consult me, but the General, knowing that I had slept none for nearly three nights, refused to allow the servant to disturb me, and demanded the towel. About daylight I was aroused, and found him suffering in great pain. An examination disclosed pleuro-pneumonia of the right side. I believed, and the consulting physicians concurred in the opinion, that it was attributable to the fall from the litter the night he was wounded. . . . The nausea, for which the cloths were applied that night, may have been the result of inflammation already begun. Contusion of the lung, with extravasation of blood in his chest, was probably produced by the fall referred to, and shock and loss of blood, prevented any ill effects until reaction had been well established, and then inflammation ensued. . . . Friday his wounds were again dressed, and although the quantity of the discharge from them had diminished, the process of healing was still going on. The pain in his side had disappeared, but he breathed with difficulty and complained of a feeling of great exhaustion. . . .

Dr. Tucker, from Richmond, arrived on Saturday, and all that human skill could devise was done, to stay the hand of death. He suf-

fered no pain today, and his breathing was less difficult, but he was evidently hourly growing weaker.

When his child was brought to him, today, he played with it for some time; frequently caressing it, and calling it his "little comforter." At one time, he raised his wounded hand above its head, and closing his eyes, was for some moments, silently engaged in prayer. He said to me, "I see from the number of physicians that you think my condition dangerous, but I thank God, if it is His will, that I am ready to go." About daylight, on Sunday morning, Mrs. Jackson informed him that his recovery was very doubtful, and that it was better that he should be prepared for the worst. He was silent for a moment, and then said, "It will be infinite gain to be translated to Heaven." He advised his wife, in the event of his death, to return to her father's house, and added, "You have a kind and good father, but there is no one so kind and good as your Heavenly Father." He still expressed a hope of his recovery, but requested her, if he should die, to have him buried in Lexington, in the Valley of Virginia. His exhaustion increased so rapidly, that at eleven o'clock, Mrs. Jackson knelt by his bed, and told him that before the sun went down, he would be with his Saviour. He replied, "Oh, no! you are frightened, my child; death is not so near; I may yet get well." She fell over upon the bed, weeping bitterly, and told him again that the physicians said there was no hope. After a moment's pause he asked her to call me. "Doctor, Anna informs me that you have told her that I am to die today; is it so?" When he was answered, he turned his eyes towards the ceiling, and gazed for a moment or two, as if in intense thought, then replied, "Very good, very good, it is all right." He then tried to comfort his almost heart-broken wife, and told her he had a good deal to say to her, but he was too weak. Colonel Pendleton came into the room about one o'clock, and he asked him, "Who was preaching at headquarters today?" When told that the whole army was praying for him, he replied, "Thank God—they are very kind." He said: "It is the Lord's Day; my wish is fulfilled. I have always desired to die on Sunday."

His mind now began to fail and wander, and he frequently talked as if in command upon the field, giving orders in his old way; then the scene shifted, and he was at the mess-table, in conversation with members of his staff; now with his wife and child; now at prayers with his military family. Occasional intervals of return of his mind would appear, and during one of them I offered him some brandy and water, but he declined it saying, "It will only delay my departure, and do no good; I want to preserve my mind, if possible, to the last." About half-past one, he was told that he had but two hours to live, and he answered again, feebly, but firmly, "Very good, it is all right." A few moments before he died he cried out in his delirium, "Order A. P. Hill to prepare for action! pass the infantry to the front rapidly! tell Major Hawks"—then stopped, leaving the sentence unfinished. Presently, a smile of ineffable sweetness spread itself over his pale face, and he said quietly, and with an expression, as if of relief, "Let us cross over the river, and rest under the shade of the trees"; and then, without pain, or the least struggle, his spirit passed from earth to the God who gave it.

Fearing for Jackson's safety when Union wagon trains were thought to be moving beyond Chancellorsville, General Lee ordered his wounded corps commander moved to Guiney Station, 10 miles south of Fredericksburg. On May 5 Jackson, in the company of Dr. Hunter McGuire, made the 17-hour ambulance trip to Fairfield, the 1,200-acre estate of Thomas C. Chandler. There he was hospitalized in a small frame house (below) where he died five days later.

MARY ANNA MORRISON JACKSON
WIFE OF LIEUTENANT GENERAL THOMAS J. JACKSON

Following the news of her husband's wounding, Mrs. Jackson, with her brother, Lieutenant Joseph G. Morrison, spent several days in an agony of suspense awaiting the repair of the railroad from Richmond to Guiney Station. Finally arriving at the little house at Fairfield on May 7, Mrs. Jackson rushed to her husband's bedside and devotedly remained there until he died, three days later.

When he left me on the morning of the 29th, going forth so cheerfully and bravely to the call of duty, he was in the full flush of vigorous manhood, and during that last, blessed visit, I never saw him look so handsome, so happy, and so noble. *Now,* his fearful wounds, his mutilated arm, the scratches upon his face, and, above all, the desperate pneumonia, which was flushing his cheeks, oppressing his breathing, and benumbing his senses, wrung my soul with such grief and anguish as it had never before experienced. He had to be aroused to speak to me, and expressed much joy and thankfulness at seeing me; but he was too much affected by morphia to resist stupor, and soon seemed to lose the consciousness of my presence, except when I spoke or ministered to him. From the time I reached him he was too ill to notice or talk much, and he lay most of the time in a semiconscious state; but when aroused, he recognized those about him and consciousness would return. Soon after I entered his room he was impressed by the woeful anxiety and sadness betrayed in my face, and said: "My darling, you must cheer up, and not wear a long face. I love cheerfulness and brightness in a sickroom." And he requested me to speak distinctly, as he wished to hear every word I said. Whenever he awakened from his stupor, he always had some endearing words to say to me, such as, "My darling, you are very much loved;" "You are one of the most precious little wives in the world." He told me he knew I would be glad to take his place, but God knew what was best for us. Thinking it would cheer him more than anything else to see the baby in whom he so delighted, I proposed several times to bring her to his bedside, but he always said, "Not yet; wait till I feel better." He was invariably

Cherished mementos attest to the abiding affection Southerners had for General Jackson. A lock of his hair and a fragment of his uniform adorn a reproduction of his last portrait (above, left). A cased bronze medallion (above, right) bearing his likeness was commissioned in England for distribution to members of the Stonewall Brigade. Although the shipment was successfully run through the blockade, the medallions apparently never reached their intended recipients.

patient, never uttering a murmur or complaint. Sometimes, in slight delirium, he talked, and his mind was then generally upon his military duties—caring for his soldiers, and giving such directions as these: "Tell Major Hawkes to send forward provisions to the men;" "Order A. P. Hill to prepare for action;" "Pass the infantry to the front," etc. . . .

Friday and Saturday passed in much the same way—bringing no favorable change to the dear sufferer; indeed, his fever and restlessness increased, and, although everything was done for his relief and benefit, he was growing perceptibly weaker. On Saturday evening, in the hope of soothing him, I proposed reading some selections from the Psalms. At first he replied that he was suffering too much to listen, but very soon he added: "Yes, we must never refuse that. Get the Bible and read them."

As night approached, and he grew more wearied, he requested me to sing to him—asking that the songs should be the most spiritual that could be selected. My brother Joseph assisted me in singing a few hymns, and at my husband's request we concluded with the 51st Psalm in verse:

"Show pity Lord; O Lord, forgive."

The singing had a quieting effect, and he seemed to rest in perfect peace. . . .

Apprehending the nearness of his end, Mr. Lacy wished to remain with him on Sunday, but he insisted that he should go, as usual, and preach to the soldiers. When Major Pendleton came to his bedside about noon, he inquired of him, "Who is preaching at headquarters today?" When told that Mr. Lacy was, and that the whole army was praying for him, he said, "Thank God; they are very kind." As soon as the chaplain appeared at headquarters that morning, General Lee anxiously inquired after General Jackson's condition, and upon hearing how hopeless it was, he exclaimed, with deep feeling: "Surely General Jackson must recover. God will not take him from us, now that we need him so much. Surely he will be spared to us, in answer to the many prayers which are offered for him." And upon Mr. Lacy's leaving, he said: "When you return, I trust you will find him better. When a suitable occasion offers, give him my love, and tell him that I wrestled in prayer for him last night as I never prayed, I believe, for myself." Here his voice became choked with emotion, and he turned away to hide his intense feeling. . . .

In order to stimulate his fast-failing powers, he was offered some brandy and water, but he showed great repugnance to it, saying excitedly, "It tastes like *fire,* and cannot do me any good." Early on Sunday morning, the 10th of May, I was called out of the sick-room by Dr. Morrison, who told me that the doctors, having done everything that human skill could devise to stay the hand of death, had lost all hope, and that my precious, brave, noble husband could not live! Indeed, life was fast ebbing away, and they felt they must prepare me for the inevitable event, which was now a question of only a few short hours. As soon as I could arise from this stunning blow, I told Dr. Morrison that my husband must be informed of his condition. I well knew that death to him was but the opening of the gates of pearl into the ineffable glories of heaven; but I had heard him say that, although he was willing and ready to die at any moment that God might call him, still he would prefer to have a few hours' preparation before entering into the presence of his Maker and Redeemer.

I therefore felt it to be my duty to gratify his desire. He now appeared to be fast sinking into unconsciousness, but he heard my voice and understood me better than others, and God gave me the strength and composure to hold a last sacred interview with him, in which I tried to impress upon him his situation, and learn his dying wishes. This was all the harder, because he had never, from the time that he first rallied from his wounds, thought he would die, and had expressed the belief that God still had work for him to do, and would raise him up to do it. When I told him the doctors thought he would soon be in heaven, he did not seem to comprehend it, and showed no surprise or concern. But upon repeating it, and asking him if he was willing for God to do with him according to His own will, he looked at me calmly and intelligently, and said, "Yes, *I prefer it, I prefer it.*" I then told him that before that day was over he would be with the blessed Saviour in His glory. With perfect distinctness and intelligence, he said, "I will be an infinite gainer to be translated." I then asked him if it was his wish that I should return, with our infant, to my father's home in North Carolina. He answered, "Yes, you have a kind, good father; but no one is so kind and good as your Heavenly Father." He said he had many things to say to me, but he was then too weak. . . .

Mrs. Hoge now came in, bearing little Julia in her arms, with Hetty following, and although he had almost ceased to notice anything, as soon as they entered the door he looked up, his countenance brightened with delight, and he never smiled more sweetly as he exclaimed, "Little darling! sweet one!" She was seated on the bed by his side, and after watching her intently, with radiant smiles, for a few moments, he closed his eyes, as if in prayer. Though she was suffering the pangs of extreme hunger, from long absence from her mother, she seemed to

"Let us cross over the river, and rest under the shade of the trees."

forget her discomfort in the joy of seeing that loving face beam on her once more, and she looked at him and smiled as long as he continued to notice her. Tears were shed over that dying bed by strong men who were unused to weep, and it was touching to see the genuine grief of his servant, Jim, who nursed him faithfully to the end.

He now sank rapidly into unconsciousness, murmuring disconnected words occasionally, but all at once he spoke out very cheerfully and distinctly the beautiful sentence which has become immortal as his last: "Let us cross over the river, and rest under the shade of the trees."

JEDEDIAH HOTCHKISS
STAFF, LIEUTENANT GENERAL
THOMAS J. JACKSON

Deeply mourning the death of his general, Hotchkiss, the civilian cartographer Stonewall Jackson had relied upon to map the Shenandoah Valley, also grieved for the loss of his comrade, Captain James K. Boswell. Writing to his wife, Hotchkiss recounted the burial of Boswell, who was killed in the same volley that felled Jackson.

I got back today from my survey of the battle-field, in which I have been engaged for more than a week past, and employ this evening in bringing up my correspondence, limited as it is, I have only written one brief note, and that to you, since the battle, for it was necessary to use all the diligence in my power to get what I had to do done and out of the way before anything else should happen. It has been very warm and very cool too, quite changeable, but still healthy. You have before this, long before, heard of Gen. Jackson's death, funeral procession and burial. —He is gone and sleeps in the Valley he loved so much. We miss him all the time and a void is made here which time can hardly fill. It seems not like our old Hd. Qrs. to any of us, and less to me than to any one else, for my tent mate is gone as well as my General. I do not know whether I shall stay here or not. I shall for the present. Gen. A. P. Hill is in command of our corps; he is an able General and will fill well the place of Gen. J. in a purely military point of view, but he is not a "man of God" like Gen. J. and wears not "the sword of the Lord and of Gideon," but still we have Gen. Lee, a good man and true, faithful in all things, and we trust Gen. Jackson "still lives" to plead our cause. Our success was a decided one, the Yankees had exhausted every appliance to make Hooker's army complete and it had the power of numbers. He could not have managed more men, and yet we routed and defeated them at every point and compelled them to seek safety in flight, and though we had a large number of men wounded, yet many of them were slight and small, less than usual for the numbers engaged, though the loss of officers was remarkably large. Some that we thought killed were only captured and will soon come back. . . . I went to the hospital where Gen. J. was taken and then to where Gen Lee was, that night after midnight, having to go a long ways, and I did not get back to look for Boswell until noon the next day; in fact the enemy had possession of the place where he was killed until about that time. I found him looking perfectly natural, a smile on his face. I have no doubt he was instantly killed, for two bullets went through his memorandum book in his side pocket and then through his heart. I got an ambulance and took his body to a nice family graveyard, Mr. Lacy's brother's and there had a grave dug, and wrapped his overcoat closely around him, putting the cape over his head, and buried him thus, in all his martial dress, lowering him to his resting place in a shelter tent I picked up on the field of battle, and then spreading it over him. Mr. Lacy made a noble prayer and we finished our sad duty just as the moon rose.

CADET JOHN S. WISE
VIRGINIA MILITARY INSTITUTE

John Wise, scion of a prominent Virginia family and future lawyer and congressman, was a young cadet at the Virginia Military Institute in Lexington when one of its own was laid to rest. Wise served as one of the honor guard attending Stonewall Jackson's body while it lay in state. Years later, Wise could still vividly remember that mournful day and would keenly feel the void left by the general's death.

*I*t was a bitter, bitter day of mourning for all of us when the corps was marched down to the canal terminus to meet all that was mortal of Stonewall Jackson. We had heard the name of every officer who attended the remains.

With reversed arms and muffled drums we bore him back to the Institute, and placed him in the section-room in which he had taught. There the body lay in state until the following day. The lilacs and early spring flowers were just blooming. The number of people who came to view him for the last time was immense: men and women wept over his bier as if his death was a personal affliction; then I saw that the Presbyterians could weep like other folks. The flowers piled about the coffin hid it and its form from view. I shall ever count it a great privilege that I was one of the guard who, through the silence of the night, and when the crowds had departed, stood watch and ward alone with the remains of the great "Stonewall."

Next day, we buried him with pomp of woe, the cadets his escort of honor: with minute-guns, and tolling bells, and most impressive circumstances, we bore him to his rest. But those ceremonies were to me far less impressive than walking post in that bare section-room, in the still hours of night, reflecting that there lay all that was left of one whose name still thrilled the world.

The burial of Stonewall Jackson made a deep impression upon the corps of cadets. It had been our custom, when things seemed to be going amiss in the army, to say, "Wait until 'Old Jack' gets there; he will straighten matters out." We felt that the loss was irreparable.

In this photograph mounted on cardboard, cadets of the Virginia Military Institute's class of 1868 gather at Stonewall Jackson's grave near the campus to pay tribute to the hero and former VMI professor—a custom followed yearly by the students for decades after the war. As he had wished, Jackson was interred at Lexington in a plot he purchased to bury his first child. Announcing the general's death, VMI's superintendent, Francis Smith, said: "Our loss is distinctive. He was peculiarly our own."

GLOSSARY

abatis—A defensive barrier of fallen trees with branches pointed toward the enemy.

adjutant—A staff officer assisting the commanding officer, usually with correspondence.

battery—The basic unit of artillery, consisting of four to six guns.

Berdan's Sharpshooters—The 1st U.S. Sharpshooters Regiment, named after its founder, Hiram Berdan, a well-known marksman.

bivouac—A temporary encampment, or to camp out for the night.

breastwork—A temporary fortification, usually of earth and about chest high, over which a soldier could fire.

butternut—The color, variously described as yellowish brown, tan, or brownish gray, of the common homespun Confederate uniform for those who could not afford to acquire cloth of the official gray. It became a general Northern term for a Confederate soldier.

caisson—A cart with large chests for carrying artillery ammunition; connected to a horse-drawn limber when moved.

canister—A tin can containing lead or iron balls that scattered when fired from a cannon. Used primarily in defense of a position as an antipersonnel weapon.

carbine—A lightweight, short-barreled shoulder arm used especially by cavalry.

case shot—*Case shot* properly refers to shrapnel or spherical case. The term was often used mistakenly to refer to any artillery projectile in which numerous metal balls or pieces were bound or encased together. See also *shrapnel*.

change front—To alter the direction a body of troops faces in order to deliver or defend against an attack.

"commissary"—A kind of whiskey issued by the army's commissary department.

corduroy road—A road with a surface of logs laid together transversely.

double-quick—A trotting pace.

dress by the colors—To arrange troops into lines according to placement of the unit's flag.

echelon—A staggered or stairsteplike formation of parallel units of troops.

enfilade—Gunfire that rakes an enemy line lengthwise, or the position allowing such firing.

flank—The right or left end of a military formation. To flank is to attack or go around the enemy's position on one end or the other.

forlorn hope—A last-ditch, desperately difficult or dangerous assignment, or the body of soldiers given such a task.

grapeshot—Iron balls (usually nine) bound together and fired from a cannon. Resembling a cluster of grapes, the balls broke apart and scattered on impact. Although references

to grape or grapeshot are numerous in the literature, some experts claim that it was not used on Civil War battlefields.

hardtack—A durable cracker, or biscuit, made of plain flour and water and normally about three inches square and a half-inch thick.

haversack—A shoulder bag, usually strapped over the right shoulder to rest on the left hip, for carrying personal items and rations.

limber—A two-wheeled, horse-drawn vehicle to which a gun carriage or a caisson was attached.

Minié ball—The standard bullet-shaped projectile fired from the rifled muskets of the time. Designed by French army officers Henri-Gustave Delvigne and Claude-Étienne Minié, the bullet's hollow base expanded, forcing its sides into the grooves, or rifling, of the musket's barrel. This caused the bullet to spiral in flight, giving it greater range and accuracy. Appears as minie, minnie, and minni.

musket—A smoothbore, muzzleloading shoulder arm.

oblique—At an angle. Units would be ordered to fire or move in a direction other than straight ahead.

picket—One or more soldiers on guard to protect the larger unit from surprise attack.

prolonge—A stout rope on a gun carriage that allowed a soldier to maneuver an artillery piece over short distances without having to attach it to a limber.

pup tent—See *shelter tent*.

rammer—An artillerist's tool used to force the powder charge and projectile down the barrel of a gun and seat them firmly in the breech. Also, the ramrod of a shoulder arm.

rifle—Any weapon with spiral grooves cut into the bore, which give spin to the projectile, adding range and accuracy. Usually applied to cannon or shoulder-fired weapons.

rifle pits—Holes or shallow trenches dug in the ground from which soldiers could fire weapons and avoid enemy fire. Foxholes.

secesh—A slang term for secessionist.

shelter tent—Also called a tente d'abri, pup tent, or dog tent, it consisted of two shelter halves (each carried by a single soldier) buttoned together and hung over a ridgepole.

shrapnel—An artillery projectile in the form of a hollow sphere filled with metal balls packed around an explosive charge. Developed by British general Henry Shrapnel during the Napoleonic Wars, it was used as an antipersonnel weapon. A fuse ignited the charge at a set distance from the gun, raining the balls down on the enemy. Also called spherical case.

skirmisher—A soldier sent in advance of the main body of troops to scout out and probe the enemy's position. Also, one who participated in a skirmish, a small fight usually incidental to the main action.

solid shot—A solid artillery projectile, oblong for rifled pieces and spherical for smooth-bores, used primarily against fortifications and matériel.

spherical case—See *shrapnel*.

sutler—A peddler with a permit to remain with troops in camp or in the field and sell food, drink, and other supplies.

tattoo—Drum or bugle call signaling the time to return to quarters in the evening. Taps, initiated in 1862, calls for lights out.

Zouaves—Regiments, both Union and Confederate, that modeled themselves after the original Zouaves of French colonial Algeria. Known for spectacular uniforms featuring bright colors—usually reds and blues—baggy trousers, gaiters, short and open jackets, and a turban or fez, they specialized in precision drill and loading and firing muskets from the prone position.

ACKNOWLEDGMENTS

The editors wish to thank the following for their valuable assistance in the preparation of this volume: Warren Adams, Cumberland County Historical Society, Greenwich, N.J.; Kim Bauer, Illinois State Historical Library, Springfield; Sheila Biles, United States Military Academy Library, West Point, N.Y.; Petie Bogen-Garrett, The Library of Virginia, Richmond; David Burgevin, Museum of American History, Smithsonian Institution, Washington, D.C.; Sue Ann Cody, William Madison Randall Library, University of North Carolina at Wilmington; Gail Miller DeLoach, Georgia Department of Archives and History, Atlanta; Conley Edwards, The Library of Virginia, Richmond; Andy Franck, High Impact Photography, Baltimore; Janice M. Frye, Chancellorsville Battlefield Visitor Center, Chancellorsville, Va.; Keith Gibson, Virginia Military Institute Museum, Lexington, Va.; Catherine Gilliam, Charlottesville, Va.; Randy W. Hackenburg, U.S. Army Military History Institute, Carlisle Barracks, Pa.; Corinne P. Hudgins, The Museum of the Confederacy, Richmond; Mary Ison and Staff, Reference Library, Prints and Photography Department, Library of Congress, Washington, D.C.; Jeff Jackson, Virginia Military Institute Museum, Lexington, Va.; Diane Jacob, Virginia Military Institute Archives, Lexington, Va.; Karen Jones, High Impact Photography, Baltimore; Norwood Kerr, Alabama Department of Archives and History, Montgomery; Diane Kessler, Pennsylvania Capitol Preservation Committee, Harrisburg; Robert E. L. Krick, Richmond National Battlefield Park, Richmond; Paul Loane, Cherry Hill, N.J.; Mary Lohrenz, Old Capitol Museum of Mississippi History, Jackson; Ira Luck, Chancellorsville Battlefield Visitor Center, Chancellorsville, Va.; Pat McGee, William Madison Randall Library, University of North Carolina at Wilmington; Jim and Judy McLean, Baltimore, Howard Maddeus, Cody, Wyo.; Lewis Micou Jr., Westfield Center, Ohio; Adele Mitchell, Carlisle, Pa.; Gerard Morin, Dyer Library, York Institute Museum, Saco, Maine; William Nixon, Cumberland County Historical Society, Greenwich, N.J.; RoseAnn O'Canas, High Impact Photography, Baltimore; George Peters, High Impact Photography, Baltimore; AnnMarie Price, Virginia Historical Society, Richmond; Pat Ricci, Confederate Memorial Hall, New Orleans; Teresa Roane, Valentine Museum, Richmond; Ruth L. Silliker, Saco, Maine; Joanna L. Smith, Stonewall Jackson House, Lexington, Va.; Larry Strayer, Dayton; Don Troiani, Southbury, Conn.; Ken Turner, Ellwood City, Pa.; William A. Turner, La Plata, Md.; David Vaughan, Atlanta; Margaret Vining, Museum of American History, Smithsonian Institution, Washington, D.C.; Michael J. Winey, U.S. Army Military History Institute, Carlisle Barracks, Pa.; Steven Wright, Civil War Library and Museum, Philadelphia.

PICTURE CREDITS

The sources for the illustrations are listed below. Credits from left to right are separated by semicolons, from top to bottom by dashes.

Dust jacket: front, The Western Reserve Historical Society, Cleveland; rear, from *An Aide-de-Camp of Lee*, edited by Major General Sir Frederick Maurice, Little, Brown, Boston, 1927.

All calligraphy by Mary Lou O'Brian/Inkwell, Inc.

6, 7: Map by Paul Salmon. 8: The Western Reserve Historical Society, Cleveland. 15: Map by Peter McGinn. 16: Massachusetts Commandery of the Military Order of the Loyal Legion of the United States and the U.S. Army Military History Institute (MASS-MOLLUS/USAMHI), copied by A. Pierce Bounds. 17: Courtesy Ken Turner, photographed by Chet Buquo (3); Library of Congress, Forbes #043. 18: Courtesy Ruth Silliker, copied by John Tillyer; collection of the York Institute Museum/Dyer Library, Saco, Maine, photographed by John Tillyer. 19: The Western Reserve Historical Society, Cleveland. 20: From *Alexander Cheves Haskell: The Portrait of a Man*, by Louise Haskell Daly, Plimpton Press, Norwood, Mass., 1934, copied by Philip Brandt George; Alabama Department of Archives and History, Montgomery. 21: Fredericksburg and Spotsylvania National Military Park, Fredericksburg, Va., photographed by Larry Sherer. 22: Museum of the Confederacy, Richmond, photographed by Larry Sherer; from "Stonewall Jackson in Winter Quarters: Memories of Moss Neck in the Winter of 1862-63," by Roberta Cary Corbin Kinsolving, in *Confederate Veteran*, Vol. 20, no. 9, pp. 24-26, Nashville, January 1912, copied by Philip Brandt George—Museum of the Confederacy, Richmond, photographed by Katherine Wetzel. 23: Virginia Historical Society, Richmond. 24: Library of Congress, Forbes #048. 26: Library of Congress, Neg. No. B8171-7576; courtesy collection of William A. Turner. 27: United States Military Academy Library, Special Collections Division, West Point, N.Y. 28: Library of Congress, Waud #724. 29: Courtesy Illinois State Historical Library. 30, 31: Drawing by John G. Keyser, courtesy Cumberland County Historical Society, Greenwich, N.J., photographed by Marty Lerario. 32: Courtesy Mrs. Adele Mitchell. 33: Courtesy Steve and Patricia Mullinax; from *Generals in Gray: Lives of the Confederate Commanders*, by Ezra J. Warner, published by Louisiana State University Press, Baton Rouge, 1959, copied by Philip Brandt George. 34: From *Two Views of Gettysburg*, by Sir Arthur J. L. Fremantle and Frank A. Haskell, The Lakeside Press, 1964, R. R. Donnelley & Sons Co., Chicago, copied by Philip Brandt George. 35: Courtesy Stonewall Jackson Foundation, Lexington, Va.; courtesy Stonewall Jackson Foundation, Lexington, Va., photographed by Les Schofer. 36:

Library of Congress, Neg. No. B8184-10365. 37: Fredericksburg and Spotsylvania National Military Park, Fredericksburg, Va. 38: Library of Congress. 41: Map by Walter W. Roberts, overlay by Time-Life Books. 43: Library of Congress, Waud #97. 44: Valentine Museum, Richmond. 45: Library of Congress, Waud #569. 46: From *A Narrative of Service with the Third Wisconsin Infantry*, by Julian Wisner Hinkley, Wisconsin History Commission, 1912, copied by Philip Brandt George. 47: Eleanor S. Brockenbrough Library, Museum of the Confederacy, Richmond; Craig T. Johnson, photographed by Larry Sherer. 48: Confederate Memorial Hall, New Orleans, photographed by Claude Levet. 49: Library of Congress, Waud #506. 50, 51: From *War Diary and Letters of Stephen Minot Weld*, privately printed by The Riverside Press, 1912; The Western Reserve Historical Society, Cleveland; Library of Congress, Waud #195. 52: Collection of C. Paul Loane, photographed by Robert J. Laramie—The Western Reserve Historical Society, Cleveland. 54: MASS-MOLLUS/USAMHI, copied by A. Pierce Bounds—courtesy New York State Archives, Division of Military and Naval Affairs, copied by Randall Perry. 55: Library of Congress, Forbes #060. 57: May by Walter W. Roberts, overlay by Time-Life Books. 58, 59: Courtesy collection of William A. Turner. 60: Library of Congress, Waud #124. 61: MASS-MOLLUS/USAMHI, copied by A. Pierce Bounds—Armed Forces Collections, National Museum of American History, Smithsonian Institution. 62: Library of Congress, Forbes #060a. 63: Library of Congress, Forbes #060b. 64: MASS-MOLLUS/USAMHI, copied by A. Pierce Bounds. 65: Valentine Museum, Richmond—courtesy collection of William A. Turner; Virginia Military Institute Archives, Lexington, photographed by Michael Collingwood. 67: Collection of C. Paul Loane, photographed by Robert J. Laramie. 68: Fredericksburg and Spotsylvania National Military Park, Fredericksburg, Va., photographed by Larry Sherer. 69: Courtesy Doug Bast/Boonsboro Museum of History, photographed by Larry Sherer; Museum of the Confederacy, Richmond, photographed by Katherine Wetzel. 71: Map by Walter W. Roberts, overlay by Time-Life Books. 72: Library of Congress, Manuscript Division, #548. 73: Library of Congress, Forbes #068. 74: Courtesy John R. White—Troiani Collection, photographed by Bob Petrasy. 75: Fredericksburg and Spotsylvania National Military Park, Fredericksburg, Va., photographed by Larry Sherer. 76: Courtesy Georgia Department of Archives and History, Atlanta. 77: The Library of Virginia, Richmond. 78: Brad L. Pruden Collection. 79: MASS-MOLLUS/USAMHI, copied by A. Pierce Bounds. 80, 81: National Archives, Neg. No. 111-

BA-2291; courtesy collection of William A. Turner. 82, 83: Library of Congress, Waud #740. 84: Hargrett Rare Book and Manuscript Library, University of Georgia Libraries, Athens, photographed by Henry L. Mintz. 85: National Archives, Neg. No. 165-JT-317—Museum of the Confederacy, Richmond, photographed by Katherine Wetzel. 86, 87: Collection of C. Paul Loane, photographed by Robert J. Laramie. 89: Courtesy Mrs. Mary Lib Walker Taylor, photographed by Henry L. Mintz. 90: MASS-MOLLUS/USAMHI, copied by A. Pierce Bounds. 91: Pennsylvania Capitol Preservation Committee, Harrisburg. 92: Collection of C. Paul Loane, photographed by Robert J. Laramie. 93: Rochester Historical Society, Rochester, N.Y. 94: Virginia Military Institute Museum, Virginia Military Institute, Lexington, photographed by Michael Collingwood. 95: MASS-MOLLUS/USAMHI, copied by A. Pierce Bounds. 96: Courtesy Lewis A. Micou Jr. 97: Virginia Military Institute Museum, Lexington. 98: Museum of the Confederacy, Richmond, photographed by Larry Sherer; courtesy Mary Stewart McGuire Gilliam, Lexington, photographed by Thomas C. Bradshaw. 99: Miriam and Ira D. Wallach Division of Art, Prints and Photographs, The New York Public Library, Astor, Lenox and Tilden Foundations. 101: Map by Walter W. Roberts. 102: Library of Congress, Neg. No. B8184-4994. 104: L. M. Strayer Collection, Dayton. 105: Fredericksburg and Spotsylvania National Military Park, Fredericksburg, Va., photographed by Larry Sherer. 106: Bessent Family Photographs, Personal Collections Section, Z. Smith Reynolds Library, Wake Forest University, Winston-Salem, N.C., photographed by Henry L. Mintz. 107: Courtesy Mrs. Guy Taylor Hardee and Miss Katherine Purdie, photographed by Henry L. Mintz, in the possession of the Bladen County Historical Society. 108: Alabama Department of Archives and History, Montgomery. 109: Courtesy Ken Turner, copied by Chet Buquo. 110, 111: Library of Congress, Waud #754. 112: Eleanor S. Brockenbrough Library, Museum of the Confederacy, Richmond. 113: Fredericksburg and Spotsylvania National Military Park, Fredericksburg, Va., photographed by Larry Sherer. 114: Collection of C. Paul Loane, photographed by Robert J. Laramie. 115: New York State Division of Military and Naval Affairs, Military History Collection, Albany, photographed by Henry Groskinsky. 116: MASS-MOLLUS/USAMHI, copied by A. Pierce Bounds; Library of Congress, Manuscripts Division, William O. Bourne Papers. 117: Special Collection Division, United States Military Academy Library, West Point, N.Y. 118: Painting by George Leo Frankenstein, courtesy Fredericksburg and Spotsylvania National Military Park, Fredericksburg,

BIBLIOGRAPHY

BOOKS

Andrews, Marietta Minnigerode. *Scraps of Paper*. New York: E. P. Dutton, 1929.

Battles and Leaders of the Civil War. Vol. 3. Ed. by Robert Underwood Johnson and Clarence Clough Buel. New York: Thomas Yoseloff, 1956.

Blackford, William W. *War Years with Jeb Stuart*. New York: Charles Scribner's Sons, 1945.

Blair, Harry C. *Dr. Anson G. Henry: Physician, Politician, Friend of Abraham Lincoln*. Portland, Oreg.: Harry C. Blair, 1950.

Borcke, Heros von. *Memoirs of the Confederate War for Independence*. Philadelphia: J. B. Lippincott, 1867.

Brooks, Noah. *Mr. Lincoln's Washington: Selections from the Writings of Noah Brooks, Civil War Correspondent*. Ed. by P. J. Staudenraus. New York: Thomas Yoseloff, 1967.

Casler, John O. *Four Years in the Stonewall Brigade*. Dayton: Morningside Bookshop, 1971.

Cooke, Jacob B. "The Battle of Kelly's Ford, March 17, 1863." In *Personal Narratives of Events in the War of the Rebellion, Being Papers Read before the Rhode Island Soldiers and Sailors Historical Society*. Vol. 5. Wilmington, N.C.: Broadfoot, 1993.

Daly, Louise Haskell. *Alexander Cheves Haskell: The Portrait of a Man*. Norwood, Mass: Plimpton Press, 1934.

Dawes, Rufus R. *Service with the Sixth Wisconsin Volunteers*. Marietta, Ga.: E. R. Alderman & Sons, 1890.

Dickert, D. Augustus. *History of Kershaw's Brigade*. Dayton: Morningside Bookshop, 1976 (reprint of 1899 edition).

Dinkins, James. *1861 to 1865: Personal Recollections and Experiences in the Confederate Army*. Cincinnati: Robert Clarke, 1897.

Fuller, Charles A. *Personal Recollections of the War of 1861*. Sherburne, N.Y.: News Job Printing House, 1906.

Galwey, Thomas Francis. *The Valiant Hours: Narrative of "Captain Brevet," an Irish-American in the Army of the Potomac*. Harrisburg, Pa.: Stackpole, 1961.

Haley, John. *The Rebel Yell and Yankee Hurrah: The Civil War Journal of a Maine Volunteer*. Ed. by Ruth L. Silliker. Camden, Maine: Down East Books, 1985.

Hall, H. Seymour. "Fredericksburg and Chancellorsville." In *War Talks in Kansas: A Series of Papers Read before the Kansas Commandery of the Military Order of the Loyal Legion of the United States*. Wilmington, N.C.: Broadfoot, 1992 (reprint of 1906 edition).

Handerson, Henry E. *Yankee in Gray*. Cleveland: Press of Western Reserve University, 1962.

Holt, Daniel M. *A Surgeon's Civil War: The Letters and Diary of Daniel M. Holt, M.D.* Ed. by James M. Greiner, Janet L. Coryell, and James R. Smither. Kent, Ohio: Kent State University Press, 1994.

Jackson, Mary Anna. *Memoirs of Stonewall Jackson*. Dayton: Morningside Bookshop, 1976 (reprint of 1895 edition).

MacCauley, Clay. "From Chancellorsville to Libby Prison." In *Glimpses of the Nation's Struggle: Papers Read before the Minnesota Commandery of the Military Order of the Loyal Legion of the United States, 1887*. Vol. 1. Wilmington, N.C.: Broadfoot (reprint of 1887 edition).

McGlashan, Peter. *Battle of Salem Church, May 3, 1863*. Savannah: Breid & Hutton, 1893.

Marshall, Charles. *An Aide-de-Camp of Lee*. Ed. by Frederick Maurice. Boston: Little, Brown, 1927.

Military Essays and Recollections: Papers Read before the Commandery of the State of Illinois, Military Order of the Loyal Legion of the United States. Vol. 2. Wilmington, N.C.: Broadfoot, 1992 (reprint of 1894 edition).

Military Essays and Recollections: Papers Read before the Commandery of the State of Illinois, Military Order of the

Loyal Legion of the United States. Vol. 4. Wilmington, N.C.: Broadfoot, 1992 (reprint of 1907 edition).

Patterson, Edmund DeWitt. *Yankee Rebel: The Civil War Journal of Edmund DeWitt Patterson.* Ed. by John G. Barrett. Chapel Hill: University of North Carolina Press, 1966.

Paxton, Frank. *The Civil War Letters of General Frank "Bull" Paxton, CSA: A Lieutenant of Lee & Jackson.* Ed. by John Gallatin Paxton. Hillsboro, Tex.: Hill Jr. College Press, 1978.

Peabody, J. H. "Battle of Chancellorsville." In *G. A. R. War Papers.* Cincinnati: Fred C. Jones, 1901.

Silliman, Justus M. *A New Canaan Private in the Civil War: Letters of Justus M. Silliman, 17th Connecticut Volunteers.* Ed. by Edward Marcus. New Canaan, Conn.: New Canaan Historical Society, 1984.

Small, Abner R. *The Road to Richmond: The Civil War Memoirs of Major Abner R. Small of the Sixteenth Maine Volunteers.* Ed. by Harold Adams Small. Berkeley: University of California Press, 1939.

Smith, James Power. *With Stonewall Jackson in the Army of Northern Virginia.* Gaithersburg, Md.: Zullo and Van Sickle, 1982.

United States War Department. *The War of the Rebellion.* 128 vols. Washington, D.C.: Government Printing Office, 1902.

Weld, Stephen Minot. *War Diary and Letters of Stephen Minot Weld, 1861-1865.* Cambridge, Mass.: Riverside Press, 1912.

White, Wyman S. *The Civil War Diary of Wyman S. White: First Sergeant of Company F, 2nd United States Sharpshooter Regiment, 1861-1865.* Ed. by Russell C. White. Baltimore: Butternut and Blue, 1993.

Wickersham, Charles I. "Personal Recollections of the Cavalry at Chancellorsville." In *War Papers Being Read before the Commandery of the State of Wisconsin Military Order of the Loyal Legion of the United States.* Vol. 3. Wilmington, N.C.: Broadfoot, 1993 (reprint of 1903 edition).

Wise, John Sergeant. *The End of an Era.* New York: Thomas Yoseloff, 1965.

PERIODICALS

Boswell, James Keith. "The Diary of a Confederate Staff Officer: Jackson's Boswell." *Civil War Times Illustrated.* April 1976.

Farley, Porter. "Reminiscences of the 140th Regiment New York Volunteer Infantry." *Rochester Historical Society,* 1944, Vol. 22.

" 'Fighting Joe' Hooker" (interview). *San Francisco Chronicle,* May 23, 1872.

"Found Miracle Cure for Rheumatism Case." *The Infantry Journal, U.S.A.,* n.d.

Hinkley, Julian Wisner. "A Narrative of Service with the Third Wisconsin Infantry." *Wisconsin History Commission: Original Papers,* September 1912.

Johnson, W. R. "Where the Flag Was a Welcome Sight." *National Tribune* (Washington, D.C.), August 9, 1883.

Kinsolving, Roberta Cary Corbin. "Stonewall Jackson in Winter Quarters." *Confederate Veteran,* 1912, Vol. 20.

McGuire, Hunter. "Account of the Wounding and Death of Stonewall Jackson." *Virginia Medical Monthly,* October 1961 (reprinted from the *Richmond Medical Journal,* May 1866).

Martin, Micajah D. "Chancellorsville: A Soldier's Letter." *Virginia Magazine of History and Biography,* 1929, Vol. 37.

Mathews, William F. [Untitled letter, May 8, 1863.] *Central Georgian,* June 3, 1863.

Moorman, Marcellus N. "Narrative of Events and Observations Connected with the Wounding of General T. J. (Stonewall) Jackson." *Southern Historical Society Papers,* 1902, Vol. 30.

[Morrison, J. G.] "Wounding of Lieutenant-General T. J. Jackson." *The Land We Love,* July 1866.

Smith, James Power. "General Lee at Gettysburg." *Southern Historical Society Papers,* August 1920.

Temple, Wayne C. "Dr. Anson G. Henry: Personal Physician to the Lincolns." *Bulletin of the 44th Annual Meeting of the Lincoln Fellowship of Wisconsin, April 12, 1987,* 1988, no. 43.

OTHER SOURCES

Armstrong, Edward H. Letter from the Thomas Armstrong Papers, 1859-1885. Wilmington, N.C.: University of North Carolina, William Madison Randall Library, Manuscript Collection.

Booth, J. Ansel. Letters, May 1863. Fredericksburg, Va.: Fredericksburg and Spotsylvania National Military Park.

Brewster, Charles H. Letter, May 10, 1863. Northampton, Mass.: Northampton Historical Society.

Dawes, Rufus. Letter, May 1, 1863, from the Rufus Dawes Papers. Washington, D.C.: Library of Congress, Manuscript Division.

Dibble, Alvin. Narrative from the William O. Bourne Papers. Washington, D.C.: Library of Congress, Manuscript Division.

Haskell, Frank A. Letter, March 31, 1863. Madison, Wis.: State Historical Society of Wisconsin.

[Haygood, W. B.] Unsigned letter, May 18. 1863, from the Edward Harden Papers. Durham, N.C.: Duke University.

Henry, Anson G. Letter, April 13, 1863. Springfield: Illinois State Historical Library.

Herbert, Hilary A. "Grandfather's Talks about His Life under Two Flags." Memoirs, 1903. Chapel Hill: University of North Carolina, Southern Historical Collection.

Hotchkiss, Jedediah. Letters, May 1861-1864, from the Jedediah Hotchkiss Papers. Washington, D.C.: Library of Congress, Manuscript Division.

McFarland, J. W. Letter, May 9, 1863, from Joseph Graham file. Fredericksburg, Va.: Fredericksburg and Spotsylvania National Military Park.

Mathews, William F. Letter. Fredericksburg, Va.: Fredericksburg and Spotsylvania National Military Park.

Mesnard, Luther B. Unpublished manuscript, n.d. Carlisle Barracks, Pa.: U.S. Army Military History Institute.

Morrison, J. G. Letter, October 29, 1863, from the Charles William Dabney Papers, ms. #1412. Chapel Hill: University of North Carolina, Southern Historical Collection.

Robinson, John S. Letter, n.d. Fredericksburg, Va.: Fredericksburg and Spotsylvania National Military Park.

Smith, James Power. "Stonewall Jackson and Chancellorsville." Address to the Military Historical Society of Massachusetts, n.d. Boston: Military Historical Society of Massachusetts.

Southerton, William B. "Chancellorsville." Unpublished memoirs, n.d. Columbus: Ohio Historical Society.

Steffan, Edward W. Letters, n.d. Fredericksburg, Va.: Fredericksburg and Spotsylvania National Military Park.

Swift, Lucius B. "An Enlisted Man in the Chancellorsville Campaign." Unpublished manuscript, n.d. Washington, D.C.: Library of Congress, Manuscript Division.

Taylor, Edward H. C. Letter, May 7, 1863, from the Edward H. C. Taylor Papers. Ann Arbor: University of Michigan, Bentley Historical Library, Michigan Historical Collection.

Todd, Westwood A. "Reminiscences of the War between the States 1861-1865." Unpublished manuscript, n.d. Chapel Hill: University of North Carolina, Southern Historical Collection.

Van Blarcom, Lewis. Address given at the 15th New Jersey Volunteers Reunion. Unidentified newspaper, n.d. Fredericksburg, Va.: Fredericksburg and Spotsylvania National Military Park.

Winn, David Read Evans. Letter, May 9, 1863. Atlanta: Emory University.

INDEX

Numerals in italics indicate an illustration of the subject mentioned

TIME® LIFE BOOKS Time-Life Books is a
division of Time Life Inc.

TIME LIFE INC.
PRESIDENT and CEO: George Artandi

TIME-LIFE BOOKS
PRESIDENT: John D. Hall
PUBLISHER/MANAGING EDITOR: Neil Kagan

VOICES OF THE CIVIL WAR

DIRECTOR, NEW PRODUCT DEVELOPMENT:
Curtis Kopf
MARKETING DIRECTOR: Pamela R. Farrell

CHANCELLORSVILLE

EDITOR: Henry Woodhead
Deputy Editors: Kirk Denkler (principal), Harris J. Andrews,
Philip Brandt George
Art Director: Barbara M. Sheppard
Associate Editor/Research and Writing: Gemma Slack
Senior Copyeditor: Donna D. Carey
Picture Coordinator: Lisa Groseclose
Editorial Assistant: Christine Higgins

Initial Series Design: Studio A

Special Contributors: Brian C. Pohanka, David S. Thomson
(text); Paul J. Birkhead, Charles F. Cooney, Steve Hill,
Robert Lee Hodge, Henry Mintz, Anne Whittle (research);
Roy Nanovic (index).

Correspondents: Christina Lieberman (New York).

Vice President, Director of Finance: Christopher Hearing
Vice President, Book Production: Marjann Caldwell
Director of Operations: Eileen Bradley
Director of Photography and Research: John Conrad Weiser
Director of Editorial Administration (Acting): Barbara Levitt
Production Manager: Marlene Zack
Quality Assurance Manager: James King
Library: Louise D. Forstall

Consultants

Brian C. Pohanka, a Civil War historian and author, spent six
years as a researcher and writer for Time-Life Books' Civil
War series and Echoes of Glory. He is the author of *Distant
Thunder: A Photographic Essay on the American Civil War* and
has written and edited numerous works on American military
history. He has acted as historical consultant for projects
including the feature film *Glory* and television's *Civil War
Journal.* Pohanka participates in Civil War reenactments and
living-history demonstrations with the 5th New York Volunteers, and he is active in Civil War battlefield preservation.

Ernest B. (Pat) Furgurson is a Virginia-born journalist, biogra-
pher, and Civil War historian, and a former officer in the U.S.
Marine Corps. He is author of *Chancellorsville 1863: The Souls
of the Brave* and *Ashes of Glory: Richmond at War.* His four-part
series on battlefield preservation in *Mid-Atlantic Country*
magazine won national awards for public service. He was a
founder of Protect Historic America, the organization of writ-
ers and historians that led the campaign to block the Disney
company's plan for a theme park alongside the Manassas
battlefield.

Robert Krick is the author of more than 100 published arti-
cles and nine books, among them *Fredericksburg Artillery* and
Lee's Colonels. His book *Stonewall Jackson at Cedar Mountain*
won three national awards, including the Douglas Southall
Freeman Prize. His most recent work is *Conquering the
Valley: Stonewall Jackson at Port Republic.*

First printing. Printed in U.S.A.
School and library distribution by Time-Life Education,
P.O. Box 85026, Richmond, Virginia 23285-5026.

TIME-LIFE is a trademark of Time Warner Inc. U.S.A.

Library of Congress Cataloging-in-Publication Data
Chancellorsville / by the editors of Time-Life Books.
     p. cm.—(Voices of the Civil War)
     Includes bibliographical references and index.
     ISBN 0-7835-4708-0
     1. Chancellorsville (Va.), Battle of, 1863—Sources.
I. Time-Life Books. II. Series.
E475.35.C46 1996
973.7'33—DC20   96-42435
                                                      CIP